THE HEALING STAGE

BLACK PERFORMANCE AND CULTURAL CRITICISM
E. Patrick Johnson, Series Editor

THE HEALING STAGE

BLACK WOMEN, INCARCERATION, AND THE ART OF TRANSFORMATION

Lisa Biggs

THE OHIO STATE UNIVERSITY PRESS

COLUMBUS

Library of Congress Cataloging-in-Publication Data
Names: Biggs, Lisa (Actor and playwright), author.
Title: The healing stage : Black women, incarceration, and the art of transformation / Lisa
    Biggs.
Other titles: Black performance and cultural criticism.
Description: Columbus : The Ohio State University Press, [2022] | Series: Black performance
    and cultural criticism | Includes bibliographical references and index. | Summary:
    "Focusing on sites in the US and South Africa, Biggs follows four ensembles of currently
    and formerly incarcerated women and the teaching artists with whom they collaborate
    to investigate how performance-based arts projects both in prison and out can effect
    positive personal, social, and political change"—Provided by publisher.
Identifiers: LCCN 2022034968 | ISBN 9780814214930 (cloth) | ISBN 0814214932 (cloth) |
    ISBN 9780814282595 (ebook) | ISBN 0814282598 (ebook)
Subjects: LCSH: Prison theater. | Women prisoners. | African American prisoners. | Women
    in the performing arts. | Performing arts—Social aspects. | Theater and society.
Classification: LCC HV8861 .B54 2022 | DDC 365/.66108996073—dc23/eng/20220902
LC record available at https://lccn.loc.gov/2022034968
Other identifiers: ISBN 9780814258569 (paper) | ISBN 0814258565 (paper)

Cover design by Angela Moody
Text composition by Stuart Rodriguez
Type set in Minion Pro

For Sherral, Dana, Marni, Rosetta,
Jafta, Nellie, and Evelyn

CONTENTS

ACKNOWLEDGMENTS

I owe a tremendous debt of gratitude to the women whose creative work is at the center of this project. Thank you for allowing me to be a witness to your artistry, your lives, and your visions for a better tomorrow.

E. Patrick Johnson, Ana Maria Jimenez-Moreno, Elizabeth Zaleski, and the entire staff at The Ohio State University Press believed in the project from the beginning and brought their insights and unfailing guidance to the work every step of the way. Thank you for your faith, vision, expertise, and patience.

When I first stepped onto the shining wood floor of the Living Stage Theatre Company in Washington DC, I could not have imagined that the lessons Oran Sandel, Rebecca Rice, Jennifer Nelson, Kristin Horton, Tanisha Christie, and Denise Kumani Gantt would teach me would not only change my life but propel and prepare me to be the scholar that I am today. The path that they helped me forge has only been deepened and expanded with the generous mentorship of D. Soyini Madison, Ramon Rivera-Servera, Michael Dinwiddie, Darlene Clark Hine, Tavia Nyong'o, Jose Esteban Munoz, Sandra Richards, Martha Biondi, Harvey Young, Nick Davis, Julie Malnig, Alycia Smith-Howard, David Blight, Rowland Abiodun, Carol Simpson Stern, Paul Edwards, Margaret Thompson Drewall, and Nitasha Sharma.

Colleagues at Michigan State University, including Geneva Smitherman, Tama Hamilton-Wray, Dylan Miner, Estrella Torres, Terese Monberg, Kevin Brooks, Anita Skeen, and Katie Wittenauer helped me expand my horizons. At

Brown University, Francoise Hamlin, Tricia Rose, Brian Meeks, Noliwe Rooks, Paget Henry, Matthew Guterl, Lundy Braun, Ainsley LeSure, Charrise Barron, Elmo Terry-Morgan, Karen Allen Baxter, Kathy Moyers, Alonzo Jones, and Dotun Ayobade provided much needed grounding and encouragement.

A manuscript workshop cosponsored by Africana Studies and the Center for the Study of Race and Ethnicity (CSREA) at Brown was invaluable to my writing process. Tricia Rose, Judith Hamera, Eunice Ferreira, Leo Bernstein, Anthony Bogues, Patricia Ybarra, Stephanie Larrieux, and Caitlin Murphy-Scott helped me identify strengths and areas in need of clarification. Through the CSREA, I also met Scott Poulson-Bryant, Karen Inouye, Christina Downs, Kevin Escudero, Sarika Chandra, Dario Valles, Michelle Rose, Mahasan Chaney, Ronald Aubert, and Akua Naru, all of whom inspired me every day with their scholarship.

I learned how to feel the world around me from my artistic mentors, including Rhodessa Jones, Holly Hughes, Wendy Woodson, Suzanne Dougan, Wendy Woodson, Peter Lobdell, and Paul Carter Harrison. Cindy Garcia, Nina Billone Prieur, Lori Barcliff-Baptista, Judi Singleton, Ashley Lucas, Munjulika Rahman, Edwin Corbin Gutierrez, Kareem Khubchandani, Chris Davidson, Charmaine Henriques, Chieko Maene, Kathleen Murphy, Geoff Swindells, Sui Zhang, and Victoria Fortuna all opened their hearts and homes to me at various points on the journey. None of this work would have been possible without the visionary artistry and leadership of Lisa Wagner-Corollo, Jacob Kaufman, Rick Riddle, Jennifer Witherspoon, Kathy Randels, Ausettua Amor Amenkum, Michaela Harrison, Sherral Kahey, Imani Walker, Lorna Hogan, Rosetta Kelly, Angela Day, and Roshnie Moonsammy. Many thanks as well to the administrators, staff, and volunteers of the Departments of Correctional Services in the US and South Africa for their support.

This book is about healing, and Maya Shewnarain, William Barnett, Sherry Balantine, Stephanie Barasch, and Ixchel Muhlberg put their healing power to work on me. Thank you for saving my back, hands, and neck, and for helping me learn how to hold what I needed to hold and to let other things go.

My parents, Beverly and James Biggs, made all these things possible.

Austin Jackson, the wind beneath my wings, thank you always for your steady guidance, expert insights, constant love, and encouragement.

INTRODUCTION

Race, Gender, Crime, Performance

The 1913 Annual Report for the New York State women's prison at Auburn, one of the oldest custodial facilities for women in the United States, lists performances of *The Colored Ladies' Political Club or The Colored Suffragettes* as one of the prison's—and by extension, the incarcerated women's—crowning achievements. On May 15, 1913, two months after the first national march for women's suffrage, women confined in Ward V presented the thirty-minute, blackface minstrelsy sketch written by Sophie Huth Perkins, a white American playwright.[1] This rare early twentieth-century theatrical work written for a large all-female cast tells the story of Mrs. Simon Pure, an impoverished African American woman who has decided to run for elected office, specifically for mayor. Set in the early 1900s when American women could not vote in political elections or hold public office, the comedy finds its humor in ridiculing the idea of Black women as political theorists, community organizers, and civic leaders. Voting rights activists, known as suffragists, were engaged in a national campaign to overturn the prohibitions that prevented women from voting and holding elected office. As white suffragists fought to secure the vote for themselves, however, they worked deliberately to exclude Black women from political power.

1. Nettie Leonard, *Annual Report of Women's Prison* (Albany: New York State Legislature, 1913), 200; Nicole Hahn Rafter, *Partial Justice: Women in State Prisons, 1800–1935* (Boston: Northeastern University Press, 1985), 154.

1

The Auburn matrons used *The Colored Suffragettes* to discipline the imprisoned Black, indigenous, and white women under their charge to behave like good prisoners and to uphold Jim Crow segregation and women's disenfranchisement. As a work of blackface minstrelsy, *The Colored Suffragettes* literalizes white Americans' belief in African inferiority and positions race as a "truly impassable boundary."[2] Moreover, the script turns Black women's dreams of full citizenship and political power into a joke. In the opening scene, we learn that Mrs. Simon Pure (pronounced "Missus, I'm impure") has invited several other politically minded African American women to her apartment for a campaign strategy meeting and fundraiser. To project an image of competence and affluence, Mrs. Pure persuades the building janitor, George Alexander Washington Horatio Anthony Webster Johnson, to play her butler for the afternoon. When her "mannish" friends finally assemble, Mrs. Pure launches into her stump speech, announcing in a faux-Black dialect, "de time has come fo'de down-trodden sex to trow off their yoke of slavedom and rise above . . . de washtub and de flatiron and all de other things what put a kink in de dispositions of us women."[3] Her political aspirations are soon dashed, however, when it becomes clear that her guests are not interested in what she has to say. Instead they mock her malapropisms and ridicule one another for being poor and culturally unsophisticated. The arrival of a final, unexpected guest brings the production to a surprising end. Mrs. Kodd Fish, a "celebrated" Greek costume performer, condescends to instruct the women how to do laundry with a surprise (modern? ethnic? social?) rhythmic dance demonstration that proves too much for the group to handle. Scandalized, they scatter to the winds, leaving Kodd Fish alone on stage with the butler, Johnson. He wheels and turns about, singing happily along to a (then) familiar minstrel tune, the selection of which was left to the director of each production. The curtain closes on this image of a white woman crossed-dressed and in blackface makeup in a caricature of a happy Black man encouraging the audience to sing along.

More than a century later, prison-arts programs continue to operate at selected women's facilities around the United States and across the world, but many people no longer believe that incarceration is an effective or appropriate response to crime. A growing number of crime survivors, prison scholars, educators, victim's advocates, and activists have called for the abolition of the system. They recognize that incarcerating people does not stop poverty, violence, or addiction, those factors that are most often identified as the causes

---

2. Benjamin Reiss, *The Showman and the Slave: Race, Death, and Memory in Barnum's America* (Cambridge, MA: Harvard University Press, 2001), 8–9.

3. Sophie Huth Perkins, *The Colored Ladies' Political Club or the Colored Suffragettes* (Chicago: T. S. Denison and Company, 1910), 11–12.

of crime. Locking people up also does not overturn bad laws or put a stop to the worst practices of police, prosecutors, or the courts, factors that critics of the criminal legal system point to that drive people into carceral facilities. While the country continues to invest in these ineffective solutions, the people who are most affected by the system cannot wait for something to change. At selected sites, women behind bars have turned to a new kind of theater to save their own lives, heal, and transform the performance of policing and of punishment.

In this book, I document a history of the policing and punishment of Black women in the United States and offer five examples of how women who have been criminalized use theatrical events and everyday acts of Black expressive culture to redress interpersonal and institutional harm, a process that I call *stage healing*. Drawing on ethnographic fieldwork I conducted between 2008 and 2018 with Demeter's Daughters, the Big Water Women's Prison Drama Club, the Medea Project: Theater for Incarcerated Women in South Africa, and Healing Justice Mamas,[4] I argue that, under the guise of rehabilitative prison arts programming, these contemporary drama clubs use performance to investigate, disrupt, and transform prevailing discourses about women's criminality. Instead of disciplining women to follow orders and adhere to dominant expectations regarding appropriate behavior, these community-engaged arts programs create opportunities for them to examine and to redress their experiences of racialized gender- and sexuality-based violence using original scenes, monologues, poetry, song, and dances that the women create and perform for audiences of other incarcerated women and correctional officials, and in some cases, for the general public. The productions, as well as the workshop and rehearsal processes that precede them, prepare women to advocate for and to enact new, fairer, more just, and more inclusive social policies and practices on both sides of the prison door. They do so because theater for incarcerated women is a vital site for healing, communal change, and cultural struggle, the combination of which is absolutely needed to end interpersonal and state violence and to meet the needs of some of the most vulnerable members of our society now.

INCARCERATING WOMEN

Women historically have constituted a small portion of the US prisoner population, less than 10 percent, but Black women have long been overrepresent-

---

4. To protect the identities of the incarcerated women at the center of this study, I use pseudonyms to identify the people, places, and settings where this research occurred. I include a full explanation of my research methods and the rationale for this choice in this introduction.

ed.[5] They were disproportionately sentenced to time behind bars at Walnut Street, the United States' first penitentiary, and have continued to be overrepresented in every other form of penal control since, from convict leasing to the reformatory movement and beyond. The most recent era of Black women's mass incarceration began in the 1970s, when lawmakers instituted changes in local, state, and federal policing and sentencing guidelines in order to mandate incarceration for those crimes that women, especially low-income Black women, are most likely to commit. Petty larceny (shoplifting), possession and consumption of illegal drugs, and sex-work crimes now carry sentences of imprisonment. As a result, in the decade leading up to the full-scale implementation of the War on Drugs alone (1970–80), the total number of women confined to state and federal prisons more than doubled, from approximately 5,800 in 1970 to over 12,300 by 1980.[6] Over the next four decades (1980–2017), the total number of incarcerated women skyrocketed over 750 percent to more than 225,000 in 2017.[7] If one factors in the parole and probation populations as well, by 2017 there were 1.3 million women under some form of correctional

---

5. W. E. B. DuBois, *The Philadelphia Negro: A Social Study* (Philadelphia: University of Pennsylvania Press, 1899); Sarah Haley, *No Mercy Here: Gender, Punishment, and the Making of Jim Crow Modernity* (Chapel Hill: University of North Carolina Press, 2016); Talitha LeFlouria. "Under the Sting of the Lash: Gendered Violence, Terror, and Resistance in the South's Convict Camps," *Journal of African American History* 100, no. 3 (2015): 366–84. See also Talitha LeFlouria, *Chained in Silence: Black Women and Convict Labor in the New South* (Chapel Hill: University of North Carolina Press, 2016); Leslie Patrick-Stamp, "Numbers That Are Not New: African Americans in the Country's First Prison, 1790–1835," *Pennsylvania Magazine of History and Biography* 119, no. 1/2 (1995): 95–128; Leslie Patrick-Stamp, "The Prison Sentence Docket for 1795: Inmates at the Nation's First State Penitentiary," *Pennsylvania History: A Journal of Mid-Atlantic Studies* 60, no. 3 (1993): 353–82.

6. This rate is twice the concurrent 167 percent growth in the men's population.

7. Data compiled from US Department of Justice, Bureau of Justice Statistics, *Historical Corrections Statistics in the United States, 1850–1984* (Rockville, MD: Westat Inc., 1986); US Department of Justice, Bureau of Justice Statistics, *Prison and Jail Inmates at Midyear 2000* (Washington, DC: Bureau of Justice Statistics, 2001); US Department of Justice, Bureau of Justice Statistics, *Jail Inmates at Midyear 2010—Statistical Tables* (Washington, DC: Bureau of Justice Statistics, 2011); US Department of Justice, Bureau of Justice Statistics, *Jail Inmates in 2015* (Washington, DC: Bureau of Justice Statistics, 2016); US Department of Justice, Bureau of Justice Statistics, *Prisoners in 1986* (Washington, DC: Bureau of Justice Statistics, 1987); US Department of Justice, Bureau of Justice Statistics, *Prisoners in 1990* (Washington, DC: Bureau of Justice Statistics, 1991); US Department of Justice, Bureau of Justice Statistics, *Prisoners in 1994* (Washington DC: Bureau of Justice Statistics, 1995); US Department of Justice, Bureau of Justice Statistics, *Correctional Populations in the United States, 1997*, NCJ 177613 (Washington, DC: Bureau of Justice Statistics, 2000); US Department of Justice, Bureau of Justice Statistics, *Prisoners in 2000*, Bulletin NCJ 188207 (Washington, DC: US Department of Justice, 2001); US Department of Justice, Bureau of Justice Statistics, *Prison Inmates at Midyear 2007* (Washington, DC: Bureau of Justice Statistics, 2008); US Department of Justice, Bureau of Justice Statistics, *Prisoners in 2010* (Washington, DC: Bureau of Justice Statistics, 2012); US Department of Justice, Bureau of Justice Statistics, *Prisoners in 2012—Advance Counts*, Bulletin NCJ 242467 (Washington, DC: US Department of Justice, 2013); US Department of Justice, Bureau of Justice Statistics, *Prisoners in 2017* (Washington, DC: Bureau of Justice Statistics, 2019).

control—approximately 111,360 in prison, 113,700 in jail, 113,724 on parole, and 918,275 on probation.[8] The numbers of women have continued to rise even though the national crime rate has been declining for decades. When the experiences of Black women are specifically considered, the impact of mass incarceration becomes even more stark. By early 1991, despite constituting just 6 percent of the US population, nearly half of the women behind bars were African Americans, and they continue to be overrepresented in the criminal legal system.[9] In 2018, the Sentencing Project and the National Association for the Advancement of Colored People (NAACP) noted that African American women were imprisoned at nearly twice the rate of white women (96 vs. 49 per 100,000) and 43 percent more often than Latinas (96 vs. 67 per 100,000).[10] They receive harsher punishments than whites or Latinas for the same crimes. Black women who fail or refuse to conform to white heteropatriarchal expectations of appropriate gender and sexual behavior receive some of the most severe punishments of all.

The simultaneous widening of the carceral net and dismantling of social safety programs in the late twentieth century hit low-income African American communities particularly hard. The Census Bureau reported in 2015 that over 28 percent of the US adult population lived in poverty, including 16.9 million women (13.4% of all women) and 11.7 million men (9.9% of men). When those data are aggregated by race as well as gender, the combined impact of racism and sexism in hiring practices becomes more apparent. One in four (23.1%) Black women and one in five (20.9%) Latinas live in poverty, at more than twice the poverty rate of Asian American women (11.7%) and whites (9.6%). While the median wealth of unmarried white women in the United States stood at just over $15,600 in 2015, it was $200 for single Black women and just $100 for Latinas.[11] Despite hard-fought struggles to elimi-

---

8. A jail is a short-term holding facility where people who have been accused of a crime are detained temporarily. After a person is arrested, they are taken to jail. The overwhelming majority of those in jail have not been convicted of any crime. A person who is tried and found guilty of an offense that carries a sentence of confinement of 364 days or less would serve out their sentence in jail. Only those who are tried, convicted, and sentenced to confinement of 365 days or more should be sent to prison. Far more people who are convicted serve their sentences in jail than in prison.

9. Tracy L. Snell and Danielle C. Morton, *Women in Prison* (Washington, DC: Bureau of Justice Statistics, 1994).

10. The Sentencing Project, "Incarcerated Women and Girls Fact Sheet," 2017, https://www.sentencingproject.org/wp-content/uploads/2016/02/Incarcerated-Women-and-Girls.pdf; NAACP, "Criminal Justice Fact Sheet," 2022, https://www.naacp.org/criminal-justice-fact-sheet/.

11. Jasmine Tucker and Caitlin Lowell, *National Snapshot: Poverty Among Women & Families, 2015* (Washington, DC: National Women's Law Center, 2016); see also the Institute for Policy Studies, "Women and the Racial Wealth Divide," accessed January 21, 2022, https://inequality.org/racial-wealth-divide-snapshot-women/.

nate racism and sexism in housing, employment, education, politics, and the public sphere, low-income African Americans continue to bear the weight of bad public policy as states and local governments for the last fifty years have pumped money into policing and away from public health, education, housing, welfare, infrastructure, and job-training programs.

These disparities are compounded by public policy decisions that over-police and underprotect Black women and girls under the pretext of ensuring public safety and justice such as the much-touted 1994 Violent Crime Control and Law Enforcement Act (Crime Bill). It authorized still more aggressive policing to control poor, urban, and Black communities as part of the War on Drugs. A central component of that sweeping legislation, the Violence Against Women Act (VAWA), importantly and for the first time allotted significant federal resources, money, and personnel to the investigation and prosecution of violent crimes against women. However, the VAWA's reliance on racist tropes about the victims and perpetrators of crime as well as on "criminal legal remedies" for gender-based violence had devastating effects on low-income women, in particular on Black women.[12]

According to the National Organization of Women (NOW), one in three women in the United States is a victim of intimate partner assault, and one in five will be sexually assaulted in her lifetime. African American women are, however, more than twice as likely as white women to experience physical abuse, which includes sexual abuse. Black women are less likely to be believed when they do report abuse and are far more likely to face serious barriers in accessing the financial, medical, law enforcement, and other life-saving resources they need to protect themselves and to heal. Because Black women and girls are mischaracterized as fundamentally immoral, hypersexual, and incapable of being raped, those few perpetrators who are held to account for harming them generally receive lighter punishments than they would have if their victims had been white. Such neglect signals to other potential abusers that Black women and girls—their hopes, their lives, their dreams, and their safety—do not matter. In 2019, more than 80 percent of women behind bars surveyed reported that they had experienced domestic violence and that, prior to their thirteenth birthdays, they had been forced into unwanted sexual activity and endured one or more sexual assaults, traumatic events for which they received neither adequate treatment nor justice. Behind bars they also find no sanctuary from abuse. Though they constitute less than 10 percent of the prisoner population, more than a third of the incarcerated people sexually

---

12. Mimi E. Kim, "Challenging the Pursuit of Criminalization in an Era of Mass Incarceration: The Limitations of Social Work Responses to Domestic Violence in the USA," *British Journal of Social Work* 42, no. 7 (2013): 1278.

victimized by corrections staff are women.[13] Their abjection is reinforced by the refusal of elected officials to allocate funding for gender-informed health care, safe housing, or for vocational, educational, and recreational programming to meet their needs.

These experiences communicate to imprisoned women that they must look outside the system for support and for healing. As Audre Lorde put it, *"The master's tools will never dismantle the master's house."*[14] In select sites, they turn to each other and to the arts, to theater, in order to *stage healing*, a practice of radical storytelling that draws upon Black expressive cultural practices to investigate, disrupt, and transform prevailing discourses about women's criminality, and in so doing create spaces where incarcerated women can begin to address interpersonal and systemic harm themselves.

PRISON THEATER

There is no single or comprehensive history of incarcerated artists or organized formal arts programs for people behind bars in the age of mass incarceration (from around 1970 until the present time). Volunteer teaching artists who work behind bars often point to the September 1971 Attica, New York, men's prison uprising as the catalyst for their work.[15] The Attica Brothers' outrage over the horrendous conditions of confinement and the violence they endured at the hands of racist staff members, when broadcast nationally on live television, moved many theater artists to consider teaching behind bars. In the last forty years, teachers, participants, and scholars of prison-based arts programs have documented their impact, writing in vivid detail about how their work breaks up deviant and destructive behavior patterns, teaches critical thinking and decision-making skills, and prepares incarcerated people to lead more productive lives in free society.[16] Examples of such work span

13. Gina Fedock, with Cristy Cummings and Sheryl Kubiak, "Incarcerated Women's Experiences of Staff-Perpetuated Rape: Racial Disparities and Justice Gaps in Institutional Responses," *Journal of Interpersonal Violence* 36, no. 17–18 (2019): 8668–69.

14. Audre Lorde, "The Master's Tools Will Never Dismantle the Master's House," in *Sister Outsider: Essays and Speeches* (Berkley, CA: Crossing Press, 1984), 107. Original italics.

15. William Cleveland, *Art in Other Places: Artists at Work in America's Community and Social Institutions* (Westport, CT: Praeger, 1992); Hart, "Historical and Social Role."

16. Michael Balfour, *Theatre in Prison: Theory and Practice* (Bristol, UK; Portland, OR: Intellect, 2004); Steven Hart, "The Historical and Social Role of the Arts in Prison," *Prison Journal* 66, no. 11 (1986): 11–25; Amy Scott-Douglass, *Shakespeare Inside* (London: Continuum, 2007); James Thompson, *Prison Theatre: Perspectives and Practices* (London; Philadelphia: Jessica Kingsley, 1998); Laurence Tocci, *The Proscenium Cage: Critical Case Studies in US Prison Theatre Programs* (Youngstown, OH: Cambria, 2007).

programs for adults and children in detention centers and jails as well as in minimum-, medium-, and maximum-security facilities, including segregated housing units (solitary confinement). The scholarship documents how important it is to carve out spaces for creative self-reflection and to build supportive communities regardless of how long a person has been or will be locked away.

Jonathan Shailor's edited anthology, *Performing New Lives: Prison Theater* (2011), comes closest to presenting a history of the field in the era of mass incarceration, surveying fourteen programs across the US for adults and young people that teach a broad range of theater practices ranging from presenting works of Shakespeare and other classic plays to developing original scripts.[17] Despite the uncertainty that attaches to almost any program designed to help incarcerated people, as in any good theater classroom the participants in the fourteen programs that Shailor features grow as artists through coursework. Actors' sense of themselves physically, emotionally, intellectually, and spiritually strengthens as they wrestle to unpack and then communicate the meaning of a text. They deepen their interpersonal and communication skills through scene and monologue work and take away a renewed sense of self-confidence, self-worth, and personal accomplishment from the process. These programs achieve these aims in spite of their surroundings, Shailor argues, by offering participants a space of *sanctuary*, where the "distractions and denigrations of the normal prison context are temporarily set aside."[18] Over time, as the prisoners continue to train as actors and begin to stage plays, the sanctuaries grow into what he calls *crucibles of transformation,* in which incarcerated people can develop "mature coping skills" such as "self-expression, listening, teamwork, critical thinking, and creative problem-solving."[19] Shailor states that these skills help people grow as individuals, build self-esteem and a capacity for empathy, and prepare them to navigate life in open society as moral citizens, thus reducing recidivism—a core concern of every corrections administrator.

In reference to programs that are allowed to bring audiences into correctional facilities to witness performances, Shailor offers his most provocative claim, that arts-in-corrections can operate on a third register as *vehicles for social (re)integration,* encouraging the "healing that needs to take place at both an individual and a communal level."[20] He explains:

> As actors facing their audiences, prisoners have the opportunity to take advantage of a liminal zone where identities and relationships are fluid and

17. Johnathon Shailor, *Performing New Lives: Prison Theater* (London: Jessica Kingsley Publishers, 2011).

18. Shailor, *Performing,* 22.

19. Shailor, *Performing,* 24–29.

20. Shailor, *Performing,* 28.

multi-dimensional, and where they can, in a very real sense, perform new lives . . . [by holding] the character in her awareness and her body. If we allow ourselves to truly see her, in all of these dimensions, if we hear her longing, then ultimately we are called not only to celebrate her performance but also to open our hearts and being to re-envision our approach to criminal justice and offender reform.[21]

Corrections arts programs provide one of the few spaces in which incarcerated people can (re)present themselves to society. Their theatrical performances afford audiences of free people an opportunity to enter into the prison and see them not as convicts and felons, but as "fellow human being[s] longing to be seen, to connect, to understand and to be understood, to be whole."[22] These encounters can be emotionally powerful at the individual level, but they are not substitutes for sweeping legislative change that would end the systemic inequalities and unjust public policies that destroy communities and put millions of poor, especially poor African Americans, behind bars. Prison arts programs can affect how the American, predominantly white, public sees the disproportionately high number of Black, Indigenous, and Latino people behind bars. However, there is a danger in equating temporary feelings of recognition, wholeness, and relief with healing. I agree with Shailor when he writes that currently and formerly incarcerated people cannot be (re)integrated into a society that has "no place for them."[23] Nor can they return to communities that have been devastated to the point that they no longer exist. The liminal space that exists between "convict" and "character" through acting on the carceral stage may provide an opportunity for audiences to recognize imprisoned individuals as fellow human beings, but it asks little else of them. At the end of a typical show, the prisoners return to their cells and the free people walk free. The question of whether incarceration itself is a fair, appropriate, or effective solution to human conflicts, crime, and public health crises goes largely unanswered. Inattention to these concerns leaves contemporary arts programs vulnerable to accusations that they operate as a "civilizing" tool designed to (re)affirm and legitimize the power and authority of the ruling class, or, as James Thompson put it, serve as a less "explicitly punitive" aspect of a prison term.[24]

---

21. Shailor, *Performing*, 31.
22. Shailor, *Performing*, 31.
23. Shailor, *Performing*, 28.
24. James Thompson, "From the Stocks to the Stage: Prison Theater and the Theater of Prison," in *Theater in Prison: Theory and Practice*, ed. Michael Balfour (Bristol, UK; Portland, OR: Intellect, 2004), 57–76.

STAGE HEALING

Stage healing emerges from communities of predominantly Black incarcerated women. It imagines healing on a far larger scale than Western medicines' cures or the rehabilitative script offered by a prison system focused on inflicting pain. Stage healing as a practice of self-repair is generated and sustained by women behind bars in collaboration with the volunteer theater artists who direct their drama clubs. The term is deeply indebted to Cara Page and the Kindred Healing Justice Collective, who characterized *healing justice* as "how we can holistically respond to and intervene in generational trauma and violence . . . to bring collective practices that can impact and transform the consequences of oppression on our bodies, hearts and minds." This "active intervention," writes Prentiss Hemphill, makes listening to and collaborating with people who are "imagining transformative responses to harm" other than "feeding Black incarceration" foundational, not only to healing work but also to Black community organizing—in their case, specifically the Black Lives Matter movement.[25] Healing justice recognizes that locating alternative, noncarceral responses to harmdoing requires finding ways to "develop and to honor practitioners of many different disciplines and modalities with capacities and skills to be with trauma, who know themselves well enough to navigate the complex terrain of emotion and guide others towards change."[26]

The theater artists who occupy the center of this book are such practitioners who are able to stand with people who have endured harm, and in many cases have perpetrated it as well, and who know themselves well enough to guide others toward change. They do so by devising and staging performances with women that give breath to aspects of life that are present in them but which are not yet fully legible in the world—memories, hopes, desires, fears, sensations, and much more. In place of stereotypes, they cultivate multiplicity, complexity, and nuance. And, in the absence of care from the state, they make time to listen, to learn, to see, to hear, to hold, and to understand. They recognize that healing does not come from anger, shame, or fear, and that it does not happen when people feel like they are being judged. Healing requires connection, love, and belief in people's capabilities. Healing work affirms that people can break up old patterns of thought and behavior that are no longer helpful or needed and replace them with new, more nurturing ways of being

25. Prentiss Hemphill, "Healing Justice Is How We Can Sustain Black Lives," *Huffington Post*, February 7, 2017, accessed September 11, 2020, https://www.huffpost.com/entry/healing-justice_b_5 899e8ade4b0c1284f282ffe.

26. Hemphill, "Healing Justice."

in the world.[27] Healing done at the personal level prepares and sustains people to work together to address those interpersonal, institutional, and social practices that cause harm.

The theater ensembles featured in *The Healing Stage* approach healing as a process of self-repair, one that requires the loving care and support of other people. This approach stands in sharp contrast to Western medicine, which understands healing as largely a process of freeing a person from an affliction of the mind or body, one directed by trained professions who learn how to investigate complaints and diagnose and manage treatment. While Western medicine has developed many powerful, life-saving practices, its underlying beliefs about who is human, who deserves (the best or any) care, what health and wellness mean, and the reliability of patients' knowledge (or lack thereof) of themselves make quality healthcare services inaccessible for far too many. In a country that largely believes, as Leah Lakshimi Piepnza-Samarsinha finds, that you are either "sick or well, fixed or broken, and that nobody would want to be in a disabled or sick or mad bodymind," people who are (chronically) "sick . . . mad . . . disabled . . . [or] neurodivergent" are seen as problems to be solved rather than as part of the human continuum.[28] So too are poor, Black, and unruly women labelled as problems, disrespected and denied the care, compassion, and support they need so that they too can flourish.

Within African American folk traditions, healing is a holistic practice that involves the physical body as well as the mind, the soul, the spiritual realm, the past, nature, and other people in an afflicted person's extended social circle. Like faith healing, which Stephanie Mitchem defines as the (rare or selective) cure of an affliction by divine intervention, folk healing emphasizes the power of relationships. Where faith healing relies upon a relationship to the divine or supernatural, folk healing passes down the accumulated wisdom and experience of community members to relieve suffering and restore equilibrium and harmony. Performance plays a critical role in the process as healing work "encompasses word, action, story, ritual, and practice."[29] Folk healers identify the causes of disease/dis-ease and relay critical information about the condition and the steps required to resolve it through story. Healing is predicated upon the creation and the telling or performance of stories. Because conditions can have historic, physical, mental, spiritual, environmental, inter-

27. Many, many thanks to Maya Shewnarain for these insights gained in conversation on January 10, 2022.

28. Leah Lakshimi Piepnza-Samarsinha, "A Not So Brief Personal History of the Healing Justice Movement, 2010–2016," *Mice Magazine*, 2016, accessed September 10, 2020, http://micemagazine.ca/issue-two/not-so-brief-personal-history-healing-justice-movement-2010%E2%80%932016.

29. Stephanie Mitchem, *African American Folk Healing* (New York: New York University Press, 2007), 25–28.

personal, and other root causes, healing is a process that takes time. As a result, where a condition is deep, painful, or feels permanent, healing work need not be immediately directed toward freeing or restoring a person to an external ideal of health or wholeness. Healing might instead mean developing reliable palliative care, locating necessary support systems or equipment, and easing immediate pain or discomfort. Knitting together or bridging a wound that cannot be eliminated is healing if it brings the sufferer greater ease. Healing can also take place in spaces where no obvious visible or felt wound exists. Sometimes a new baby can do this work for families. The baby's arrival can evoke a sense of hope, joy, and completion in spaces where people do not even know they need it. Old injuries can suddenly seem less important. People put aside past conflicts and work together in ways that had previously seemed impossible. Here healing acquires new transformative and affirmative connotations with broad implications for individuals, families, and whole communities. Finally, in addition to its restorative, palliative, and liberatory work, healing can also mean advancing or promoting the well-being, welfare, safety, and prosperity of families, communities, institutions, nations, lands, waters, plants and animals, environments, and much more.

Stage healing stages healing. It establishes the conditions for individual and communal self-repair drawing upon Black expressive cultural practices. The practice stands in stark contrast to the rehabilitative discipline imposed behind bars which Ashley Lucas describes as little more than a three-step process in which the convicted are expected to *reflect* upon their past wrongdoing, *confess,* and then *express remorse.*[30] Day in and day out, the "corrected" (compliant) prisoner is neither nurtured nor cared for, but instead trained to perform these three steps on demand. Mastery of this *rehabilitative script* is essential for both survival behind bars and securing one's future freedom. Imprisoned men and women learn to perform it, or else risk additional detention and punishment until they comply or are rendered insane or dead. Women behind bars know they need more, and in some sites, they have turned to theater to get it.

Stage healing is grounded in real and fictional characters and the play of make-believe, and it is serious work. It is distinct from self-help courses and from individual or group drama therapy led by a licensed clinical practitioner, although its outcomes can also alleviate suffering. The drama clubs featured in *The Healing Stage* offer an invaluable space in which women may reflect on, process, distill, and creatively share their experiences and their wisdom

---

30. Ashley Lucas, "When I Run in My Bare Feet: Music, Writing, and Theater in a North Carolina Women's Prison," *American Music* 31, no. 2 (2013): 135.

so that they and others might see, hear, understand, and grow from what they know. Through their collective work, the women reveal and disrupt old, problematic ways of being in the world and bring to light the roots of human conflicts. They do so because they recognize that if human behavior—performance—is the site of harm, oppression, or even social death, so too can it be "the site of its redress."[31] These practitioners encourage Black women—all women—behind bars to deploy their wit and wisdom to intervene in and address some of the most pressing social problems we face. As these seemingly small moments of antiracist, antisexist, queer-inclusive community accumulate, they can create significant change in the participants' lives and the culture and practice of incarceration.

To do the work, practitioners tap into the wellspring they know of Black expressive cultural practices. *Expressive culture* encompasses the wide range of everyday practices that people enact to constitute, understand, critique, transform, and disseminate social norms and values, including both public and hidden, stated and unstated, codes of behavior. This continuum includes quotidian practices such as preparing food, styling hair, engaging in conversation, and playing sports and as well as behavior that might be more commonly read as rituals or special occasions such as attending a baby shower or going to the theater.

Black expressive cultural practices comprise the quotidian ways in which people of African descent make, break, and remake social values, norms, and practices. While I use the terms *Black* and *African American* interchangeably, I recognize that African American culture is not monolithic and that African Americans are not the only Black people in the world. Moreover, I know that Black expressive cultural practices are not the exclusive property of people of African descent. A quick scan of social media will reveal millions of people the world over singing and dancing to house music despite never having set foot on the Southside of Chicago. Granted, culture is an embodied, performed practice, something that people do. Culture is often imagined as rooted in specific communities, time periods, and spaces, but actually overflows physical, geographic, temporal, political, economic, and social boundaries. Approaching culture in this way as performance disrupts notions of ethnic and racial purity and reframes culture into an ever-changing continuum of learned human behaviors that builds, sustains, disrupts, and transforms communities.

Elite influencers have certainly wielded culture as a hegemonic educational and disciplinary project to force others to behave in ways that are most

---

31. Christen A. Smith, *Afro-Paradise: Blackness, Violence and Performance in Brazil* (Urbana: University of Illinois Press, 2016), 24.

profitable and pleasurable to themselves. As Stuart Hall argues, though, people are not "dopes" or "passive" receptacles, they are always aware and critical of how political, social, and economic elites attempt to structure and manipulate their lives.[32] The forces of domination and subordination arising from racism, misogyny, and heteropatriarchy should not be underestimated. Yet the study of popular culture, specifically the culture of the marginalized and oppressed who constitute the majority of humanity, demonstrates that elites do not have absolute power. Hall has found instead that "there is a continuous and necessarily uneven and unequal struggle by the dominant culture constantly to disorganize and reorganize popular culture."[33]

Harvey Young makes the point that Black people learn "how to be themselves *as black people.*" Families, other community members, events, and institutions teach people from birth how to locate themselves within the social world and how to fulfill prescribed social roles. Over time, as a person masters the script, they forget they are performing, a process akin to learning to ride a bike. The *habitus* or learned patterns and practices of being in the world become second nature. Those practices, inculcated by families and through everyday events, rituals, and ordinary expressive cultural practices, gradually "convey a sense of belonging to a larger community comprised of individuals with similar claims of blackness . . . and similar black experiences."[34] E. Patrick Johnson observes that "arguably ritual is the cornerstone of the performative process through which African Americans come to understand, reinforce, and reflexively critique who they are in the world."[35] In citing "ritual," Johnson alludes not only to faith practices but also to the ritualistic yet humble practices of gesture, speech, joking, attire, dress, eating, movement, dance, gathering, and more that constitute, sustain, reinforce, and animate Black habitus and sociality.

Not all Black expressive practices encourage change for the better. Johnson also observes that "Black performance has the potential of simultaneously forestalling and enabling social change." How many times have Black organizations been derailed by colorism, classism, homophobia, misogyny, ageism, or biases against people with criminal histories? Like any other culture, Black culture can be a site of resistance to oppression on the one hand and an obstacle to change on the other. Even seemingly liberatory practices can

---

32. Stuart Hall, "Notes on Deconstructing 'the Popular,'" in *Stuart Hall: Essential Essays,* ed. David Morley (Durham, NC: Duke University Press, 2018), 352.

33. Hall, "Notes," 354.

34. Harvey Young, *Embodying Black Experience: Stillness, Critical Memory, and the Black Body* (Ann Arbor: University of Michigan Press, 2010), 21.

35. E. Patrick Johnson, "Black Performance Studies: Genealogies, Politics, Futures," in *The Sage Handbook of Performances Studies,* ed. D. Soyini Madison and Judith Hamera (Thousand Oaks, CA: Sage Publications, 2007), 447–49.

harbor requirements to suppress emotions and desires deemed socially inappropriate.[36] Black people are not alone in living with these contradictions. To understand and investigate the most pressing concerns about human life and well-being Black people, like everyone else, turn to the arts, to theater. Theater is one of the chief cultural sites where Black people debate social norms and expectations.

Theatrical performances exist on a continuum of expressive cultural practices. Commonly understood as "special occasions," plays are set aside from the flow of daily life in time and space, but like funerals, graduations, and other special events, they are a regular part of the everyday. Although often dismissed today as elite or taken-for-granted as frivolous entertainment, theatrical performances serve a ritualistic function that brings people together as members of specific cultural, temporal, and geographic communities. Today, the arts operate as one of the primary mediums through which ideas about "race, class, gender, or other dimensions of identity are inculcated, debated and resisted."[37] Human beings use theater to engage in a special kind of knowledge exchange made possible in part by the playful frame of the stage and the proscenium arch that sets the audience apart from the actors and production staff. On stage, performers have permission to act out real-life struggles and make them available for collective analysis, public debate, and action without suffering the same consequences they would endure in "real" life. While the playful frame establishes the parameters of the event and signals to all participants when the play begins and when it ends, like other significant social events, the actual lived experience invites participants to investigate human sociality and community dynamics long after the lights come down. By studying the interplay between special events like theatrical productions and everyday social behaviors, researchers can discern the political struggles at work in a community.

The Healing Stage focuses on theater for incarcerated women to recenter their voices in the struggle over justice, equality, punishment, accountability, and healing. My work specifically responds to E. Patrick Johnson's call to researchers to "go about creating an ethics of black performance studies without policing boundaries, silencing opposing or dissenting voices, while at the same time holding true to a politics of social change and transformation that moves us forward in the liberation of black peoples."[38]

---

36. Johnson, "Black Performance Studies," 447.

37. Oluwakemi M. Balogun and Melissa Graboyes, "Everyday Life in Africa: The Importance of Leisure and Fun," in *Africa Every Day: Fun, Leisure, and Expressive Culture on the Continent,* ed. Oluwakemi M. Balogun, Lisa Gilman, Melissa Graboyes, and Habib Iddrisu (Athens: Ohio University Press, 2019), 4.

38. Johnson, "Black Performance Studies," 461.

METHODOLOGY

I selected Demeter's Daughters, the Big Water Drama Club, the Medea Project in South Africa, and Healing Justice Mamas based on their shared community-engaged theater practices and several additional criteria. These included organizational longevity (each has operated for more than ten years); continuity in women's leadership and staffing; sustained access to the women's correctional facility where they work; emphasis on devising and staging original performances with prisoners; commitment to postincarceration support of participants; and proximity to major metropolitan areas with significant Black populations. Each arts program was founded by a woman and, more than twenty years later, continues to be led by women. Taken together, their work invites us to consider why women are the fastest growing segment of the global prison population. They encourage us to question why prisons have become the solution for managing victim-survivors of racism, sexism, poverty, homo- and transphobia, sexual assault, domestic violence, addiction, mental health diseases and disorders, and homelessness. While these programs affirm that those who have done harm must somehow be held accountable, they also insist that the onus for change cannot be placed solely on the shoulders of the incarcerated. They ask us to participate in a much larger process of both individual and communal growth, a process in which they—we—all engage in stage healing to move human society beyond incarceration. Tapping into Black expressive cultural practices rooted in ritual practice, prison theater programs encourage us to invest in art-making to transform individuals, institutions, culture, and entire societies. Their aim is no less than to constitute the more fair, more just, and more equitable world we all deserve.

Because incarceration carries a heavy stigma, it is necessary to protect the identities of the incarcerated women at the center of the project, so I use pseudonyms to identify all of the people, places, and programs enrolled in the US portion of the project, as mandated by the Institutional Review Board, the administrative body of the US Department of Human Health and Services that protects the welfare, rights, and privacy of human research subjects. Most importantly, the participants in this study and the corrections administrators who allowed me to work in their facilities entrusted me with their stories in part because I guaranteed that I would not reveal who they are. Disclosing their identities could lead to retaliation against the incarcerated women, including the loss of privileges (e.g., time outside of their cells or family visits) and disruptions to valued work and housing assignments. The physical safety and mental health of those involved could be jeopardized and future decisions regarding sentencing, parole, probation, and clemency could be negatively impacted. So too could the theater programs, teachers, corrections officers, and administrators face repercussions such as the loss of status, funding, or work. All of these concerns shaped both my research methods and the writing of the ethnography. As such, no legal names, nicknames, street names, or aliases were utilized, nor were any of the study participants allowed to select their own pseudonyms. I assigned pseudonyms to all of the incarcerated study participants and to the theater programs, prisons, and jails. Pseudonyms are also used to identify all of the directors, teachers, corrections officials, prison and jail staff members, and volunteers.

The one exception to this policy relates to the Medea Project in South Africa, which was permitted to present the women's work in the public sphere. Their performances in Johannesburg and Pretoria were covered extensively by local media, which published the women's names and images in print and online with the permission of South Africa's Department of Correctional Services and of the women themselves. In that case I have decided to disclose the participants' identities in keeping with South African practice, but out of an abundance of caution I refer to the participants only by their first names. News cycles are short and internet archives often unstable, but the stigma of incarceration endures. While this decision cannot altogether preclude negative repercussions, I hope that it might mitigate some of the worst effects.

In place of specific identifiers, I use thick description to immerse readers in the research sites. For those who desire more visuals, a limited archive of images taken during my fieldwork is available on the web page for this book, https://ohiostatepress.org/books/titles/9780814214930.html. As a performance studies scholar and critical performance ethnographer, I write about this work using an expansive notion of text, one that allows me to draw upon the original play scripts and performances as well as everyday Black expressive cultural practices that include gesture, attire, speech, oral histories, storytelling, dance, ritual, song, and faith practices. This rich and varied repertoire of knowledge does not stand in opposition to traditional archival approaches or materials, but serves to complement them as it reveals and interrupts academic disciplinary concerns and customary judicial processes related to evidence, truth, and history. For me, this was the only way to study theater behind bars.

Women are allowed to bring only their bodies to prison. While they may be able to access journals, paper, pens, and now even tablets to connect to the internet, they are rarely able to keep that material, much less to disseminate it beyond the prison walls. What women write is carefully scrutinized, heavily censored, subject to confiscation and destruction at all times, and rarely if ever preserved. Women behind bars as such keep very, very few papers. What the prison system maintains, much less makes public, about them often amounts to little more than an inmate number and a mug shot as well as each woman's race, sex, arrest and conviction record, current status (e.g., prisoner, parolee, probationer, active offender, discharged, escaped, or absconded), and location. These records demonstrate the administrative functioning of the prison as an institution but tell us little about the inner lives of the women themselves. Only by traveling to, participating in, and observing the drama club programs and performances, interviewing participants where allowed, and speaking with program directors and administrators as well as with corrections staff, could I complete this project.

My access varied at each site but in general I participated in rehearsals, workshops, performances, planning meetings, and other formal and informal events staged by my case studies as appropriate. I accompanied program facilitators to the women's correctional facilities where they taught. I was interviewed by the arts program directors in advance, and I underwent some form of volunteer training or visitor orientation at each penal facility. Once allowed into a prison or jail, experiences as a participant/observer—a witness—helped me gain important insights into the context out of which these programs emerge, the specific challenges they faced, and the means by which they addressed obstacles in their paths. Most importantly, I met the women they served.

My research focused on people who were confined to correctional facilities for women, recognizing that departments of correctional services use their own metrics to determine people's sex. I did not conduct research with transwomen confined to corrections facilities for men. With only a few exceptions, all the participants in the project identified themselves to me as cisgender women. One or two participants disclosed that they were transmen, and I have noted their gender identities where I believed it was appropriate. I realize that this approach risks misgendering some of the study participants. I believe it also limits the possibility that additional disciplinary action might be taken against those still behind bars should they be inadvertently identified through my writing.

I use the terms "women," "women behind bars," "incarcerated women," "women prisoners," and "imprisoned women" rather than *convicts, inmates, offenders,* or *perpetrators* to continually evoke the participants' status as people first and their political relationship to the state as gendered subjects secondarily. *Offender, perpetrator, convict, inmate,* and *prisoner* are widely, interchangeably, used by the general public, by imprisoned people, and by officers and prison administrators. As Megan Sweeney writes, however, each word denotes a "different political charge."[39] *Offender* and *perpetrator* con-

---

39. Megan Sweeney, *Reading Is My Window: Books and the Art of Reading in Women's Prisons* (Chapel Hill: University of North Carolina Press, 2010), 271.

note someone who has transgressed a norm or violated a law, not necessarily someone who has been convicted of wrongdoing or sentenced to serve time behind bars. In fact, you also do not have to have broken a law to become an *inmate,* a person confined to a prison, jail, mental hospital, or other institution. The majority of the people in local county jails have not been convicted of any crime, nor have the approximately 22,000 people with mental health diseases or disorders detained involuntarily in American psychiatric hospitals and civic commitment centers each year. *Inmates* differ from *convicts,* people who have been found guilty and convicted of a crime. Conviction, however, does not automatically mean incarceration.

The Prison Policy Institute reported that 2.3 million people were imprisoned in American correctional facilities in 2018, while another 3.7 million people who had broken the law were free on probation, a form of court supervision. The word *prisoner* specifically means a *person deprived of liberty,* which is a key concept in American judicial and penal practices, evoking the image of a person held against their will behind bars. Nina Billone theorizes that the terms *imprisoned* and *incarcerated* highlight the state's act of enclosing a person away from free society. *Imprisoned* and *incarcerated,* she continues, also signify the simultaneous "process of cancellation" that moving a person from a state of citizenship to the status of a prisoner *deprived of liberty* confers.[40]

During my fieldwork, I regularly heard incarcerated women referred to as "ladies" or "females." While I believe corrections staff members and volunteers considered these terms to be a politer way of referring to the women prisoners, I felt that they unavoidably carried derogatory connotations that I prefer not to repeat. "Female" reduces adult women to biology and erases important gender, race, class, and penal disciplinary practices at work in our society, while "ladies" points to (even mocks) the gap between an idealized symbol of upper-class, white femininity and the real-life circumstances of the majority low-income Black women who enrolled in the arts programs I studied. Like Sweeney and Billone, I believe that referring to study participants who were held behind bars as "imprisoned women," "incarcerated women" and "women prisoners" ensures that I "foreground their status as women and denote their physical confinement without conferring on them an existential or fixed identity as criminals."[41]

Fieldwork experiences framed the interviews I conducted later with the program facilitators, with the participants, with women graduates of the programs who remain connected, and with other key interlocutors. Opportunities to attend meetings, support performances produced by the arts program

---

40. Nina Billone, "Performing Civil Death: The Medea Project and Theater for Incarcerated Women," *Text and Performance Quarterly* 29, no. 3 (2009): 263.

41. Sweeney, *Reading,* 271.

directors on the outside, and participate in everyday activities like house parties, pot lucks, public policy briefings, public protests, and other events enriched my understanding. It was never easy.

KEEPIN' STILL AND MINDIN' THINGS

Working—being—in prison or jail was—is—hard, every day and all the time. Carceral facilities are designed to inflict pain and suffering, and on most days being inside felt, to paraphrase one young poet, like an unrelenting "walk in grief."[42] Spaces are cramped by design, dark, and often dingy. The air is stuffy and the walls are high and intimidating. Officers are on edge as are the imprisoned people you meet. You are always working with people for whom this is one of their worst days. The task of conducting research behind bars is further complicated by security concerns that limit when and where you can move, with whom you can you speak, the questions you can ask, and what you can bring with you (e.g., no cameras, phones, or video or tape recorders).

Research in carceral settings is also ghosted by the abuses of previous investigators. Imprisoned people have long been the preferred subjects of researchers because the conditions of confinement make it easier to dictate and control scientific variables. They continue to be subjected to gross exploitation at the hands of officers, state governments, and corporations who use their labor to cover their budgets and in some cases to bolster their profits.[43] In the 1970s, US lawmakers began passing legislation that curtailed the use of imprisoned people for experiments and implemented more rigorous standards to prevent abuse and exploitation behind bars. I underwent rigorous IRB training and drew upon my lived experiences as an actor, playwright, and teaching artist to serve as a participant/observer at each case study site. I accompanied the Healing Justice Mamas program facilitators to their sites to take weekly classes. I repeated this practice with Demeter's Daughters as well, but as their workshop moved toward performance, I remained to assist in the scripting and staging of their performance. In South Africa with the Medea Project, I served as the assistant production coordinator, working long hours for weeks at a time in the women's prison and making multiple trips to Johannesburg when in 2012 the Department of Correctional Services allowed the production to move to Pretoria for public performances. Finally, with the Big

---

42. Anonymous teenage poet, "Walk in the Day," Living Stage Theater Company, Washington, DC, unpublished manuscript.

43. Allen Hornblum, *Acres of Skin: Human Experiments at Holmesburg Prison: A True Story of Abuse and Exploitation in the Name of Medical Science* (New York: Routledge, 1998).

Water Drama Club I focused primarily on its history and development, as the warden prohibited me from access to all aspects of the program except the one and only performance of *Beauty Coming 'n Going*.

To navigate the ever-changing and often unpredictable demands of corrections officers, I found myself relying heavily upon my training in community-engaged theater, particularly in improvisation. The life-changing years (1999–2001) during which I worked as an actor and teaching artist at the Living Stage Theater in Washington, DC, were invaluable to my approach. Founded in 1966 by Robert Alexander, and then under the artistic direction of long-time company member Oran Sandel, Living Stage utilized a critical method of theater-making in which improvisation, in particular the practice of spontaneous, collaborative composition, was used to investigate complex social problems. Our ensemble of four to six actors plus a musician trained in the technique daily, running through exercises developed by Alexander, Sandel, Viola Spolin, Augusto Boal, and Keith Johnstone as well as past and present members of the Living Stage ensemble. Assistant director Tanisha Christie called the company a "laboratory for life" because it gave ensemble members and workshop participants alike the freedom to "play people who are not ourselves and do things that we ourselves have not done."[44]

For communities that never saw themselves, their histories, their strengths, or their dreams on stage, the opportunity to shape the outcome of a character's life by suggesting action or dialogue in an improvised scene, or by taking over a role, was exhilarating.[45] Longtime company member Rebecca Rice, an African American theater artist, described Living Stage's work as a process of "dissolving the borders that define us" so that we might "come together as equals and dream the future."[46] There I learned deep listening and collaboration skills, mindfulness, nonjudgmental witnessing, critical generosity and jazz, and how to be flexible in the moment to meet shifting needs while fulfilling stated goals. I learned how to pay attention by improvising scenes and how to play in the moment with people aged 3 to 103, from preschoolers to senior citizens, elementary and high school students, kids in foster care and people with developmental disabilities.

Workshops with women enrolled in a group called Crossing the River, which provided comprehensive drug and alcohol treatment to mothers, most directly prepared me for this project. Sitting in Crossing the River circles, I

---

44. Quoted in "Why Walk . . . When You Can Fly!," The Living Stage Documentary, 1999, https://www.youtube.com/watch?v=OpgwtC6rdUk.

45. Susan C. Haedicke, "The Challenge of Participation," in *Audience Participation: Essays on Inclusion in Performance*, ed. Susan Kattwinkel (Westport, CT: Praeger, 2003), 71–87.

46. Quoted in "Why Walk . . . When You Can Fly!"

quickly realized that, but for a few incidents, opportunities, and decisions, any one of us could have been sitting in another woman's place. Those Black women had some stories to tell! Working with them confirmed for me that cultivating the ability to narrate one's life and tell your own stories is essential for healing and liberation. Most importantly for this research, Living Stage taught me to hear and respect my own interiority, "the inner reserve of thoughts, feelings, desires, fears, ambitions that shape a human self" that Kevin Quashie calls *the quiet,* that untouchable center of the mind/body/spirit that operates as a "stay against the social world."[47] *The quiet* is a metaphor for an interior space where one can be unconcerned with the public, with racial subjectivity, or any other external social expectations. These skills that foster listening, paying attention, collaborative play, and respect for *the quiet* helped me navigate correctional settings.

Into the work, I brought with me the eyes and ears of an actor and the heart of a mover and improviser. My background helped me cultivate trust and stand in close proximity to the free and incarcerated artists working behind bars to witness their work. It also fortified within me a willingness and readiness to act, and a sense of *response-ability,* which Kelly Oliver defines as both the *ability to respond* and the *sense of obligation or duty to act.*[48] As a critical ethnographer working as a dialogic or coperformative witness, I ought not only to do what my interlocutors were doing in the drama workshops and other field sites, but to do so with a view to understanding "the materiality of their struggles and the consequences."[49] With such proximity comes vulnerability, which, Bryant Keith Alexander writes, can "democratize . . . human sociality by closing the gaps between the known and the unknown, between self and others, and between the borders and boundaries of differently lived experiences."[50] My fieldwork began from a place of ethical responsibility. As D. Soyini Madison explains, critical ethnographers approach research with "a compelling sense of duty and commitment based on the principles of human freedom and wellbeing." They understand that, in partnership with the interlocutors at their field sites, they can put their ethnographic research to use to "address processes of unfairness or injustice within a particular lived domain." I felt I had an ethical responsibility first to "make a contribution towards changing those conditions towards greater freedom and equity" by support-

47. Kevin E. Quashie, *The Sovereignty of Quiet: Beyond Resistance in Black Culture* (New Brunswick, NJ: Rutgers University Press, 2012), 21.

48. Kelly Oliver qtd. in Della Pollock, *Remembering: Oral History Performance* (New York: Palgrave MacMillan, 2005), 4.

49. D. Soyini Madison, "Co-Performative Witnessing," *Cultural Studies* 21, no. 6 (2007): 829.

50. Bryant K. Alexander, "Performance Ethnography: The Reenacting and Inciting of Culture," in *The Sage Handbook of Qualitative Research,* ed. Norman Denzin and Yolanda S. Lincoln, 3rd ed. (Thousand Oaks, CA: Sage Publications, 2005), 411–41.

ing the work of the teaching artists and the incarcerated participants in the classroom.[51] Because I did not know how jails and prisons operated, I asked the teaching artists whom I accompanied to teach me how to behave and how to get around. Following procedures was essential to the success of my project, and demonstrating a willingness to comply with corrections regulations helped me gain and maintain access. I also knew that maintaining access would require flexibility. When obstacles, such as a delay at the front security gate preventing class from starting on time, or the sudden cancellation of a workshop in the context of an unexplained lockdown occurred, I persisted because I knew how life-affirming the work could be. When corrections officers scoffed, "Drama? Why do they need drama?" my improv training prepared me to meet their scorn with a playful retort, "What? You don't have any drama in here??? Pleeeeease. You got drama. I'm just trying to direct it." Funny quips like that usually caught them off guard, earning me a laugh and some respect. Working behind bars is dreary work all day, every day, including for those in uniform. Week to week, I tried to remember the officers' names, ask how they were doing, and talk sports or the weather—anything to push past the darkness that tempered every surface no matter how hard staff worked to "brighten" their surroundings. Once inside a workshop, I was comfortable doing the exercises with the incarcerated women, writing and improvising, singing or moving, and sharing my stories, but took care not to be the focus of attention or take up too much space. I was present, but approached fieldwork in the close quarters of a prison workshop as a practice of *keepin' still and mindin' things,* a model that I borrowed from one of the first African American women to successfully sue for her freedom, Elizabeth "Mum Bett" Freeman.

In 1780 "Mum Bett" Freeman identified a path to freedom for herself and others using knowledge she acquired in her position as an enslaved and exploited laborer on the margins of white slave-holding society. The widow of a Revolutionary War soldier, enslaved from birth, she played the role of a diligent and devoted servant, which was expected of her in western Massachusetts. Local leaders met in the home of her enslaver to debate declaring independence from the British and to prepare to go to war. Later, they returned to debate the contents of the Massachusetts state constitution, which declared "all men are born free and equal." As Freeman did her job, cooking, cleaning, and waiting upon them, she paid attention to their conversations. When the opportunity arose to sue for her own freedom, she seized it and successfully used what she had overheard to argue that she and other enslaved Black people had a "legal and constitutional right" to freedom. In 1781, Freeman

---

51. D. Soyini Madison, *Critical Ethnography: Method, Ethics, and Performance,* 3rd ed. (Thousand Oaks, CA: Sage Publications, 2019), 4.

became "the first New World African woman to win her freedom through the courts." When asked how she knew so much about the rights granted US citizens, Freeman replied that she learned by "keepin' still and mindin' things."[52]

I approached the study of theater for incarcerated women with knowledge of and an enthusiasm for Black women's culture, including a deep appreciation for how African American women have leveraged their marginalized position in American society to gain valuable knowledge, often by "keepin' still and mindin' things." As one of the few witnesses to this work who was able to crisscross the boundaries of correctional facilities with relative ease, I was asked by the program facilitators and incarcerated artists I worked with to take responsibility for what I saw and for what I learned as well as what they taught me. At various points throughout the ten-year process required for me to write this book, I shared my writings with the program facilitators, and where possible with some of the incarcerated women, to solicit their feedback. Their insights have been invaluable. Any oversights or misrepresentations are mine.

I envision *The Healing Stage* contributing to ongoing discourses about and debates over the criminal legal system, especially regarding the treatment of women. I hope it will expand public knowledge and understanding of the conditions of confinement as well as the factors that contribute to women's criminalization, their wrongdoing, and their incarcerations. This book will reveal how incarcerated artists use performance as a healing practice to encourage self-repair and broader societal change. Because I locate the theater and performance practices I witnessed within Africanist epistemologies, I hope readers will understand that incarcerated women's art is not a static object but a doing, a verb, an action that makes something occur in the world by shifting reality now and for the future.[53] In carceral settings around the country, incarcerated women artists are doing the work of self-repair and of institutional, social, and societal transformation. Their lives depend upon it.

THE ACTS

I frame my ethnographic chapters with chapter 1, "She Was No Rosa Parks: A Black Women's History of Mass Incarceration in the United States." With it, I

52. A. Yemisi Jimoh and Francoise N. Hamlin, *These Truly Are the Brave: An Anthology of African American Writings on War and Citizenship* (Gainesville: University Press of Florida, 2015), 29–30. See also Xiomara Santamarina, "Elizabeth Freeman," in *African American Lives*, ed. Henry Louis Gates Jr. and Evelyn Brooks Higganbotham (Oxford: Oxford University Press, 2004), 317.

53. Rowland Abiodun, "Ase: Verbalizing and Visualizing Creative Power through Art," *Journal of Religion in Africa* 24, no. 4 (1994): 309–22.

look back to the grounding precepts of white supremacy and Black women's inferiority that anchored the American colonial system and that continue to serve as the basis for the criminal legal system. This gendered history of racialized policing and incarceration argues that the US judicial system is fundamentally designed to control and contain Black women under the guise of policing and redressing crime.

Chapter 2, "How to Stage Healing," recounts how Black women performing artists have redressed gender-based, racialized violence against African American women in the twentieth century, putting antilynching plays and imprisoned women's blues from the 1930s and 1940s in conversation with select post-1970 visual and theatrical pieces. The chapter argues for the importance of two alternative catalysts for present-day prison-based theater programs, the trial of political prisoner Angela Y. Davis in 1972 and the 1975 prosecution of Joan Little, a young rape survivor who killed the corrections officer who attacked her. The work that visual artist Faith Ringgold at the Women's House of Detention in New York undertook to support Davis and the acapella musical group Sweet Honey in the Rock's advocacy on behalf of Little affirmed the value of Black lives and Black culture in an era when mass incarceration was just beginning to build its baleful momentum. Their projects point to how Black women at the end of the Civil Rights Movement and the dawn of mass incarceration articulated visions of a more fair, more just, and more equitable future. The chapter unearths powerful examples of Black women artists/activists who devise and deploy creative work to express their dissent from the repressive norms upheld by America's criminal legal system.

Chapter 3, "Bad Bad Bad Bad Bad Bad Woman: Making Theater in a Midwestern Jail," introduces readers to my first case study and to stage healing as a process of self-repair. It recounts key moments from the eighteen months of study I conducted at the Midwestern jail with Demeter's Daughters where opportunities to joke, write, and share their work forged sisterly bonds among the participants. I argue that sisterly support was vital to the women's well-being as individuals because it enabled them to name what they had experienced and issue through their final performance a poignant, unmistakable, demand for radical structural change.

Chapter 4, "The Pink Dress," offers an example of how incarcerated women use performance to stage healing to ignite institutional change. In 2010, Big Water women's prison was assigned a new warden, who imposed "the pink dress policy." Any Black lesbian, bi-, trans-, queer or, gender-nonconforming person who wore their uniform in "too masculine" a fashion was punished, stripped, and forced to wear the pink dress. In response, the Big Water Drama Club used a once-a-year opportunity to present an original play that challenged the "pink dress" policy by attacking the anti-Black, homophobic logic that underlay it. The chapter demonstrates how incarcerated women's creative activism can stage healing to improve the quality of life for all people behind bars.

Chapter 5, "Bring Me My Machine Gun: The Medea Project in South Africa," centers on an artistic collaboration between the San Francisco–based Medea Project: Theater for Incarcerated Women and an ensemble of women confined in Johannesburg, South Africa, at the Sun City prison from 2009 to 2012. In 2012, their show, *Serious Fun at Sun City,* staged healing on a cultural scale with performances at the State Theater in Pretoria. I argue that by subverting national expectations of appropriate prisoner behavior and redeploying indigenous African expressive cultural practices the ensemble exposed the harmful, masculinist, cultural practices that devalued and criminalized women. Through monologue, song, and dance, they further issued a collective warning to the country about what could happen should the needs of women continue to go unaddressed.

Chapter 6, "It Has Been My Healing to Tell the Dirty Truth," returns to the US as its setting and follows the Healing Justice Mamas as they connect their jail arts program to advocacy for policy changes at the national level to mitigate state violence using poetry and personal narrative performances. Their artistic/activist practice reminds us that unless and until the most vulnerable among us are protected, none of us is truly safe, well, or free.

Finally, with "Beyond Incarceration," the conclusion to *The Healing Stage,* I reiterate the importance of attending to the needs of women in the era of mass incarceration and beyond, arguing that unless and until their experiences and their wisdom are included in discourses about safety, accountability, and justice, we will continue to waste valuable time, resources, and human lives merely to build a safer world for the most privileged. Incarcerated women artists are not waiting for that day to come. They are doing the work and making it happen now.

Discourses about crime and justice rarely incorporate the perspectives of survivors behind bars, but contemporary public policies designed without their input are doing little to keep Black women safe. The arts may not seem like an obvious source of answers to the pressing problems that women behind bars identify. Yet incarcerated Black women have embraced the arts— poetry, theater, dance—to tell their stories. In small collectives, they share their work and together name the violence they have endured as well as the harm they themselves have done, with the long-term goal of finding new ways to reduce harm and protect people. While the theater cannot single-handedly transform systems of oppression or force anyone to change, the arts programs that operate behind bars that I showcase in this book bring women together to examine our human dilemmas, to test our approaches, and to imagine new possibilities. The exchange of artistic expression can change people's perspectives and their hearts, and with these changes can come changes in individual behavior, in relationships, and in families, and with them changes in public policy, communities, and more.

I intend this book to contribute to ongoing discourses about crime, justice, healing, decarceration, and prison abolition. The theater programs for incarcerated women at the center of this study are committed to ending the silences surrounding women's lives and to building a better future. Some five decades after the Combahee River Collective issued its call for radical action to protect the lives of Black women, these programs and others like them are committed to creating practices and institutions that serve and protect those in need. They recognize that all of our fates are linked and that when Black women are safe, we all may be.[54]

---

54. The Combahee River Collective issued "The Combahee River Collective Statement" in April 1977; see Keeanga-Yamahtta Taylor, ed. *How We Get Free: Black Feminism and the Combahee River Collective* (Chicago: Haymarket Books, 2017).

CHAPTER 1

"She Was No Rosa Parks"

A Black Women's History of Mass Incarceration in the United States

On August 27, 1974, a rape and a homicide occurred at the Beaufort County Jail in Washington, North Carolina, events that would galvanize a national movement to end sexual violence against Black women and affirm their right to bodily integrity. Evidence of the killing was readily apparent. A sixty-two-year-old white corrections officer, Clarence Alligood, was found dead at daybreak, lying—pants down, half naked—in a pool of his own blood. Clenched in Alligood's right hand was the ice pick he normally kept in his desk. It had been used to kill him in the cell of the jail's only imprisoned woman, Joan (pronounced "Jo Ann") Little. A discarded bra and purple nightgown lay near the body, but Little, a petite twenty-year-old African American woman and first-time offender, was nowhere to be found.[1]

Born and raised in Washington, a North Carolina coastal town of fewer than nine thousand residents on the banks of the Pamlico River, Little had been convicted and sentenced to an exorbitant seven-to-ten-year bid for breaking into and stealing items from local trailer homes. It was her first conviction but not her first tangle with the law. The child of a blended family, Little had a history of running away and truancy as a teenager and had spent

---

1. Danielle L. McGuire, "Joan Little and the Triumph of Testimony," in *Freedom Rights: New Perspectives on the Civil Rights Movement*, ed. Danielle L. McGuire and John Dittmer (Louisville: University of Kentucky Press, 2011), 191; see also Angela Davis, "Joan Little: The Dialects of Rape," *Ms. Magazine* (June 1975), 74–77, 106–8.

time in the Dobbs Training School, a juvenile detention facility. By the time she was nineteen years old, she had dropped out of high school and struggled to find work. In the months leading up to her burglary conviction, she had been accused of shoplifting several times, but all the associated charges were dismissed for lack of evidence. The local rumor mill suggested that she was involved with an African American man twice her age who owned a local Black tavern. He allegedly was the architect of a burglary and prostitution ring. Folks in Washington thought Little was trouble and her unsavory reputation immediately made her the prime murder suspect—that, and the fact that she had run, taking Alligood's keys and some clothes she found in the jail with her. The state charged Little with murder, launched a manhunt, and invoked an antebellum fugitive slave law that authorized North Carolina police and civilians to shoot and kill her on sight.[2]

When she reemerged after nearly a week in hiding, Little admitted to killing Alligood although she knew she faced the death penalty if convicted. In statements to her attorneys and to the police she also charged Alligood with rape, revealing that, in the months leading up to his death, he and other Beaufort County jailers targeted her in a steady and unrelenting campaign of sexual harassment. Her complaints about their abuse went unanswered, and she realized no one would help her. When Alligood entered her cell with the ice pick to rape her, she fought back.

Little's testimony galvanized a broad coalition of civil rights, Black Power, women's rights, antirape, and prisoners' rights advocates to free her and set a new legal precedent. Their movement anthem, "Joan Little," penned by former Civil Rights Freedom Rider Bernice Johnson Reagon and sung acapella by Sweet Honey in the Rock, educated listeners about the case and attacked prevailing discourses depicting Black women as criminals in an effort to bridge the gap between this young woman and the rest of society. Its rousing refrain, "Joan is you / Joan is me / Our prison is the whole society," reframed and rehumanized her, building empathy in listeners as it urged them to act on her behalf.[3] These lyrics communicated that freeing Little meant more than obtaining an acquittal. The entire criminal legal system had to be held accountable. With Little's case, coalition partners sought to affirm for the first time in US history that Black women had the right to bodily integrity and self-defense, rights that included the use of deadly force against a white man

---

2. Christina Greene, "'She Ain't No Rosa Parks': The Joan Little Rape-Murder Case and Jim Crow Justice in the Post-Civil Rights South," *Journal of African American History* 100, no. 3 (2015): 428.

3. Bernice Johnson Reagon and Sweet Honey in the Rock, *We Who Believe in Freedom: Sweet Honey in the Rock . . . Still On the Journey* (New York: Anchor Books, 1993), 30–31.

in uniform. The effort would prove an uphill battle. In the minds of many in Washington and across the country, Little was undeserving of their support. As they said, "She was no Rosa Parks."[4]

Washingtonians contrasted Little's behavior with that of Rosa Parks, at the time the embodiment of respectable Black womanhood and nonviolent civil disobedience, to make a point. By the 1970s, Parks, a middle-class Black woman known for her work as a seamstress and an organizer with deep ties to the Black church, was widely revered for her carefully choreographed resistance to unjust Alabama transportation laws some twenty years earlier. Parks and women like her deserved protection.[5] In contrast, Little was dangerously unbound by social conventions. Black and white North Carolinians called her "loose" and a common criminal, one who had disrespected and done harm to the Black community long before she slew Alligood. They discounted the rape and sided with the prosecution, which argued that a Black woman like Little would have lured Alligood into her cell with promises of sex and then killed him so she could escape. So widespread was the presumption of her predatory, licentious sexuality that the judge assigned to the case openly questioned whether Little *or any Black woman* could be raped.[6]

In the decades since Little's acquittal, despite the groundbreaking precedent set by her case, the number of Black women behind bars has grown astronomically.[7] In this chapter, I recount a brief history of the policing and incarceration of Black women in the United States as an institutionalized practice of racialized, gender-based violence, one designed to enforce white, capitalist, heteropatriarchal norms and compel Black women's submission. Understanding that the performance of policing and incarceration is always influenced by the counteractions of those who resist violation, drawing their own moral codes and standards of right behavior, I chronicle how Black women have responded to efforts to define them as criminals. This includes explaining how Black women have fought the forces of control and punishment that have sought to dictate their value and the trajectories of their lives. I argue that when criminalized Black women refuse to conform to debasing

---

4. Greene, "She Ain't," 428–47.

5. Parks was chosen for this role over other African American women and girls who also protested prejudicial treatment on Montgomery buses. The most well-known, Claudette Colvin, was passed over because she was a pregnant and unwed teen at the time of her arrest. Local Black leaders felt her age, pregnancy, and social standing would undermine the effectiveness of their campaign. See Daina Ramey Berry and Kali Nicole Gross, *A Black Women's History of the United States* (Boston: Beacon Press, 2020), 163–64.

6. McGuire, "Joan Little," 212.

7. The efforts of local and national activists resulted in Little's surprising acquittal but not her release. She was forced to serve out the remainder of her sentence for shoplifting at a North Carolina women's prison, the facility she should have been sent to after her conviction.

social norms they reveal the scripts of domination used to coerce their subjection. In the US, such scripts are designed to create a convict social class whose existence justifies the violence deployed against them.

Investigating criminalized African American women's acts of resistance large and small broadens and deepens our understanding of the practices of hegemony and justice in the United States. It reveals how state and interpersonal violence cohere and mutually reinforce each other to create a convict class always already raced as Black, gendered as women, and deemed sexually deviant. Further, it demonstrates how society wields the justice system to force Black women to accept their degraded status or else pay a steep price. Most importantly, in this chapter I describe how many have used performance to assert the value of their own lives and to create spaces where they can form and cultivate their own families and communities, and think, rest, heal, and dream about the future.

The forces responsible for Black women's incarceration remain inextricably tied to many overlapping forces that extend beyond them. It is impossible to understand Black women's prison experiences without discussing the interlocking matrices of slavery, capitalism, and racial violence. I am therefore less concerned about chronological or taxonomic neatness than about relaying key moments that contextualize the current crisis and provide radically new ways to (re)read the hegemonic state-sponsored narratives about incarcerated Black women's experiences.

THE SITUATION

Very few people in the 1970s would have predicted that the United States would embrace mass incarceration. When Joan Little was put on trial, there were fewer than 6,000 women imprisoned in state and federal institutions. In many rural prisons and jails, on any given night there were no women at all.[8] Yet, by 2008, when this study began, 7.3 million people were under some

8. The US Department of Justice Bureau of Justice Statistics (BJS) reports that, when its survey was conducted in 1970, there were 357,292 people behind bars. That includes 160,863 in jails, 176,391 in state prisons, and 20,038 in federal prisons. See US Department of Justice, Bureau of Justice Statistics, *Historical Corrections Statistics in the United States, 1850–1984* (Rockville, MD: Westat Inc., 1986), Table 4-4: "Place of Incarceration of Persons Reported Present on a Given Day During the Year," 79; "Prison Population Growth: Rate (per 100,000 resident population) of Sentenced Prisoners under Jurisdiction of State and Federal Correctional Authorities on December 31, by Sex, 1925–2012," Table 6.28.2012, *Sourcebook of Criminal Justice Statistics,* University of Albany, 2013, https://www.albany.edu/sourcebook/tost_6.html#6_a. These data are compiled from US Department of Justice, Bureau of Justice Statistics, *Prisoners in 1925–81,* Bulletin NCJ-8586, (Washington DC: Bureau of Justice Statistics, 1982); US Department of Justice, Bureau of Justice Statistics, *Prisoners in 1998,* Bulletin

form of correctional supervision, whether that involved probation, parole, or time behind bars.[9] Of the 2.1 million adults incarcerated in the United States in 2008, 207,700 were women (9.89%).[10] At just under 10 percent of the total incarcerated population, these numbers may not seem significant today, but they represented a sea change, one that resulted from changes in laws, in policing, and in sentencing that mandated more time behind bars for those crimes that women were mostly likely to commit.

When the experiences of Black women are analyzed specifically, however, the injustices of the system become more apparent. Fewer Black women than Black men are behind bars, so they are often left out of discourses and research about policing and incarceration. Yet according to the Department of Justice, by 2020, African American women were incarcerated at almost twice the rate of white women. Low-income women like Joan Little were incarcerated more than any other group. Most often, they were arrested, tried and convicted for behavior undertaken to survive poverty and other forms of oppression; such behavior included shoplifting, writing bad checks, sex work, and illicit drug use related to untreated trauma and mental health diseases or disorders. Sentencing guidelines introduced in the context of the War on Drugs in the 1980s and '90s mandated that they serve more time than ever before. As a result, between 2008 and 2020 the number of women serving life sentences without parole (LWOP) increased 43 percent. This increase occurred during a time when the overall crime rate was in decline and there was a steep drop in the number of incarcerated men. For some forty years women have comprised one of the fastest growing segments of the US adult prison population.

How did we get here?

NCJ 175687 (Washington DC: US Department of Justice, 1999); US Department of Justice, Bureau of Justice Statistics, *Prisoners in 2000*, Bulletin NCJ 188207 (Washington, DC: US Department of Justice, 2001); US Department of Justice, Bureau of Justice Statistics, *Prisoners in 2012—Advance Counts*, Bulletin NCJ 242467 (Washington, DC: US Department of Justice 2013); US Department of Justice, Bureau of Justice Statistics, *Correctional Populations in the United States, 1994*, NCJ-160091 (Washington, DC: Bureau of Justice Statistics, 1996); US Department of Justice, Bureau of Justice Statistics, *Correctional Populations in the United States, 1997*, NCJ 177613 (Washington, DC: Bureau of Justice Statistics, 2000).

9. Heather West and William J. Sabol, *Prison Inmates at Midyear—Statistical Table, 2008* (Washington, DC: Bureau of Justice Statistics, 2009).

10. At year-end 2007, an additional 987,400 women or so were on probation and another 98,900 were on parole; see Lauren E. Glaze and Thomas P. Bonczar, *Probation and Parole in the United States, 2007—Statistical Tables* (Washington, DC: Bureau of Justice Statistics, 2008).

COLONIAL PRECEPTS OF RACE AND LAW

The roots of the contemporary US prison system lie in the colonial era. European society and its systems of governance rested upon the presumption of a divinely inspired, natural order. English, French, Dutch, Spanish, and Portuguese colonists may have disagreed about the exact nature of God's law and struggled to communicate the relationship between obedience and sin, will, forgiveness and grace. However, their collective worldview maintained a purposive, divinely ordered universe in which elite European men were the pinnacle of the natural order. Cedric Robinson writes, "the measure of mankind was the European," for "Europe was God's world, the focus of divine attention; the rest of mankind belonged for the moment to Satan."[11] The bonds that they forged through their shared relationship to this divine authority were the basis of the ethical relationships between and among European colonists. Sylvia Wynter writes that these communities or "universes of obligation" proscribed colonists' behavior toward both those within their circles and those without. Those within the circle understood that they had "reciprocal obligations to protect each other" because of their relationships to the same divinity. Those who did not follow the same faith, the dominant group cast aside as "strangers" who could be abused and exploited.[12] This sense of community enabled Europeans to present a united front when it came to stealing indigenous Americans' land and enslaving millions of Africans despite otherwise competing political and economic interests.

European fantasies about Africans and indigenous Americans cast them as primitive and dangerous, even demonic, creatures put on Earth for whites to dominate. George Yancy found that "the normative construction of the Black body as evil had already begun as early as the fifth century in the European Christian church" and was widely accepted by the 1500s when European colonists begin to disembark on the shores of North America.[13] Beliefs in race, in Blackness as a sign of sin, and in white superiority formed the basis of colonial culture and the bedrock of their legal codes. These concepts of race and of Black inferiority and white supremacy evolved into powerful legal precepts, general rules meant to guide and regulate American colonists' thoughts and

11. Cedric J. Robinson, *Black Marxism: The Making of the Black Radical Tradition,* 2nd ed. (Chapel Hill: University of North Carolina Press, 2000), 86, 99.

12. Sylvia Wynter, "'No Humans Involved:' An Open Letter to My Colleagues," *Forum N.H.I. Knowledge for the 21st Century* 1, no. 1 (1994): 44–45.

13. George Yancy, *Black Bodies, White Gazes: The Continuing Significance of Race in America,* 2nd ed. Kindle Edition (Lantham; London: Rowman & Littlefield Publishers, 2017), loc. 477.

behavior.[14] In the absence of standing police forces and courts in the new territories, elite white men were expected to enforce social codes, arbitrate disputes, and mete out justice. Over time, through repetition in law, media, commerce, religion, and other areas of everyday life, the precepts became naturalized and were adopted as common knowledge and social custom.

To establish and maintain this racial and patriarchal hierarchy, British colonists, whose legal system later became the basis of the US legal code, instituted one set of laws for whites and another—the Slave Codes—for Africans and indigenous Americans. Virginia's General Assembly passed the first set in 1705, and it soon became a model for other territories. It rendered African people, including all children born to an enslaved woman, into white property—slaves—for life and authorized enslavers to discipline and control them in any way they saw fit. Built upon the 1669 Casual Killing Act issued by the English monarchy, the Slave Codes affirmed that should an enslaved African resist "correction" and die, no felony charges would be brought against the killers. The political and economic elites responsible for writing and enforcing the Slave Codes assumed that no white man (or woman for that matter) would purposefully destroy their enslaved property. Africans were too valuable. The wealth of the colonies and later the US was built on the backs of millions of enslaved men, women, and children. By 1860, on the eve of the Civil War, "80 percent of the nation's gross national product was tied to slavery."[15]

Under this system, should an enslaved African be killed as a result of excessive discipline, the law treated the death as if it had never happened. This decision to immunize white people made perfect sense. If the law had held white persons responsible for killing Africans, it would have conferred upon Black people a privilege whites hoped to reserve for themselves. In the Black/white, master/slave binary, for white life to be valued, to be innocent and to require protection and safeguarding, Black life had to be disposable.[16] Outside of the master/slave relationship, Africans could have no intrinsic value. African personhood threatened and undermined the logic of the slavocracy. Not only could Africans have no value except as enslaved property, they could have no ownership over anything, including themselves. They could not have agency or selves, much less selves worth defending.

---

14. A. Leon Higginbotham Jr., *In the Matter of Color: Race and the American Legal Process*, 4th ed. (Oxford: Oxford University Press, 1980), 20–25.

15. Carol Anderson, *White Rage: The Unspoken Truth of Our Racial Divide* (New York: Bloomsbury Publishing, 2017), 7.

16. Robert Beverley, *The History and Present State of Virginia, 1705*, ed. Louis B. Wright (Chapel Hill: University of North Carolina Press, published for the Institute of Early American History and Culture, Williamsburg, VA, 1947), book 4, chapter 10: 271–74; accessed September 24, 2020, http://nationalhumanitiescenter.org/pds/amerbegin/power/text8/BeverlyServSlaves.pdf.

To enforce the racist hierarchy, the Slave Codes outlined a code of conduct and series of punishments that applied only to Blacks. The codes prohibited Africans from owning property of any kind and from arming themselves. It prohibited them from leaving their enslavers' property without written permission and set strict curfews to further limit their movement. It stated that conversion and baptism into Christianity would not free Africans from perpetual servitude, and it prevented them seeking protection under the law by bringing suits or testifying against whites. Concerned about the possibility of slave insurrections, the colonies outlawed gatherings of more than a half dozen enslaved people without a white person present and condemned those who broke the law to the lash.[17] Even simple acts such as learning to read or consuming discarded scraps of food were deemed criminal and met with torture and deprivation. To prevent these and other actions, the colonies decreed that enslaved men and women could be whipped for offending or defying a white's sense of propriety. Black women could be and were punished for failing to give way on the streets, raising their voices, laughing too loudly, looking a white person in the eye, wearing too fine apparel, or for simply having a dog without permission. Mississippi deemed Black talk that might in any way promote discontent or insubordination punishable with years of hard labor or death. Louisiana imposed the death penalty on Black people who struck a white person with only one exception—defense of an enslaver or an enslaver's property.[18] Colonists envisioned slavery as a totalizing institution, and the Slave Codes were designed to ensnare African Americans in its inescapable noose. Free and enslaved people were expected to uphold the system. This included the small population of free Black people in the colonies. For them, the punishment for defiance was slavery.

White Americans relied upon slavery to regulate, punish, and exploit Black laborers but used the local jail system as a backstop to manage unruly and disobedient Black people outside of the system. Hastily organized slave patrols and citizen militias patrolled territories to keep order and hunt runaways. When caught, they would lock Black prisoners in a local jail or in holding cells in a nearby home, bar, or inn until they could be collected, punished, or sold.[19] There they encountered people awaiting trial, debtors, the indigent, and people who engaged in lewd or disorderly conduct such as public intoxi-

---

17. *Extracts from the American Slave Code* (Philadelphia: Philadelphia Female Anti-Slavery Society, 1820): 1–3, https://www.loc.gov/item/12030696/.

18. Dwight Conquergood, "Lethal Theatre: Performance, Punishment, and the Death Penalty," *Theatre Journal* 54, no. 3 (2002): 343.

19. Mary Bosworth, *Explaining U.S. Imprisonment* (Thousand Oaks, CA: Sage Publications, 2009), 24.

cation and sex work or who were suffering from mental health diseases or disorders. Law enforcers used jails to confine enslaved people who disobeyed or defied white orders as well as runaways and those awaiting sale until their owners dealt with them.

PERFORMING JUSTICE AND MERCY

These examples demonstrate that justice then, as now, is a powerful and elusive idea, not a fixed or stable object. As Dwight Conquergood reminds us, justice is "a spirit that commands tremendous faith, power, and huge investments both economic and emotional," but which "lives only in performance" and "can be seen only when it is acted out." Justice is a performative, an idea that has meaning and effect only in "the doing." [20] Laws do not just exist, and people do not obey them simply because they are there. Public rituals are required to bestow authority upon law enforcers to enact laws and to make them enforceable.

Understanding crime through the Judeo-Christian framework of sin, to mete out justice colonists erected "theaters of mercy," public sites where community members could gather around a pillory, dunking chair, whipping post, or gallows to witness and participate in the ritual of disciplining the accused. [21] These choreographed spectacles compounded the physical pain and suffering of the accused with the additional weight of public shaming to help them repent and thus cleanse the larger community of sin. Because these public punishments were also religious rituals, they were staged not only to punish wrongdoing but also to affirm the authority of the monarchy. They consolidated power in the hands of local white male political and religious leaders, the monarchy's agents, and enforced a racial and a gendered hierarchy in the New World.

In one of the earliest recorded cases of public punishment, in September 1630, the white Virginian Hugh Davis was ordered to be "soundly whipped before an assembly of negroes and others for abusing himself to the dishon[o]r of God and shame of Christianity for defiling his body in lying with a negro." Davis was punished for having sex with an unnamed, ungendered, possibly free, possibly enslaved Black person. They deemed his actions a crime and further equated them with bestiality to underline the notion of Black inferiority. Ten years later, the court punished Robert Sweat, another white colonist, for

---

20. Conquergood, "Lethal Theatre," 343.
21. Conquergood, "Lethal Theatre," 345–46.

a similar offense after he impregnated an unnamed Black woman, the servant of a Lt. Sheppard. Sweat was ordered to perform "penance" at a local church while the pregnant Black woman was publicly "whipt at the whipping post."[22] Though they were found guilty of the same crime, the court extended to Sweat the privileges of white masculinity in assigning him a far less brutal punishment. As a white man, he could be saved, meaning rehabilitated to adhere to colonial laws and expectations. The whipping of the pregnant Black woman served another goal.

Control over sexuality was essential to the economic success of the colonies as well as to individual slaveholders. Colonial elites could not ignore the increasing numbers of Anglo-Africans, Anglo-Indians, and Afro-Indians in the territories. They evidenced a complicated "array of social and sexual relationships," writes Kathleen Brown, relations that threatened to "undermine . . . the legal basis for racial distinction."[23] Colonial society depended upon Black women's labor on their hands, on their knees, and on their backs, writes Jennifer Morgan, as workers in the fields, as domestics (e.g., cooks, maids, seamstresses), and as sexual slaves. It authorized American slaveholders to transform the perceived "grotesquerie" of African women into a profitable commodity. Colonial enslavers "appropriated" Black women's "reproductive lives by claiming [their] children as property . . . and defining a biologically driven perpetual racial slavery through the real and imaginary reproductive potential of women whose 'blackness' was produced by and produced their enslave-ability."[24] The formation of intimate bonds among enslaved people, and between the enslaved, the indigenous population, and white workers, undermined the racial hierarchy. A Black woman giving birth to the child of a white man did not produce as much anxiety as the prospect of a white woman giving birth to a child by an indigenous or Black man, free or enslaved. But by punishing the Black pregnant woman in a manner that her co-defendant, Sweat, did not experience, the court communicated that she, and by extension other Black women, had no control over their lives, their bodies, or their progeny. Whiteness as an identity and the privileges and protections that came with it would cohere and be "viable," Brown concludes, only "so long as [they] remained exclusive."[25]

22. Higginbotham, *In the Matter of Color*, 20–22.

23. Kathleen M. Brown, *Good Wives, Nasty Wenches, and Anxious Patriarchs: Gender, Race, and Power in Colonial Virginia*. Published for the Omohundro Institute of Early American History and Culture, Williamsburg, Virginia (Chapel Hill: University of North Carolina Press, 2012), 212.

24. Jennifer L. Morgan, *Laboring Women: Reproduction and Gender in New World Slavery* (Philadelphia: University of Pennsylvania Press, 2004), 1.

25. Brown, *Good Wives*, 212.

As the sociocultural fiction of race hardened during the seventeenth and eighteenth centuries, American society all but eliminated the possibility of justice for Blacks as it increasingly defined freedom as exclusively white and whiteness as the freedom to dominate and to control. Public officials used the occasion of a public punishment like that inflicted upon the unnamed Black woman in the Sweat case not only to discipline the accused but also to issue stern warnings to onlookers about the wages of sin and thus deter future wrongdoing. The stage they set for these spectacles invited community members to scour the condemned for signs of supernatural influence and demonic possession—what they understood to be the causes of crime—so they might identify the taint of sin on themselves or on others. As witnesses to the events, onlookers had a critical role to play in maintaining social order. Public punishments in "theaters of mercy" established and perpetuated the new white American epistemic order by training spectators to perform the *white gaze,* what George Yancy defines as a "distortional way of 'seeing' . . . [that] evolves out of and is inextricably linked to various raced and racist myths, white discursive practices, and centripetal processes of white systemic power and white solipsism."[26] Spectators had to be persuaded that a crime had occurred and that the accused was guilty. But perception, as Judith Butler reminds us, is not a "passive process" or a "simple act of seeing," it is "a process of interpellation, a process of hailing."[27] Colonial criminal legal rituals instructed onlookers to perceive wrongdoing through the overlapping lenses of race, gender, and sexuality.

Enslavers had a vested interest in outlawing—criminalizing—all expressions of Black agency because they upset the constructed master/slave binary. To be *criminalized,* explains Lisa Cacho, means more than being stereotyped as a lawbreaker: "To be criminalized is to be prevented from being law-abiding."[28] Black people are presumed always to be involved in criminal behavior regardless of what they are doing. American society assumes that if they are not in the midst of wrongdoing, they are coming from a crime or on their way to doing something wrong. The Slave Codes denied Africans independent thought and agency except during the commission of a crime. This arrangement outlawed Black defiance and justified the violence enacted against them to compel their submission. Further, it protected individual enslavers from being held liable for any wrongdoing an enslaved person might

---

26. Yancy, *Black Bodies, White Gazes,* loc 424–26.

27. Judith Butler quoted in Yancy, *Black Bodies, White Gazes,* loc 706.

28. Lisa Cacho, *Social Death: Racialized Rightlessness and the Criminalization of the Unprotected* (New York: New York University Press, 2012), 4.

commit.[29] Saidiya Hartman illustrates this point by citing the case of Celia, a young Black woman who in 1855 killed her enslaver, Robert Newsom, to stop his repeated rapes. The Missouri court decided that, as an enslaved woman, Celia had no right to self-defense as she had no self to defend. It executed her for murder after she gave birth to her/Newsom's third child, a boy whose life the court protected because he was considered Newsom's property even in death. Under colonial and later US law, enslaved women could "neither give nor refuse consent, nor offer reasonable resistance" to white demands, but they could be found "criminally responsible and liable" and condemned. The same racist legal system that refused to protect Celia, and millions of others just like her, would kill her in the name of justice.[30] Because criminality and Blackness are so closely linked in the popular imaginary, Cacho concludes, "criminal activity" without a Black body is often "unrecognizable;" the "Black body is necessary for an audience to recognize criminal activity," and without it, often "the same action [is] interpreted as a (white) survival strategy."[31] Through public rituals of punishment, white subjects learned to interpolate Black people as their inferiors and as criminals. The tiered system of justice forged in the "theaters of mercy" enforced this hierarchy through public displays and corporeal punishments.

Community members' sense of right and wrong also shaped discourses around sin and right behavior and the practices of justice. While the colonial justice system relied upon "theatres of mercy" to execute punishments and enforce the racial and gender hierarchy, most people mitigated conflicts privately. Public trials did not always end in justice. These public acts at times revealed the excesses, vulnerabilities, gaps, and fissures in elites' claims to superior knowledge, morality, and the authority to lead. Onlookers perceived when errors had been committed—insufficient evidence of wrongdoing, the wrong person accused, or a punishment that simply did not fit the crime—and refused to condemn the accused. Laws and rulings perceived to be unjust were met with resistance. Spectators responded by mocking and interrupting the proceedings, throwing food and rocks at the authorities, even intervening on behalf of the accused to set them free.[32] These examples demonstrate that legal precepts, like play scripts, invite but do not dictate human behavior.[33]

29. Saidiya Hartman, "Seduction and the Ruses of Power," *Callaloo* 19, no. 2 (1996): 540.

30. Hartman, "Seduction," 540.

31. Cacho, *Social Death*, 2.

32. Conquergood, "Lethal Theatre," 350–52.

33. Robin Bernstein, *Racial Innocence: Performing American Childhood from Slavery to Civil Rights,* Kindle ed. (New York: New York University Press, 2011), loc 330.

By the late 1700s, it was increasingly difficult for colonial elites to impose their will over the multitudes of enslaved, indentured, and independent workers. Enslaved and free laborers lived in close proximity and worked together under equally deplorable conditions. They were at constant risk of death by exposure, overwork, starvation, injury, and disease. Matters only grew worse as the population of the British colonies ballooned in the years leading up to the Revolutionary War, and elites deemed poverty, homelessness, and mental illness threats to the social order. Lawmakers imposed increasingly severe punishments for crimes that enslaved and free workers as well as the destitute were most likely to commit. On the eve of the War for Independence, nonviolent offenses such as the first-time theft of food or livestock could cost even a white worker their life.[34] Frustration over colonial laws such as this helped ignite the Revolutionary War.

RISE OF THE PENITENTIARY

Establishing an alternative judicial and penal practice was necessary to distinguish the United States from its former British colonial masters. The authority of the new nation was predicated upon its ability to establish and enforce laws. David Garland explains that, in the late 1700s and early 1800s, emerging modern nation-states like the US wrested the power of "policing, prosecuting, and punishing of criminals" away from the competing "private, secular and spiritual authorities" that had enforced social norms under colonial rule. People settled disputes privately where they could; however, early US lawmakers established their authority by consolidating their powers through "new institutions of criminal justice," including "institutions of police and punishment."[35] They maintained the use of corporeal punishment to discipline enslaved people but introduced the new institution of the penitentiary. In Pennsylvania, then the nation's capital and a model for the rest of the fledgling country, these transformations coincided with the decision to gradually abolish slavery and for the first time use imprisonment to punish African Americans.

Inspired by Enlightenment thinkers, including Cesare Beccaria and Jonathan Bentham, early US penal reformers insisted that the penitentiary was a

---

34. Jennifer Graber, *The Furnace of Affliction: Prisons and Religion in Antebellum America* (Chapel Hill: University of North Carolina Press, 2011), 17.

35. David Garland, *The Culture of Control: Crime and the Social Order in Contemporary Society* (Chicago: University of Chicago Press, 2001), 30. For more on the history of policing, see Dennis C. Rousey, *Policing the Southern City: New Orleans, 1805–1889* (Baton Rouge: Louisiana State University Press, 1996).

more rational, predictable, and measured way of correcting wrongful behavior among white male citizens in a democracy bound by a social contract. Reformers in the Quaker-led state legislature pushed lawmakers to build these expansive carceral facilities where white men could be rehabilitated into upstanding citizens through hard labor, silent contemplation, and isolation. The Quaker System gradually replaced the "theaters of mercy" in the city and across the nation, but instead of solely rehabilitating whites, lawmakers quickly filled newly built penitentiaries with African Americans, including a disproportionately high number of Black women. Although their presence has largely been overlooked in histories of the US prison system, free Black women were among the first to be confined at Philadelphia's Walnut Street penitentiary and in other facilities the state subsequently erected. The decision to punish Black women with incarceration became one of the new penal system's defining features.

The 1780 Gradual Abolition Act initiated a substantial change in Black people's status, transferring them from legal nonpersons in the state into a new status as free people with no legal rights or protections. Leslie Patrick-Stamp writes that the Act set in motion a slow, deliberate process whereby African Americans might one day be fully emancipated after they and their children had served decades of their lives as slaves. It also eliminated Pennsylvania's "racially specific courts and penal practices" that dated back to 1700 and replaced them with "an apparently uniform penal code" that was on the surface devoid of race-specific language, a code that theoretically applied to all.[36]

As soon as the newly expanded Walnut Street Prison opened in 1790 to "rehabilitate" the worst white offenders, the number of African Americans imprisoned began to climb. Just four years later, 20 percent of the prisoners were Black (15 out of 61 in 1792–93 and 12 out of 61 in 1793–94) even though African Americans composed just 2.3 percent of Pennsylvania residents and a mere 4.5 percent of Philadelphians.[37] Lawmakers confined and punished African Americans at Walnut Street, but they had no intention of rehabilitating them. Christopher R. Adamson explains that the idea of rehabilitative confinement for Black people undercut the ideological basis of white supremacy, the foundation of US settler colonialism, and racial capitalism. US lawmakers believed that Black people were incapable of living up to the responsibilities of citizenship. Penal reformers championed the penitentiary as a reform that would be superior to public torture, but "whereas the white felon was punished for violating norms of freedom," African Americans "were punished for

---

36. Leslie Patrick-Stamp, "Numbers That Are Not New: African Americans in the Country's First Prison, 1790–1835," *Pennsylvania Magazine of History and Biography* 119, no. 1/2 (1995): 99.

37. Patrick-Stamp, "Numbers," 101.

rejecting the rules of bondage."[38] Lawmakers introduced the new system with white men in mind, but they used it to force the growing number of free and enslaved African Americans to submit to white authority in the new nation.

Black men bore the brunt of the punishments, but the changes in policing and sentencing soon led to the imprisonment of Black women. While the number of women imprisoned at Walnut Street was always substantially lower than that of the men, with white women constituting a slim majority of women prisoners, Black women were disproportionately targeted for confinement, comprising an incredible 48 percent of the women prisoners in the institution's thirty-five-year history.[39] The overincarceration of Black women was evident almost from the start. The 1795 Walnut Street prison-sentencing docket, the oldest intact, recorded the arrival of just four women that year, all of them Black. The first two were convicted of larceny, one specifically for running away and stealing clothing from her employer. The third, Diana Oakley, was imprisoned for "keeping a disorderly house," a euphemism for sex work or running an establishment where drinking, gambling, and other "immoral" socializing took place. The last, freeborn twenty-one-year-old Catherine Coleman, was imprisoned for allegedly killing her newborn daughter by "suffering said child to perish through neglect."[40] Faced with an all-white, all-male judge and jury, and prohibited from mounting a defense or testifying on her own behalf, her guilty plea was the only utterance the court recorded.

Lawmakers exploited popular myths about Black predation to justify their imprisonment, downplaying the perilous conditions of their lives and the fervor that lawmakers brought to restricting their freedom. White Pennsylvanians may have opposed slavery, but they considered Black people to be their inferiors and discriminated against them in employment and every other area of social life. As Pennsylvania gradually abolished slavery, whites expected African Americans to accept the degraded status assigned to them. They refused. Thavolia Glymph reminds us that Black women thought that "freedom gave [them] the right to be mothers, workers, friends, and companions . . . [as well as] the right to citizenship and to dignity."[41] They were unwilling to accept the unequal oppressive conditions taking root, conditions that scripted their degradation and exploitation. They recognized that white Americans

---

38. Christopher R. Adamson, "Punishment after Slavery: Southern State Penal Systems, 1865–1890," *Social Problems* 30, no. 5 (1983): 557.

39. Patrick-Stamp, "Numbers," 106.

40. Leslie Patrick-Stamp, "The Prison Sentence Docket for 1795: Inmates at the Nation's First State Penitentiary," *Pennsylvania History: A Journal of Mid-Atlantic States* 60, no. 3 (1993): 357.

41. Glymph, *Out of the House*, 17; see also Martha S. Jones, *Birthright Citizenship: A History of Race and Rights in Antebellum America* (Cambridge: Cambridge University Press, 2018).

read any and all signs of Black self-determination, self-sufficiency, or independent sociality as an affront. Nonetheless, Black women resisted oppression through direct resistance and by forging new relationships, creating moments of joy and connection through faith practices and artmaking, building homes, loving another person, raising a child, or speaking out about injustice. In these ways, Black women fashioned and advanced alternative, oppositional moral codes and social practices steeped in Africanist epistemologies that reaffirmed the value of their lives. They communicated these values through everyday acts of living, working, and caring for themselves and for others, and through Black expressive practices such as folktales, songs, dance, and humor.

As they forged a new Black culture in the US, Black women understood that many whites read independent Black thought and action as insurrection and might bring the full force of the law and the courts to bear against them. The early sentencing records from Walnut Street confirm their observations. Nonviolent property-related crimes accounted for almost 93 percent of Black convictions between 1790 and 1835 in Pennsylvania. Nearly 84 percent of Black men and women serving time at Walnut Street were convicted of larceny, often for allegedly stealing from an employer. I say "allegedly" because again we cannot know how investigators reached these conclusions. Whenever something was misplaced, whites blamed a Black person, even when the item was later recovered. Clothing, fabric, money, food, and tools were most often alleged to have been taken. Despite widespread concerns about Black predation, white law enforcers found little evidence of violent crime. Assaultive crimes such as murder, rape, and infanticide constituted less than 4 percent of Black convictions. Still fewer people were convicted of "nuisance" charges such as keeping a "disorderly or bawdy house," a euphemism for prostitution, or for bigamy or sodomy.[42]

The convictions evidence the precarity of Black life and the limited means of recourse available for African American women to provide for and protect themselves. Free Black women faced bleak economic realities that made them among the poorest of the poor. What work they could obtain paid extremely poorly and subjected them to regular abuse. Domestic work cooking, cleaning, sewing, laundering, nursing, and providing childcare for white families was low-paying, backbreaking, largely unacknowledged, and unrewarding. Working in white homes, Black women were exposed and subjected to constant verbal, psychological, and physical violence, including sexual harassment and sexual assaults. White racism further prevented them from benefiting

---

42. Patrick-Stamp found that arson "was the only property-related offense" for which more Black women were sentenced to incarceration than Black men (17 women vs. 10 men) ("Numbers," 123).

from local relief initiatives. Joyce Appleby writes that the lack of care meant that "life expectancy was not high . . . [the] black infant mortality [rate was] twice that of white babies . . . and tuberculosis, yellow fever, and cholera . . . took their terrible toll."[43] To survive people took food and small personal items for personal consumption or sale, in some cases compensating themselves when employers withheld what they were due. Under these conditions, the urban sex economy may have offered women greater financial stability and opportunity for social mobility than domestic work, despite the associated stigma and danger.

In Oakley's case, concerns about the seductive power of independent Black women may have overlapped with Quaker intolerance for pleasurable pastimes.[44] Historically, Pennsylvania Quakers considered such activities relatively minor offenses that could be redressed through short stints at hard labor or through fines. After the Revolution, however, Black sociality raised the ire of white Quakers and activated fears of the spread of vice and the possibility of insurrection. Moreover, the specter of Black community and family formation, or art and spirituality practiced outside of the tightly regulated dance of the master/slave binary, threatened what whites believed were their exclusive claims to humanity, freedom, and prosperity. As Koritha Mitchell reminds us, "success is often the 'offense' that will make [Black people] a target" of white violence to "mark who belongs" and reinforce "existing hierarchies."[45] The social choreography of white supremacy insisted that Black people act like they were inferior and criminalized much of what they did to survive white oppression and the ways in which they expressed their freedom.

Once Pennsylvania began to punish Black people through incarceration, the practice never stopped. Soon, not only did Walnut Street teem with Black men and women convicted of crimes of poverty such as larceny and sex work, its accompanying Vagrancy Docket was filled with African Americans who refused to obey white employers' orders. In the 1800s, white citizens relied ever more heavily upon the institution to dissuade Blacks from liberating themselves and defining freedom on their own terms.[46] To punish and control more people, lawmakers built bigger and bigger prisons. Reformers realized their penitentiary dreams of panopticon discipline also in Philadelphia, just two miles from the Walnut Street Prison, at the Pennsylvania State Peni-

---

43. Joyce Appleby, *Inheriting the Revolution: The First Generation of Americans* (Cambridge, MA: Harvard University Press, 2000), 163.

44. Neglely K. Teeterly, *The Cradle of the Penitentiary: The Walnut Street Jail at Philadelphia, 1773–1835* (Philadelphia: Pennsylvania Prison Society, 1955), 5.

45. Koritha Mitchell, "Keep Claiming Space!" *CLA Journal* 58, no. 3/4 (2015): 229.

46. Jack D. Marietta and G. S. Rowe, *Troubled Experiment: Crime and Justice in Pennsylvania, 1682–1800* (Philadelphia: University of Pennsylvania Press, 2006), 258.

tentiary for the Eastern District (hereafter simply "Eastern") in 1829. Clerks assigned men to solitary cells where they ate, slept, and worked. For the first time they categorized people based on their convictions and referred to them by numbers affixed to their new, mandatory uniforms. A strict timetable regulated all prisoners' sleep, movement, meals, and work hours.[47]

Racism and sexism combined to ensure that four Black women were the first women imprisoned at Eastern—Amy Rogers, Henrietta Johnson, Ann Hinson, and Eliza Anderson.[48] In Eastern's 142-year history, Black women would be disproportionately counted among its approximately 800 women prisoners. Lawmakers sentenced African American women convicted of felony offenses to Eastern while sparing white women found guilty of similar crimes. Black women's labor spent cooking, cleaning, and doing laundry was essential to the daily operations of the facility, but it did not ensure that things ran smoothly. Solitary confinement induced severe anxiety, depression, hopelessness, self-hatred, paranoia, and hallucinations, resulting in violent outbursts and daily acts of defiance. People began to self-harm and become suicidal. For those with preexisting mental health conditions, the isolation could be a death sentence. Penal administrators did not, however, see evidence of prisoner suffering as a failure. It meant that the system was working as designed. The Quaker model, and later the somewhat modified Auburn (New York) prison model, became the standard. Lawmakers used it to severely punish Black women. By midcentury women comprised just 4 percent of prisoners in the fifteen state prisons and penitentiaries surveyed by the federal government, yet Black women accounted for 61 percent of them (109 of 180). A broader count of prisons and penitentiaries in 30 states and the District of Columbia taken in 1850 revealed that 43 percent of imprisoned women were Black (87 of 202).[49] Over the next hundred years Black people would continue to be overrepresented in every carceral institution built. Black women would do more time than any other group of women.

INCARCERATING WOMEN

In the nineteenth century carceral facilities began proliferating across the country as the new ideas about control and punishment spread. States con-

---

47. For more on the disciplinary practices of the penitentiary, see Michel Foucault, *Discipline and Punish: The Birth of the Prison,* trans. by Alan Sheridan (New York: Vintage Books, 1995).

48. Leslie Patrick-Stamp, "Ann Hinson: A Little-Known Woman in the Country's Premier Prison, Eastern State Penitentiary, 1831," *Pennsylvania History: A Journal of Mid-Atlantic Studies* 67, no. 3 (2000): 363.

49. J. D. B. DeBow, *Statistical View of the United States* (Washington, DC: B. Tucker, 1854).

tinued to use corporeal punishments, deprivation, threats of sale, and executions to discipline and control enslaved and free African Americans. However,
a small but growing number of women convicted of felonies, many of them
Black women, began to serve time in penitentiary facilities designed for men.
Women sentenced to prison were afforded none of the accommodations, privileges, or protections of antebellum white femininity. They were most often
thrown together in the attic above the prison's kitchen, herded together in
a single cell at the end of a cell block, or locked in a storeroom where they
could be easily forgotten. They were forced to do traditional women's work
such as sewing uniforms, washing laundry, ironing, farming, and cooking
for the staff and other prisoners.[50] Their labor, combined with sales of the
goods they produced, off-set the costs of running the facility and eased men's
time behind bars.[51] Women were regularly subjected to sexual harassment and
physical assaults to compel their submission to the guards and to discipline
them to comply with dominant gender roles. At the mercy of the male guards
for everything from food and water to a place to sleep, threatened with the
possibility of severe deprivation and violent punishments should they refuse,
many were forced to have sex to survive. Black women were particularly vulnerable to such attacks.

Antebellum cultural logics rendered African Americans vulnerable to
white touch, manipulation, display, and penetration in ways that bodies covered by whiteness could not be. As the emergence of the cult of domesticity or True Womanhood (re)defined what being a woman meant, Blackness
acquired and was recognized as embodying the potential to transverse normative, white-centric sex and gender roles. C. Riley Snorton writes that bodies
raced Black could interrupt, defy, and exceed the emerging gender binary system that arranged white male-masculine-man in opposition to white female-
feminine-woman.[52] In medical discourses and throughout popular culture,
white Americans circulated images of Black women as uncivilized, promis-
cuous, and hyper-heterosexual, more akin to animals who have sex only for
procreation than to people capable of creating and sustaining familial relationships. These discourses, enforced under the law, justified violence enacted
against Black women to teach them their place. Just as the Slave Codes authorized individual enslavers to "correct" their human property without restraint
to the point of death, so guards and administrators in the nation's first prisons
were granted almost unlimited license to use force to make prisoners obey

50. Nicole Hahn Rafter, "Prisons for Women, 1790–1980," *Crime and Justice* 5 (1983): 141.

51. Rafter, "Prisons for Women," 135.

52. C. Riley Snorton, *Black on Both Sides: A Racial History of Trans Identity* (Minneapolis: University of Minnesota Press, 2017).

both their orders and dominant society's expectations of them as racialized and gendered subjects. Sexual violence was so prevalent that stories of imprisoned women giving birth behind bars circulated regularly. In Southern states, incarcerated African American women like those at the Louisiana State Penitentiary between 1835 and 1862 endured regular sexual assaults and the additional injustice of seeing their young children sold away from them to profit the prison, in some instances to the same white male guards and administrators who had raped them.[53] The American public accepted these arrangements because it considered women who broke the law to be especially dangerous, and Black women's defiance all the more a danger to the social order and the nation.

THE REFORMATORY MOVEMENT

Incarcerated women—Black or white—did not take this treatment sitting down. Locked out of political power, relegated to the dirtiest jobs, and stigmatized by the violence done to them, they rebelled. Just as they had fought against unfair and exploitative treatment on the outside, so they refused to be abused and exploited behind bars. Their disobedience and lack of deference was met with harsh punishment. In 1826, medical staff at the Auburn prison in Upstate New York ordered a young Irish woman called Rachel Welch to be mercilessly whipped for becoming pregnant while in solitary confinement. While we cannot confirm today whether or not Welch had consensual sex, like the case of Joan Little more than a century later, the uneven power dynamics at Auburn made Welch dependent upon the men around her for her very survival, a scenario that compromised her agency and her ability to refuse their sexual demands. Records confirm that she was blamed for the pregnancy and punished so severely that she never recovered. She gave birth in December and died soon after. When in 1843 the staff at the women's unit at Sing Sing prison in Ossining, New York, could not stop the eighty-five women in their custody from talking or "making contact with male prisoners at work in the nearby quarry," they deployed straight-jackets, gags, solitary confinement, deprivation diets of bread and water, and "shower baths that bombarded prisoners with water until they came close to drowning" to reinstate order. Conditions were so bad at Auburn that one pastor declared that being a woman in prison was a fate worse than "death."[54]

---

53. Brett Josef Derbes, "'Secret Horrors': Enslaved Women and Children in the Louisiana State Penitentiary, 1833–1862," *Journal of African American History* 98 (2013): 283–85.

54. Rafter, "Prisons for Women," 135–40.

Welch's case lit a fire among prominent women reformers who began to campaign for women's-only correctional facilities or reformatories where women might be corrected in homosocial settings run by upstanding white matrons. As they built their case, from 1843 to 1899, US-based Roman Catholic charities opened thirty-nine Magdalene Laundries from Boston to Seattle, including two houses in 1892 for Black women and girls, one in Philadelphia and the other in Baltimore.[55] The American Magdalene Laundries, like their European counterparts, were state-supported private institutions for "fallen" women run by orders of nuns. The residents were often low-income women, many of them newly arrived European immigrants, who had borne children out of wedlock and thus failed to adhere to dominant expectations that they exhibit modesty, meekness, chastity, and domesticity. While not official prisons, the laundries functioned in every regard as such, sentencing primarily white single mothers and women suspected of sex work to a lifetime of washing "society's dirty laundry."[56]

To restore "fallen" white women to True Womanhood, penal reformers advocated for the construction of reformatories. These facilities would mirror New England college campuses with cottage-like buildings scattered around the prison grounds. Women administrators known as matrons were tasked with instilling sexual restraint and domesticity in "wayward but redeemable" white women, often newly arrived poor European immigrants convicted of nonviolent property crimes. Penal reformers believed the reformatories would prepare them to be good wives, mothers, and domestic servants, and thus fulfill their visions of a well-ordered society.

The Michigan Department of Corrections opened what is considered the first official state reformatory in 1868, Detroit's House of Shelter, which became a model for women's facilities nationwide. Built like a well-appointed middle-class home, the Shelter featured individual bedrooms rather than solitary cells. Emma A. Hall, its first matron, lived on-site full time to oversee every aspect of the experiment, which included "a program of domestic arts education and cultural activities designed to impart marketable skills and a refined character." The women, most of whom were convicted of sex work, ate "family-style meals" together "at a table set with good china and table linens," learned to sew, and attended mandatory Bible study. Concerned that the prisoners did not know how to socialize appropriately, Hall introduced structured

---

55. Michelle Jones and Lori Record, "Magdalene Laundries: The First Prisons for Women in the United States," *Journal of the Indiana Academy of the Social Sciences* 17, no. 1 (2017): 170–71, 173–74; see also James M. Smith, *Ireland's Magdalen Laundries and the Nation's Architecture of Containment* (Notre Dame, IN: University of Notre Dame Press, 2007).

56. Jones and Record, "Magdalene Laundries," 171.

recreational programs including "singing, playing the parlor organ, embroidery, and a Thursday night tea with prose and poetry recitations. At least one woman learned to read." These innovations reinforced women's traditional roles in society, drawing Michigan officials' high praise: "Culture of this kind, amid such surroundings, cannot fail to be productive of great good in preparing those who receive it for useful home life."[57]

Lawmakers praised Hall's work, but her approach did not ameliorate the overarching issues that brought women before the courts. Instead, Hall subjected them to a rehabilitative script that taught them to adhere to dominant norms and expectations of appropriate female behavior as if they were unaware. Instead of taking the women's concerns about poverty, sexism, racism, and anti-immigrant rhetoric and policies seriously, lawmakers blamed the women for their own stigmatization and infantilized them. Those who would not or could not comply with Hall's standards of feminine domesticity suffered her abuse. Their refusals or failures to perform as required revealed the limitations of Hall's methods and the underlying logics of the reformatory project. The women would not be the only ones to see the gaps and fissures in this approach. Within a decade, Hall's methods would come into question as the inspirational rhetoric and promises of miracle cures fell short and evidence of excessive cruelty toward "difficult" prisoners mounted.

Despite the failures of the House of Shelter, in 1870, at the first national gathering of professional American penologists and prison reformers in Cincinnati, Ohio, conveners issued a Declaration of Principles that urged the construction of separate reformatory prisons for women nationwide. They argued that at these single-sex facilities "fallen" "girls" could receive better care and gender-specific discipline administered by model prison matrons. As advocates campaigned for these changes, their efforts were bolstered by the writings of Cesare Lombroso, an Italian physician and researcher, and later by pioneering sexologist Havelock Ellis. Lombroso's 1876 pseudo-scientific textbook *Criminal Man* argued that outlaws belonged to a "lower," evolutionarily backward, race of human beings identifiable by their behavior and visible physical characteristics. Lombroso claimed the body could be read for signs of criminality using physical traits such as an "apelike forward thrust of the lower face," "wide or underdeveloped cheekbones," and "overly large wisdom teeth."[58] A little more than a decade later, in 1890, the British medi-

---

57. Laura Bien, "In the Archives: Criminal Girls," *Ann Arbor Chronicle*, May 2, 2014, 1–2. See also *Pauperism and Crime in Michigan 1872–73: Message of Governor John J. Bagley* (Lansing, MI: W. S. George & Co., State Printers and Binders, 1873), 26.

58. Cesare Lombroso, "Criminal Craniums," in *The Origins of Criminology: A Reader*, ed. Nicole Hahn Rafter (New York: Routledge, 1999), 168–70.

cal researcher Havelock Ellis expanded upon Lombroso's findings in the first English language criminology textbook, *The Criminal*, to answer questions regarding white criminality. Recognizing that illegal behavior was prevalent within the white population, especially among those he termed the "lesser" white ethnics (e.g., the Irish, Italian, and Polish populations), Ellis insisted that white outlaws were not born criminals but had somehow suffered an "arrest of development" that impeded their natural racial superiority. With the appropriate interventions, they might be resocialized and taught to act more like respectable, upper-class, white Americans. Those who failed to respond positively to treatment or whose physical "deformities" rendered them undesirable or burdensome, however, would have to be removed from the public sphere, cloistered in long-term asylums, and sterilized to ensure future generations would not inherit their degenerate traits and disabilities.[59] These new regulatory categories fueled a rise in policing as municipalities created standing police forces and a women's prison-building boom. Reformatories were erected to "save" redeemable white women as part of a tiered system of social control across multiple institutions that placed them alongside the asylums, prisons, chain gangs, and convict leasing systems. Together these institutions would regulate, control, and, if need be, exterminate marginalized populations as part of a larger eugenics program to purify the nation and eliminate crime.

Indiana followed Detroit in opening its state reformatory in Indianapolis in 1873, and in 1877 Massachusetts inaugurated the Reformatory Prison for Women at Sherborn. The pace of building would continue fitfully over the next four decades, with just four facilities opening between 1877 and 1912, all in New York. But soon after the turn of the century, fifteen new institutions were built between 1913 and 1933 from New Jersey to California.[60]

The South, far less willing to incarcerate white women, would continue to focus its law enforcement efforts on enslaved Black people and rely on plantation justice to enforce the social hierarchy. The Civil War upended these practices so, to restore order, Southern elites reformulated plantation justice under a new penal system they called convict leasing.

CONVICT LEASING

Emancipation transformed African Americans' legal status, but the culture of white supremacy and the everyday practices of white mastering did not disap-

59. Havelock Ellis, "The Results of Criminal Anthropology," in *The Origins of Criminology: A Reader*, ed. Nicole Hahn Rafter (New York: Routledge, 1999), 184–85.

60. Rafter, "Prisons for Women," 148.

pear. As Sarah Haley observes, the "transition from slavery to a 'free' southern economy based upon coerced wage or contract labor was a historical process in which the hierarchy of bodies had to be reconstituted, reconsolidated, and reasserted."[61] African Americans devised new ways of being in the world while their former enslavers sought to reestablish control.

Determined to undermine the rights of the country's newest citizens, white lawmakers refashioned old Slave Codes into new (anti-)Black Codes that exploited the exception clause of the Thirteenth Amendment, which prohibits slavery and involuntary servitude "except as a punishment for a crime" of which one has been duly convicted. From Mississippi to Maryland, South Carolina to Illinois, African American men and women trying to build new lives in freedom were charged and incarcerated for invented offenses only Black people could commit that ranged from idleness, unemployment, and vagrancy to disturbing the public order. Lawmakers most aggressively persecuted those who dared renegotiate historical labor contracts, criminalizing them for demanding better wages and working conditions, or for simply refusing to work for whites at all. In one of the most egregious examples, in early July 1920, Arthur and Violet Scott, Black sharecroppers from Paris, Texas, lost two sons to a lynch mob while three of their daughters were gangraped by some twenty white men in a nearby jail following a labor dispute with a local white farmer. Once freed, the Scott's three girls, Cora, Millie, and Eulah, ranging in age from fourteen to twenty years old, escaped north with their remaining family. A photograph published by the *Chicago Defender* of the survivors arriving months later at Chicago's Union Station became one of the enduring images of the Great Migration. Yet the Scott case was but one of the over 2,400 lynchings and mass gang rapes that occurred in the United States between 1865 and 1965.[62]

African American men were the primary targets of law enforcers, who used the courts and vigilante lynch mobs to maintain white control, especially in the South. The Scott case, however, exemplifies how regulating Black women's behavior became essential to the performance of law enforcement in the post–Civil War era. Rape had long been an accepted practice under slavery to break Black women's bodies, destroy their self-esteem and self-worth, and reproduce the enslaved population. Many white men expected their license to rape Black women to continue unabated. Post-Emancipation, Black women continued to be vulnerable to sexual assaults at work, in particular when

61. Sarah Haley, *No Mercy Here: Gender, Punishment, and the Making of Jim Crow Modernity* (Chapel Hill: University of North Carolina Press, 2016), 25.

62. "Family Driven from South by White Mob," *Chicago Defender,* September 4, 1920, Big Weekend edition.

labor disputes arose. Danielle McGuire found that, well into the twentieth-century, rape "served as a tool of psychological and physical intimidation that expressed white male domination and buttressed white supremacy."[63] Because rape and other forms of sexual assault are crimes of intimacy that often occur behind closed doors, the number of Black women who have been sexually assaulted by whites is incalculable. Hazel Carby laments that, as a result, and despite its prevalence, "the institutionalized rape of Black women has never been as powerful a symbol of black oppression as the spectacle of lynching."[64]

To reestablish Southern white control over the Black labor force, tens of thousands of African Americans were arrested and sold as convict laborers to work for white, privately owned brickyards, turpentine farms, timber farms, plantations, coal and clay mines, and ditch-digging, road-surfacing, and iron smelting operations. In some states, lawmakers actually staged neo-slave auctions on the steps of county courthouses to make it clear that white supremacy would endure. The new (anti-)Black Codes had devastating effects. By 1880, the overwhelming majority of prisoners in the South forced to work in convict leasing operations were Black. Every state that had adopted convict leasing put Black women to work alongside Black men.

Few Black women were able to completely avoid domestic or agricultural work post-Emancipation, but their freedom threatened white authority and the historical scripts of white supremacy. In the 1860s, large numbers of married Black women abandoned white people's kitchens and fieldwork to "focus on the interests of their households and to fulfill their maternal obligations."[65] The mass exodus shocked white Southerners. While whites valued the home, the family, and women's domesticity, they believed Black people were incapable of forming long-lasting loving relationships, parenting, and maintaining their own homes. They interpreted Black women's refusals to work as domestic laborers as deeply disrespectful, high-and-mighty behavior. In response to the shortage of domestic laborers, white communities banded together to make it illegal for Black women to refuse to work for whites. One South Carolina newspaper put it succinctly in an article titled "Negro Women to Be Put to Work."[66] Those Black women who turned down work or who resisted exploitation and abuse on the job found themselves at the mercy of individual employers, white mobs, and the courts.

---

63. Danielle L. McGuire, "'It Was Like All of Us Had Been Raped': Sexual Violence and African American Freedom," *Journal of African American History* 91, no. 3 (2004): 907.

64. Hazel V. Carby, *Reconstructing Womanhood: The Emergence of the Afro-American Woman Novelist* (New York: Oxford University Press, 1987), 39.

65. Talitha LeFlouria, "The Hand That Rocks the Cradle Cuts Cordwood: Exploring Black Women's Lives and Labor in Georgia's Convict Camps, 1865–1917," *Labor* 8, no. 3 (2011): 49.

66. "Negro Women to Be Put to Work," *Greenville News*, October 2, 1918, 4.

In Southern and Midwestern states with convict leasing operations, Black women were forced to work alongside the men building roads and other vital infrastructure to connect rural and urban communities and make Southern industries profitable once again. In addition, they were required to perform traditional "women's work" such as cooking, cleaning, sewing, and laundry to support camp operations. Because their labor was needed to keep the prisoners and guards fed and clothed, women were distributed across all of the camps, not held in a single central location. This dispersal exacerbated their vulnerability. Women who had already endured too much were now subjected to sexual exploitation by guards and other male prisoners who assumed they were also there for sex.[67] Black women fought back against this maltreatment with fists and words, talking back, breaking tools, attacking their attackers, falling sick, feigning illness, and, where possible, running away. Camp overseers made examples of defiant Black women by staging violent scenes of punishment that echoed the worst excesses of the lethal theaters of mercy of the colonial era and the antebellum plantations.[68] Rather than submitting to the new regime, many Black women left the South, seeking greater freedom for themselves in the North, West, and Midwest.[69]

FREEDOM?

At the turn of the twentieth century, a growing number of low-income white and Black American women along with newly arrived European immigrant women began living and working outside of the home. As they acquired a measure of financial autonomy in rapidly industrializing urban areas beyond the traditional control of the church and family, they overturned the social order. Women who defy gender and sexuality norms have always existed. William Eskridge writes that what differed in the late 1800s and early 1900s was the "publicness and self-consciousness" of women's deviations from traditional gender and sexual roles, and "society's anxious perception that many people shared their inclinations."[70] Social purity advocates feared these changes heralded the end of civilization and the white race. They set out to adjust young white women's attitudes toward work and to impose a "single

67. LeFlouria, *Chained in Silence*, 103–39; Haley, *No Mercy Here*, 67–68.
68. Talitha LeFlouria, "'Under the Sting of the Lash': Gendered Violence, Terror, and Resistance in the South's Convict Camps," *Journal of African American History* 100, no. 3 (2015): 366–84.
69. Darlene Clark Hine, "Rape and the Inner Lives of Black Women in the Middle West," *Signs* 14, no. 4 (1989): 912–20.
70. Eskridge found that until the late 1800s, American society "gave same-sex intimacy no sanction" but also did not aggressively pursue "legal penalties." See William Eskridge, *Gaylaw: Challenging the Apartheid of the Closet* (Cambridge, MA: Harvard University Press, 2009), 17–19.

standard of sexual behavior and morality on all" that required "chastity before marriage and fidelity within it" to "produce healthier, physically stronger and morally superior [white] offspring."[71] Purity-movement activists allied themselves with anti-vice agents to aggressively target "fallen women" who deviated from heteronormative gender and/or sexuality. The "fallen woman" label was purposefully broad so that it might include sex workers as well as women who had children out of wedlock, drank in public, used lewd or vulgar language, wore men's clothing, had sex with and formed lasting relationships with other women, and comported themselves in other "unladylike" ways.[72] Positivist criminologists and other proponents of biological determinist theories of crime attributed wrongdoing as well as a host of other social problems such as poverty and homelessness to defects they imagined were transmitted genetically from mother to child. It was a patently racist and sexist approach, utterly baseless in its claims, but purity and reformatory advocates embraced it nonetheless and used it to develop and impose a new regulatory system based on race, class, gender, and sexuality.

The forced and voluntary migrations of Black women out of the South also restructured the development of policing and prisons in the twentieth century. As they moved, Black women carried with them their values, hopes, dreams, and determination to forge new ways of life for themselves and their families. The rising numbers of African American migrants and Black immigrants from other parts of the African diaspora transformed the landscapes of cities like New York, which epitomized many African American's freedom dreams. Saidiya Hartman writes that there, social elites and their yellow journalist allies triggered a moral panic in the early 1900s with stories about the perils of the influx. They fabricated wild tales about white slavery and the looming threats posed by pimps, pushers, and other predators (men they insisted were of Jewish, Black, or Asian descent) who had also rushed to the city.

Policymakers most feared that young white women would be victimized, but recognized that Black women were also at risk because of their limited economic opportunities, putative lack of civility, and the "licentious training" they charged that Black women had received under slavery that left them bereft of morality. Early twentieth-century sociological theories elaborating on the impact of environment and biology on gender and sexuality determined

---

71. John D'Emilio and Estelle B. Freedman, *Intimate Matters: A History of Sexuality in America,* 3rd ed. (Chicago: University of Chicago Press, 2012), 165, 168.

72. Women labeled "fallen" faced far more serious consequences than men who committed similar offenses. They were stigmatized and outcast and faced a lifetime of discrimination. See Eskridge, *Gaylaw,* 26–30; Estelle Freedman, *Their Sister's Keeper: Women's Prison Reform in America, 1830–1930* (Ann Arbor: University of Michigan Press, 1984), 14–16.

that Black women were more masculine, more violent, and more criminally minded than white women. Henry Yu explains that popular media and scientific discourses at the time adopted "spatial metaphors to map . . . racial identity," resulting in "notions of place that were highly racialized."[73] People believed that cultures were "self-contained objects with clear physical boundaries" and that ethnic and racial identities were heavily shaped by the physical environment.[74] Harlem, the Southside of Chicago, Detroit, Oakland, and other African American urban enclaves were understood to encourage deviance on many levels, producing aggressive behavior, gender nonconformance, criminality, and homosexuality in Black women, qualities that they spread like a contagion to vulnerable others.[75]

To contain Black women, policymakers imposed stricter regulations and expanded the police. Hartman explains that, soon, "moving about the city as they pleased and associating freely with strangers, young [Black] women risked harassment, arrest, and confinement."[76] Newly passed Wayward Minor laws criminalized their everyday behavior much like the Southern (anti-)Black Codes they had left behind. While walking home from work, a cabaret, or a bar after dark, a Black woman could be seized and charged with solicitation. If she were found to have previous sexual experience, children out of wedlock, a sexually transmitted disease, intimate relationships with "lowlifes" or with other women, clothing that did not align with her sex, or simply to reside in a house of ill repute, conviction was likely. Law enforcers aggressively policed spaces where Black women gathered to socialize and work among themselves. Black women were most susceptible to running afoul of the law when they exercised their freedom in the labor market, which upper-class people and white laborers sought to regulate to their advantage.[77]

The perception that some African American women engaged in criminal behavior was not completely without merit, but they were no more likely to do so than whites. In growing urban areas, the informal economy opened up a world of possibilities, offering financial incentives, flexibility, and dynamism that agricultural, skilled trade, and domestic work could not. LaShawn Harris writes that, in New York, temporary, short-lived, and in some cases downright dangerous work in various trades as numbers-runners, sex workers, stolen-

---

73. Henry Yu, *Thinking Orientals: Migration, Contact, and Exoticism in Modern America* (New York: Oxford University Press, 2001), 54.

74. Yu, *Thinking Orientals*, 54.

75. Estelle B. Freedman, "The Prison Lesbian: Race, Class, and the Construction of the Aggressive Female Homosexual, 1915–1965," *Feminist Studies* 22, no. 2 (1996): 401.

76. Saidiya Hartman, *Wayward Lives, Beautiful Experiments: Intimate Histories of Riotous Black Girls, Troublesome Women, and Queer Radicals* (New York: W. W. Norton, 2020), 220.

77. Hartman, *Wayward Lives*, 220–24.

goods fences, and psychics offered Black women a means to transform their socioeconomic and social standing by occupying public and private spaces in ways that had historically been prohibited. Hustling was heavily stigmatized, and Black women who opted to pursue work in the illicit economy often encountered opposition from family, friends, and community members who feared they were putting themselves in harm's way. African American elites decried such work for fear that it would undermine their efforts to "uplift" the race. Rooted in the Black church and in newly established women's organizations, racial-uplift programs strived to mitigate poverty and provide mutual aid and protection at a time when other American institutions would not. For many people with limited resources and few alternatives, though, work in the illicit economies offered a pathway to economic and social independence that "respectable" pursuits did not. To all those unwilling to labor endlessly at poorly paying, demoralizing jobs as cooks, maids, nannies, and washerwomen, the underground economy offered the possibility of pleasure, spontaneity, flexibility, and real social and economic mobility, benefits that many felt far outweighed the risks.[78] Black women who chose to work under the table not only challenged white American society's presumptions about what was possible for them, they upset their own community's expectations about appropriate, respectable behavior.

Knowing when and how to project respectability did not always translate into economic stability, and it certainly did not translate into justice or freedom. Dissembling enabled some women to face "the pervasive stereotypes and negative estimations" levied against them and function in a hostile world as laborers in white households.[79] The ability to switch between embodying respectability and refusing to "behave" evidenced Black women's intimate knowledge of dominant social expectations and the importance of their own moral codes, codes that they applied and acted upon in the moment to suit their needs. They needed these skills to navigate American society and, as time went on, to increasingly use performance to disrupt racist, sexist practices and live their freedom.

Law enforcers, social workers, and a host of other social reformers objected to the choices Black women and other women made about how to live, including some members of the African American community. Pioneering Black sociologist W. E. B. DuBois countered biological determinist theories about Black crime in his groundbreaking publication, *The Philadelphia Negro: A Social Study* (1899), but was unsparing in his characterizations of Black women prisoners, whom he disparaged as "generally all prostitutes from

---

78. LeShawn Harris, *Sex Workers, Psychics, and Numbers Runners: Black Women in New York City's Underground Economy* (Urbana-Champaign: University of Illinois Press, 2016).

79. Hine, "Rape and the Inner Lives of Black Women," 912–20.

the worst slums."[80] His and other ad hominem attacks obscured how racism and patriarchy rendered Black women socially and economically vulnerable. Such fears about the decay of the social order, evidenced by working women's unruly behavior, spurred the development of the new regulatory regime and with it more prisons for women. Hartman concludes that "those who dared refuse the gender norms and social conventions of sexual propriety—monogamy, heterosexuality, and marriage—or failed to abide by the script of female respectability were targeted" for arrest and incarceration.[81]

THE END OF THE REFORMATORIES

Rather than serve as less severe alternatives to penitentiaries, reformatories used the same, failed rehabilitative scripts of isolation, deprivation, neglect, and violence imposed on penitentiary men to make women conform to prevailing racialized gender and sexual norms. Regina Kunzel writes that reformatory advocates championed their ability to force poor and working-class white women to act like proper housewives and mothers in quiet, isolated rural settings that mirrored the design of women's colleges. Social science literature from the early 1900s depicts reformatories as safe domestic spaces where matrons and their fragile, child-like, white "fallen" charges cared for one another's welfare.[82] Women who had learned as girls to cook, clean, wash clothes, farm, and sew, and who in many cases were employed as domestics when they were arrested, were "trained" as cooks, seamstresses, laundresses, farm laborers, and maids.[83] Matrons reinforced this education with highly structured recreational activities that they believed would instill sexual restraint. Church services, choral singing, nature walks, and performances of blackface minstrelsy like *The Colored Suffragette* were introduced to return the "fallen" to "traditional female roles."[84]

Imprisoned women disagreed with the program. They rebelled against the infantilizing treatment, violence, backbreaking labor, isolation, deprivation, and boring recreation programs and pushed back against matrons' limited

---

80. W. E. B. Du Bois, *The Philadelphia Negro: A Social Study* (Philadelphia: University of Pennsylvania Press, 1899), 255.

81. Hartman, *Wayward Girls*, 220–21.

82. Regina Kunzel, *Criminal Intimacy: Prison and the Uneven History of Modern American Sexuality* (Chicago: University of Chicago Press, 2008), 117.

83. Sarah Potter, "'Undesirable Relations': Same-Sex Relationships and the Meaning of Sexual Desire at a Women's Reformatory during the Progressive Era," *Feminist Studies* 2 (2004): 395; see also Nicole Hahn Rafter, *Partial Justice: Women in State Prisons, 1800–1935* (Boston: Northeastern University Press, 1985), 33–35.

84. Eskridge, *Gaylaw*, 20.

analyses of the circumstances of their lives and the causes of crime. They met matrons' contempt for working people and immigrants' cultures with equal disdain and gave no respect to people who would not respect them. They turned instead to each other. Prison administrators and researchers soon realized that one of the unanticipated outcomes of anti-vice/social-purity policing and the reformatory system was the formation of close-knit, homosocial communities among incarcerated women, out of which incidences of "undesirable relations" began to emerge.[85] Sarah Potter notes that bourgeois Victorian norms had historically tolerated "chaste expressions of love" in "romantic friendships" between elite white women or girls.[86] Prison administrators initially theorized that the couplings they observed between white women were like the "school girl crushes" of elites, utterly harmless—a "benign form of situational homosexuality . . . more romantic than sexual."[87] This characterization reflects the power of early reformers' belief in the restorative power of the family and of domestic spaces for white women prisoners. Whiteness was equated with heteronormativity, and reformers' efforts were geared toward restoring "fallen" white women to their socially determined roles as wives and mothers. However, this approach obscures the fact that the "fallen woman" category included lesbians, bisexuals, and other queer folks who did not practice dominant heterosexuality, as well as many people whose gender presentation was masculine, trans or nonbinary. Police enforced sumptuary laws that required people to appear in public wearing clothes that aligned with the sex they were assigned at birth and regularly raided spaces where women who desired or were in same-sex relationships socialized. These strategies ensured that a significant percentage of the people held in women's prisons were confined for their homosexuality and queer gender presentation.

Despite the enthusiasm of lawmakers and their social purity movement allies for these institutions, the reformatory era was ultimately short-lived. It came to an end in the mid-twentieth century as a result in part of the dissolution of convict leasing and chain gangs in response to white labor organizing, which successfully argued that convict labor undercut white men's ability to find work to provide for themselves and their families. These changes forced states to move men off public and private work crews back into men's prisons. To accommodate the demand for more beds, states transferred women with felony convictions out of predominantly male facilities where they had been held and into the reformatories. The increased presence of women convicted of felonies, many of whom were African Americans, changed the culture as

85. Potter, "Undesirable Relations," 394.
86. Potter, "Undesirable Relations," 405.
87. Kunzel, *Criminal Intimacy*, 114.

well as the perception of the reformatories. Policymakers and penal administrators feared that "mannish" Black lesbians would seduce innocent, presumably heterosexual, white reformatory "girls" into intimate relationships and lives of crime from which they (the white women) would never recover. To save those innocent whites, corrections administrators delegated their limited resources to support programming for white women, developing a segregated system of work and housing that ensured that Black women lived and labored apart from them and under the harshest conditions. Gone were the bucolic "nature walks over the reformatories' rolling hills" and other group recreational activities designed to instill sexual restraint.[88] Increased security protocols enforced the color line to limit white women's exposure to Black women whom society deemed real criminals.

In an already segregated world, Black women were now forced to serve white women prisoners and administrators just as they had been forced to service convicted men and guards in men's prisons and in convict leasing and chain gang operations. Soon, every state in the nation had built at least one separate custodial prison for women where administrators reinforced the racial and gender divide. Those who disrupted operations or refused or failed to comply with orders were pathologized and punished. Rather than protect women by addressing economic exploitation, racism, homophobia, and sexism through laws and public policies, civic leaders, penal experts, and their public health allies attributed poverty and a host of other "social ills" to Black women. To truly gain their freedom and disrupt the brutal practices of the US criminal legal system, Black women would have to end the violence enacted against them by the state.

TURNING THE TABLES: POLICING THE POLICE

Spurred on by their own experiences with Jim Crow segregation and inspired by the anticolonization struggles of emerging African nations in the wake of World War I and World War II, African Americans expanded the fight against structural racism in the twentieth century. They mounted nationwide campaigns to end Jim Crow and secure the right to vote. James Forman writes that, in addition, to remedy the ravages of segregation, community leaders advocated for a "Marshall Plan for urban America" that would develop better housing, schools, and employment opportunities while raising wages and expanding access to quality and effective health services. These interventions

---

88. Rafter, "Prisons for Women," 166.

would improve the quality of life for African Americans and other marginalized communities.[89] With them, radical changes in policing, the courts, and the prisons were required.

Sustained organizing resulted in the repeal of Jim Crow and the passage of sweeping civil rights and voting rights legislation (1960–68) buoyed by large-scale social unrest. In 1967 alone, there were uprisings in over a hundred municipalities across the country, the largest of which occurred in Detroit and was ignited by the police raid on a party at an unlicensed, Black-owned bar.[90] Black activists and community leaders consistently told white elected officials, business leaders, and the media that to quell the violence they had to end Jim Crow and meet people's demands for radical changes in housing, education, employment, policing, and governance. As white elected officials passed legislation to dismantle Jim Crow, they feared that angry, militant "Negros" would continue to incite violent protests. Prominent national policymakers also regularly mischaracterized and pathologized the causes of Black community problems. The influential Moynihan Report (1965) published under the Johnson administration to address "race relations" was rife with plantation-era myths about the disorganized, broken, and dangerous nature of the Black family. While the report noted the debilitating effects of slavery and segregation, it ultimately placed responsibility for Black poverty on the shoulders of Black women, in particular working single mothers whom Moynihan accused of failing to adhere to upper-class, white, heteropatriarchal norms.[91] Fear, shame, and old social scripts that stigmatized women for the violence enacted against them made it almost impossible to address police-perpetrated sexual violence or other forms of racial and gender-based discrimination. But something had to be done. Federal officials embedded within the 1968 Civil Rights legislation to end housing discrimination the Anti-Riot Act, which outlawed traveling to "incite, promote, encourage, participate in or carry on a riot." Law enforcers used it and subsequent legislation to undermine Black political organizing and set the stage for the greater militarization of police.[92] Thus, as the nation on the one hand lurched toward expanding Black freedom, counterforces on the other side simultaneously moved to limit its possibilities.

---

89. James Forman Jr., *Locking Up Our Own: Crime and Punishment in Black America* (New York: Farrar, Straus and Giroux, 2017), 12–13.

90. See Herb Boyd, *Black Detroit: A History of Self-Determination* (New York: Amistad, 2017).

91. Daniel Patrick Moynihan, *The Negro Family: The Case for National Action*, US Office of Policy Planning and Research (Washington, DC: United States Department of Labor, 1965).

92. Radley Balko, *Rise of the Warrior Cop: The Militarization of America's Police Force* (New York: Public Affairs, 2013).

Black women also faced challenges from within their own communities. As they worked, the predominantly male Civil Rights and Black Power leadership largely overlooked Black women's concerns regarding the role of police in perpetrating gender and sexual violence. On Black women's legislative agenda were ending gender-based police brutality, injustice in the courts, domestic violence, sexual assault, and workplace discrimination, issues that they had worked for decades to move out of the shadows and into the public sphere. Police violence against Black women was endemic, but only rarely spurred public protests. Black women activists noted, however, that police stood by as Black girls who integrated historically white public elementary and high schools were harassed and physically assaulted by white teachers, parents, elected officials, and their fellow students. They felt when police turned fists, dogs, hoses, guns, flashlights, and batons on nonviolent protestors fighting to end Jim Crow and everyday Black folks minding their own business. Long before Rosa Parks rose to prominence as the face of the Montgomery Bus Boycott, she worked for decades in Alabama to document and stop sexual violence against women in police custody and deter patrolling officers from picking Black women up for sex as they walked home from work, church, and other social events.[93] She was not alone in identifying police as a major impediment to Black freedom.

In a rare moment of public outcry, the 1963 Detroit police murder of Cynthia Scott, a twenty-four-year-old African American woman, became a local cause when civil rights organizers linked her death to a larger pattern of police violence aimed at Black men. Scott was gunned down during what the Detroit Police Department (DPD) called an arrest on *suspicion* of street prostitution before multiple eyewitnesses, many of whom—including Scott's date that evening—contradicted patrolman Theodore Spicher's claim that he had acted in self-defense.[94] The NAACP, the Nation of Islam, and other local and national organizations disputed the Detroit police and white mainstream media's justifications for Scott's death, calling the preemptive arrest for suspicion of prostitution illegal and railing against their decision to publicly label her "a known prostitute." Whether or not she was involved in sex work, she was a woman who did not deserve to die in that way. The coalition linked her death to a long history of police harassment, illegal arrests, torture, and

93. Danielle L. McGuire, *At the Dark End of the Street: Black Women, Rape and Resistance—A New History of the Civil Rights Movement from Rosa Parks to the Rise of Black Power* (New York: Vintage Books, 2010).

94. Dan Beck and Hal Cohen, "Cynthia Scott: 9 Versions of How She Died," *Detroit Free Press,* July 21, 1963, 3.

executions that targeted African Americans in the city. An educational flyer produced by UHURU, a student-led, proto-Black Power organization based at Wayne State University, detailed three instances of excessive force against Black men in the months leading up to Scott's killing.[95] UHURU linked the Scott killing to these cases to make a point. The violence was not an anomaly, it was targeted. Scott's murder was not the consequence of there being a few poorly trained "bad apple" or rogue cops on the DPD. Detroit police were corrupt. There was a pattern of anti-Black policing, and it was purposeful, systematic, and designed to terrorize and punish. As one Detroiter put it, DPD was a "low-down vicious anti-Negro machine" paid for by the state and local governments to harass, intimidate, and kill.[96]

In one of the most memorable national confrontations over the issue, Student Nonviolent Coordinating Committee (SNCC) organizer Fannie Lou Hamer relayed to a rapt audience of delegates at the 1964 Democratic National Convention and television viewers at home how Winona, Mississippi, police called her a "bitch," beat her, and repeatedly tried to "pull [her] dress over [her] head and try to feel under [her] clothes" to stop her from registering Black voters. Hamer told this story again and again "until the day she died" as "testimony of the sexual and racial injustice of segregation."[97]

Throughout the 1960s, communities across the United States charged police with brutality, identifying what Micol Siegel calls a "continuum of violent expressive cultural practices" they used from the "immediate thunk" of a fist, boot, or gun butt to the "most attenuated inflections of discursive, epistemic, symbolic, psychic and economic injury."[98] Police who terrorized Black communities could not be counted on to investigate, much less stop, racist, homophobic, and/or gendered violence. As Ruth Wilson Gilmore writes, police were the "cause of premature deaths" everywhere.[99] They overlooked harmful behavior in communities deemed deserving of protection and used violence against the marginalized to protect elites. They were the problem. By the end of the decade, many women understood that true Black liberation required ending the policing of gender and sexual expression.

95. Matthew D. Lassiter and the Policing and Social Justice HistoryLab, "UHURU Flyer," *Detroit Under Fire: Police Violence, Crime Politics, and the Struggle for Racial Justice in the Civil Rights Era* (Ann Arbor: University of Michigan Carceral State Project, 2021), accessed January 3, 2022, https://policing.umhistorylabs.lsa.umich.edu/s/detroitunderfire/item/4928.

96. "Police Brutality," *Illustrated News* 3, no. 15 (July 22, 1963), 2; Lassiter, "UHURU Flyer."

97. McGuire, "'It Was Like All of Us Had Been Raped,'" 910; see also Keisha N. Blain, *Until I Am Free: Fannie Lou Hamer's Enduring Message to America* (Boston: Beacon Press, 2021).

98. Micol Siegel, *Violence Work: State Power and the Limits of Police* (Durham, NC: Duke University Press, 2018), 10–11.

99. Ruth Wilson Gilmore, qtd in Siegel, *Violence Work*, 11.

IN DEFENSE OF BLACK WOMANHOOD

By the 1970s it was clear in the minds of many Black women that, despite decades of work, massive organizing efforts were still required to address their concerns about gender discrimination and sexual violence. Across the United States, Black women from every socioeconomic and political background engaged in political and social organizing. Although they each took their own path, much of the work was buoyed by a determination to end ineffective public policies and improve women's livelihoods. Whether working within existing Black civil rights and Black nationalist organizations, collaborating with white feminist groups, or initiating their own collectives, they organized. One of the most successful movements, which sought welfare reform, fought demeaning stereotypes and invasive, harmful practices of social workers tasked with policing welfare recipients to disqualify them from aid.[100] Women also worked to end food insecurity and malnutrition, advocated for better housing, schools, and working conditions; fought to prevent sexual assaults and domestic violence while protecting reproductive rights; and acted to ensure unfettered access to quality, affordable health care. Others initiated and promulgated new research into Black women's history, arts, and culture. Some devoted themselves to the grassroots while others such as Shirley Chisholm ran for and won public office. They formed international coalitions as well to protect Black lives around the globe. One of the most successful, the campaign to end apartheid in South Africa, built on previous generations' support for African independence.[101]

In July 1971, President Richard Nixon declared a war on drugs to delegitimize the broad coalition of organizations comprising the radical left that advocated for poor people's rights, an ending to the Vietnam War, women's rights, LGBTQ equality, and Black liberation. Presidents Reagan, Bush, and Clinton heard his dog whistle and built on Nixon's policies. The 1968 federal Omnibus Crime Control and Safe Streets Act, another piece of legislation passed to stop "urban crime," coupled with the Rockefeller antidrug laws in New York, laid the foundation for the 1980s-to-1990s War on Drugs, an all-out assault on low-income, Black and Brown, predominantly urban communities. Long-established antipoverty programs that had only recently begun to

---

100. Daina Ramey Berry and Kali Gross, *A Black Woman's History of the United States* (Boston: Beacon Press, 2020), 195.

101. See Pamela Brooks, *Boycotts, Buses and Passes: Black Women's Resistance in the US South and South Africa* (Amherst: University of Massachusetts Press, 2008); see also Nicholas Grant, *Winning Our Freedoms Together: African Americans and Apartheid, 1945–1960* (Chapel Hill: University of North Carolina Press, 2017).

support African Americans were soon co-opted and reformulated into anti-crime initiatives that aggressively policed low-income people seeking social services.[102] Drug commitments and arrests for nonviolent property offenses soared. The 1994 Violent Crime Control and Law Enforcement Act (Crime Bill) established sentencing guidelines that eliminated local judges' discretion and mandated long sentences for the same nonviolent crimes of poverty that Black women were most likely to be arrested for and convicted of committing. The surge was also spurred by the expansion of police powers under the Crime Bill. The Crime Bill included the Violence Against Women Act (VAWA), which affirmed that gender-based crimes such as rape and domestic violence violated women's civil rights. It was hailed as a success, but critics warned that the so-called gender-neutral policing guidelines it mandated would not translate into race- or class-neutral policing. These shifts in policy, Beth Richie explains, "privilege[d] gender-specific analysis while virtually ignoring how race, class, and sexuality can create particular vulnerability to violence," including state violence.[103] As Kali Gross notes, "Black women [were] twice as likely to be killed by a spouse" as white women, but they were never, ever imagined as being worthy of state protection.[104] The coalition of mainstream feminist organizations, lawmakers, and police who urged the bill's passage expanded police powers without truly safeguarding some of the most vulnerable women. VAWA thereby contributed to a dramatic increase in the incarceration of Black and Brown women as police responding to domestic violence calls began to arrest everyone on site. Not only did these policies fail to stop violence, they often resulted in additional charges against women whom the police deemed unworthy of protection. Although Black women were no more likely than whites to use illegal drugs, and the national rate of illegal drug use was in decline in the 1970s, drug-related arrests of low-income Black women rose in the 1980s and '90s at three times the rate of arrests of white women and twice that of Black men. By 2011, one million women were under some form of state control (e.g., incarcerated, paroled, or on probation), most of them Black, and almost all (85%–90%) reported that they were survivors of domestic violence *and* sexual assault, a trend that continues today.[105]

---

102. Michelle Alexander, *The New Jim Crow: Mass Incarceration in the Age of Colorblindness* (New York: New Press, 2012).

103. Beth Richie, *Arrested Justice: Black Women, Violence, and America's Prison Nation* (New York: New York University Press, 2012), 102.

104. Kali N. Gross, "African American Women, Mass Incarceration and the Politics of Reform," *Journal of American History* 102, no. 1 (2015): 32.

105. Gross, "African American Women," 29.

More than a decade later, state policies seemingly designed to immiserate and impoverish have left African American men, women, and children more likely to be hungry and malnourished, to rent and not own a home, to face eviction, and to lack access to high-quality education and affordable health care. Racialized gender-based violence in the home coupled with discriminatory practices embedded in state laws have contributed directly to Black women's social and economic vulnerability. The 2008 Great Recession precipitated by the predatory home mortgage lending crisis wiped out most Black families' assets.[106] By 2019, the wealth of the average white household, defined as the difference between assets and debt, was $983,400, nearly seven times greater than the wealth of the average Black household ($142,500). When the numbers are aggregated by race and gender, the disparity in economic status becomes starker still. According to the Brookings Institute, "The median wealth of single white men under the age of 35 ($22,640) is 3.5 times greater than that of single white women ($6,470), 14.6 times greater than that of single Black men ($1,550), and 224.2 times greater than that of single Black women ($101)." State violence in the performance of policing and in the form of social and economic policies has directly contributed to Black women's overrepresentation in the nation's prisons and jails. As designed, these measures repress and immiserate.

RESPONDING TO THE CRISIS

Over the last fifteen years, justice-involved people—currently and formerly incarcerated men and women, children impacted by foster care and juvenile courts, their families, and their allies—have worked tirelessly to pull the cover off of repressive policing and draconian sentencing practices nationwide. Often organizing today under the #BlackLivesMatter banner, they have challenged the normative operations of police, courts, prosecutors and defense attorneys, social workers, school counselors, and health-care providers who, over the last fifty years, have increasingly understood their jobs as policing low-income, African American and, increasingly, Latino (some of whom are also Black) communities. Performance has been integral to activist efforts to reveal, disrupt, and shut down policing as we know it, from the embrace of the "Hands

---

106. Emily Moss, Kriston McIntosh, Wendy Edelberg, and Kristen Broady, "The Black–White Wealth Gap Left Black Households More Vulnerable," The Brookings Institute (December 8, 2020), accessed September 16, 2021, https://www.brookings.edu/blog/up-front/2020/12/08/the-black-white-wealth-gap-left-black-households-more-vulnerable/.

Up, Don't Shoot" surrender/prayer/accusation/indictment gesture undertaken to confront police on the streets of Ferguson, Missouri, to Patrisse Cullors's 2020 solo performance at the Broad Museum in Los Angeles in protest of the Los Angeles Police Department's mistreatment of her brother, *Prayer to the Iyami*.[107] Artists, activists, and healers alike have used performance in the streets and on stage to end policing and punishment as we know it.

Through performance these activists also demand the implementation of less harmful, more effective alternatives to the punitive system that is currently in place. The stigma associated with incarceration, drug abuse, sex work, domestic violence, sexual assault, and poverty makes direct action for many incarcerated people difficult to imagine, much less achieve. Yet they do want things to change. Theater programs behind bars offer opportunities for women to work through their questions in ways that they find meaningful and healing.

In the next chapter, I share a history of incarcerated women artists that bridges the late 1800s and the invention of the blues to the contemporary era of theater behind bars. I document how the artists used performance as a tool to understand their experiences and communicate what they learned to others. I consider the effects and impact of their work and what we might learn from them.

---

107. Thomas F. DeFrantz, "The Black Beat Made Visible: Hip Hop Dance and Body Power," in *Of the Presence of the Body: Essays on Dance and Performance Theory,* ed. André Lepecki (Middletown, CT: Wesleyan University Press, 2004), 64–81; Patrisse Cullors, *Prayer to the Iyami* (Los Angeles: Broad Museum, 2020), accessed September 16, 2021, https://www.youtube.com/watch?v=bco10-TKNlg.

CHAPTER 2

How to Stage Healing

Although often overlooked in discourses about crime, punishment, rehabilitation, art, and education behind bars, criminalized and incarcerated women make art. They have used the visual and performing arts to enter into the public sphere and tell their own stories. Nicole Fleetwood writes that incarcerated visual artists' work is shaped by the "conditions of unfreedom," governed by "immobility, invisibility, stigmatization, lack of access, and premature death."[1] So too the performance work of incarcerated women is impacted by prison life. The content and form of theater pieces is limited by the state, but incarcerated actors, playwrights, and designers find innovative ways to make work that reflects their experiences in and outside of prison. Many reflect upon the past while others make work to slip, sabotage, and escape the institutions that confine them. Often, the work critiques US institutions of justice and the everyday cultural practices of the nation. Through performance, some even imagine and enact—stage—alternative, more loving and supportive societies in which racism, sexism, and economic exploitation are no more.

In this chapter I gather examples of primarily Black criminalized and incarcerated women visual and performing artists whose creative work connects racialized, gender-based oppression in the home to unjust laws and oppressive cultural practices nationwide. Beginning the late 1800s and mov-

---

1. Nicole Fleetwood, *Marking Time: Art in the Age of Mass Incarceration* (Cambridge, MA: Harvard University Press, 2020), 25.

ing chronologically, the collection of songs, plays, visual art works, and theater pieces I discuss here unveil the artists' understandings of the violent under-pinnings of American society, in particular its heavy reliance on *misogynoir*, what Moya Bailey defined as the "co-constitutive racialized and sexist violence that befalls Black women as a result of their simultaneous and interlocking oppression at the intersection of racial and gender marginalization."[2] In addi-tion to chronicling misogynoir, this assembly demonstrates how some crimi-nalized and incarcerated women have used their creative work to *stage healing*, which I define as setting the conditions for self-repair to restore a sense of wholeness and well-being to individuals and their communities using Black expressive cultural practices.

NOBODY'S "ROSIE"

Little has been written about arts programs for or artistic work by crimi-nalized and incarcerated women in the United States. Most of the scholarly attention on incarcerated artists has focused on men. Men have comprised the majority of the incarcerated. Yet from the beginning, women, especially low-income Black and immigrant women, have always constituted a small but significant percentage of the prison population and of the incarcerated artists producing work. Racism, sexism, and class biases coupled with the stigma associated with incarceration have prevented many of them from publicizing their work. But, to truly understand how hegemonic stories about women's lives authorize racist and sexist policing and punishment, we must look to women's creative work.

The limited published history of incarcerated women's art locates the blues as one of the earliest forms to which they turned to share their artistry and their stories. The blues first emerged in the late 1800s following Emancipation and quickly became known as the sound of hard-won Black freedom. That freedom for the first time included the ability to travel, to work for a wage, to build businesses and homes, and to determine one's own intimate and familial relationships. Although castigated as "the devil's music" for its secular, often raunchy lyrics and roots in "disreputable" poor Black communities, the blues, as Shana Redmond writes, provided a space, a shelter, for Black women where they could meet, vocalize their experiences, and socialize on their own terms. Ostracized from mainstream white society and the male-dominated Black

---

2. Moya Bailey, *Misogynoir Transformed: Black Women's Digital Resistance*, Kindle ed. (New York: New York University Press, 2021), 1.

public sphere, Black women built supportive spaces around the blues where they could express themselves freely decades before the civil rights, women's, and gay liberation movements began.[3]

The trials and tribulations of heterosexual romantic relationships are the subject of many classic blues songs, but early recording stars Gertrude "Ma" Rainey (1886–1939) and Bessie Smith (1894–1937) rose to prominence for their impassioned vocality and sonic challenges to some of the most pressing issues of the day. In an era when heterosexual "love and domesticity were supposed to constitute the outermost limits of [women's] lives," and "full membership in the public community was the exclusive domain of men," Angela Y. Davis writes that blueswomen challenged popular notions about Black women's place in society.[4] Rainey and Smith aired all their disappointments with the status quo *and* their dirty laundry in songs that challenged dominant norms about gender and sexual expression, often by disclosing men's bad behavior. Smith recorded many songs that addressed the unjust conditions. Her "Washwoman Blues" dealt with economic exploitation, while "Jail House Blues" and "Send Me to the 'Lectric Chair" both critiqued unjust laws and patriarchal violence. Rainey's songs followed a similar pattern. In her well-known "Chain Gang Blues," a woman is sentenced to the chain gang for nothing. It ends with the haunting lyric: "Ain't robbed no train, ain't done no hanging crime / Ain't robbed no train, ain't done no hanging crime / But the judge said I'd be on the county road a long, long time." Her "Hustlin Blues" recounts a Black sex worker's struggles with her abusive pimp. These songs offer no commentary about the morality of "disreputable" women but focus on the woman's precarious position. Unlike white women, Black women were "not exempt by virtue of their gender" from the violence of the US criminal legal system. It treated them like predacious prostitutes deserving of no mercy.[5] Blues songs like these memorialized the brutal conditions under which they lived and labored and condemned the society that relegated them to such lives.[6] Black listeners, Black women in particular, would have recognized the impossibility of the women's situations. They turned to the blues because the music affirmed their experiences. The opportunity to come together in venues where blues songs were sung or where they might listen to recordings also encouraged and uplifted Black women's sociality, including in some cases, their romantic love

3. Shana Redmond, *Anthem: Social Movements and the Sound of Solidarity in the African Diaspora* (New York: New York University Press, 2013).

4. Angela Davis, *Blues Legacies and Black Feminism: Gertrude 'Ma' Rainey, Bessie Smith and Billie Holiday* (New York: Vintage Books, 1999), 9–10.

5. Davis, *Blues Legacies,* 123, 127–28.

6. Davis, *Blues Legacies,* 121.

for one another. Listeners valued songs like Rainey's "Prove It on Me Blues," which voiced the secret pleasure of lesbian relationships, and supported her, Smith, and other blueswomen because their songs named, affirmed, and at times even celebrated Black women's lives and experiences.

When Rainey and Smith sang these songs, public support for survivors of domestic violence, same-sex relationships, and sex workers was virtually nonexistent. Violence in the home was considered a private matter to be addressed by a man and his wife, in some instances with help from their extended families. It was not public business. Same-sex sex was unmentionable, and women who challenged gender norms through sex work and other disreputable occupations were stigmatized, ostracized, and policed. Blueswomen's sonic interventions made "oppositional stances to male violence" and to these other expressions of heteropatriarchy "culturally possible at least at the level of individual experience." Their songs unveiled how some men, including some African Americans, used deprivation, verbal abuse, and physical violence to control and police women to assert and perpetuate male dominance. In so doing, these singers moved what were considered to be private concerns into the public sphere where they could be analyzed and acted upon by individual listeners and more broadly by community members. Their songs became hits precisely because they told the truth and sought to influence the performance or doing of everyday life for the better.[7]

Captive Black women also turned to the blues to unpack, refute, and transform the twisted logics of racism and patriarchy, as well as to enter the public sphere as artists and as social and political actors. A set of rare recordings by a cohort of women confined at Mississippi's infamous Parchman Farm state penitentiary offers one of the earliest examples of such artistry. Recorded by the ethnomusicologists John A. Lomax in 1936 and Herbert Halpert in 1939 and released in 1988 by Rosetta Records on the album *Jailhouse Blues*, the songs detail how Black women experienced and contested sexism and racism in their personal lives and at the prison farm. Sarah Haley has written definitively about the compilation, detailing how, across a mere two dozen tracks, the singers—including Mattie Mae Thomas, Eva White, and Alma Lewis—represent the law as a tool for Black exploitation and themselves as both victims of the legal system and agents of its undoing. On the album, these Parchman women sing songs of their choosing, the blues as well as old work songs, gospel, and secular tunes rife with sexual innuendo and play, demonstrating the breadth and the depth of their knowledge and artistry. They rework existing performance forms and suture onto them new practices with the intent

---

7. Davis, *Blues Legacies*, 29.

of communicating the urgency of the present and insisting on the need for more. Taken together, the songs counter popular images of women behind bars as licentious whores and thieves, or as "Rosies," what Haley describes as an idealized embodiment of imprisoned men's hopes and fears as they look forward to reuniting with wives, girlfriends, and other loved ones.[8] Through song, the Parchman women reveal themselves to be neither "Rosies" nor any of the other labels assigned to them.

Instead, the Parchman women use song to remind listeners that they too are targets of the law. Their songs counter their erasure in the public sphere by ripping the cover off the legal system's claims to impartiality, fairness, and justice. Two songs that exemplify the difference between how women are characterized and how they understood themselves in relationship to the law are "No More Freedom," sung by Mattie Mae Thomas and Eva White, and "Penitentiary Blues," which the group sings. Both acapella songs accuse lawmakers of arresting and convicting women as a pretext for exploiting them as unpaid prisoner laborers. They lyrically indict law enforcers from police to juries, judges to prison guards, for upholding anti-Black Jim Crow laws. Specifically, these songs narrate the lives of women who were arrested and imprisoned for innocuous actions such as "standing on the corner," defending themselves against an attacker, or for no reason at all.[9] The lyrics accuse lawmakers of inventing crimes to justify exploitation and to punish Black women for daring to be free. The songs communicate the unfairness of a legal system built to criminalize Black life and the sense of foreboding associated with the inevitability of punishment.

Not only do the Parchman women's songs articulate how the law is used to further economic exploitation, they also reveal how incarceration is performed through violent practices in explicitly raced and gendered ways. One of the most poignant testimonies is found in Alma Lewis's "Long Line," which catalogues prison conditions: "Let me tell you girls it aint no mercy here / Lord catching this long line is killing me / It's so many women / Here and so many different kind / Some high yellows but I'm a chocolate Brown / This long line is killing me."[10] Parchman forced women and men to work from sunup to sundown. Their unpaid labor funded camp operations and turned a profit for their keepers and the state. Women performed gender-specific labor, including cooking, canning, sewing, laundry, and fieldwork. In the sewing room where these songs were recorded, they made uniforms for the camp's

---

8. Sarah Haley, *No Mercy Here: Gender, Punishment, and the Making of Jim Crow Modernity.* Kindle ed. (Chapel Hill: University of North Carolina Press, 2016), loc 4748.

9. Haley, *No Mercy Here,* loc 4608.

10. Haley, *No Mercy Here,* loc 4723.

approximately 3,000 prisoners, plus mattresses, bedding, and the sacks used to harvest cotton, Parchman's primary crop.[11] The "long line" of imprisoned Black women conveyed in the song represents the unending nature of the work and the inescapability of prison life for far too many.[12]

In addition to unveiling and criticizing the exploitation of their labor, women used these songs to trouble the "Rosie" portraits of heterosexual love. Like Rainey and Smith before them, the Parchman blueswomen voice the sorrows and suffering of relationships gone wrong and use their performances to address the problem of sexual violence. Mattie Mae Thomas's acapella solo, "Dangerous Blues," opens *Jailhouse Blues* with these pressing concerns, relating the struggle of a solitary woman who refused to conform to gender norms and as a result was driven or cast out of her home to "walk the road." The song begins with an early boast in the voice of the woman protagonist: "You keep talking 'bout the dangerous blues / If I had a pistol, I'd be dangerous too / You may be a bully, but I don't know / But I'll fix you so you won't gimme no mo' trouble in the world I know."[13] Her swagger, directed at an unknown (presumably male) antagonist, however, is soon replaced with lyrics that confide the repercussions of her alienation. The second verse, sung from the perspective of the singer's (male?) partner, details her faults and their consequences: "She won't cook [mah or no] breakfast, she won't wash no clothes / Said that woman don't do nothing but walk that road."[14]

The ability to move, to travel, was one of the hallmarks of emancipation, but life without the protection of family or community made Black women particularly vulnerable to economic and physical abuse. The protagonist pays a high price for her inability or refusal to do women's work to her partner's satisfaction. She confesses in the next verse that she has not only been cast out but also badly injured: "My knee bone hurt me and my ankles swell / Said I may get better, but I won't get well." These injuries may appear slight, but they feel unrecoverable to the singer. The final verses educe why. They reveal that the singer has become a prisoner and a mother against her will: "Say, Mattie had a baby, and he got blues eyes / Say, must be the Captain, he keep on hanging around / He keep on hanging around, keep on hanging around." Mattie's baby was presumably fathered by a white man, "the Captain," likely a prison guard. Long after the birth, he continues "hangin' around," an ominous

---

11. Bernice Johnson Reagon and Rosetta Rietz, "Liner Notes," *Jailhouse Blues* (New York: Rosetta Records, 1988).

12. Haley, *No Mercy Here,* loc 4730.

13. Haley, *No Mercy Here*; Parchman Farm Women Singers, *Jailhouse Blues* (New York: Rosetta Records, 1988).

14. Haley, *No Mercy Here,* loc 4856.

presence that cannot be shook and that Haley suggests signifies that the sex was not consensual and that the singer was still not safe. Thomas's repetition of the last line, "keep on hangin' around," "conveys the inescapability of rape" for them.[15] Rape was the rule. The final words ring with hints of loss, regret, and perhaps a desire for retaliation, and are a far cry from the song's boastful opening notes. "Dangerous Blues," coupled with other songs on the album, sonically identify racialized, gender-based violence as among the most pressing issues facing incarcerated and free women.

Under these conditions it is no wonder that several songs on the album encourage escape and call for the total destruction of the prison system. "Evil Superintendent" and "Ricketiest Superintendent," two versions of the same song, are the most explicit:

If I make it to the bushes, the sergeant can't do me no harm . . .
First chance I get I'm gonna make a start for home . . .
When I leave this place I will sure have something to tell . . .
I can tell the world just what is meant by hell . . .
What you gon' do babe when they tear your jailhouse down
What you gon' do babe when they tear your jailhouse down
Go get me a wick and a blanket and jailhouse on the ground."[16]

Haley explains that the song authorizes individual escapes "to the bushes" and calls for the destruction of the prison itself with an arsonist's "wick and a blanket" to light the flame. The singers sonically linked the need for individual freedom with "the destruction of systems and structures of power," understanding that it was the overarching system of misogynoir penality that had to be destroyed whether it expressed itself in the home or in other institutions.[17] To get there, the singers endorse myriad methods for bringing about change, from the musical accusations sung in protest on *Jailhouse Blues* to physical acts of sabotage and escape.

Raising awareness of the brutality of the system and stopping interpersonal violence was vital to the women at Parchman, but voicing their concerns was only part of the struggle. For women to "get well" meant eviscerating the judicial system in which guilt and innocence meant nothing. It meant ending patriarchal violence. The songs on the album *Jailhouse Blues* are performative utterances not intended simply to describe conditions or inform listeners

15. Haley, *No Mercy Here*, loc 4866.
16. Haley, *No Mercy Here*, loc 4889.
17. Haley, *No Mercy Here*, loc 4910.

about a pressing issue. As Thomas DeFrantz writes, they were supposed to "incite action."[18]

Defending imprisoned Black women's lives required repealing racist laws and ending misogynoir. Most importantly, it required establishing new ways of being in the world. Until the latter part of the twentieth century, incarcerated women like those confined at Parchman received little public support for their efforts to undo the American legal system and transform the culture. The confluence of civil rights, labor, antiwar, prisoners' rights, women's liberation, and LBGTQ organizing would put the criminal legal system on the chopping block. In the meantime, other marginalized artists joined them in defending Black lives through performance. Among of the most poignant early interventions were antilynching plays.

ANTILYNCHING PLAYS

Like their sister blueswomen, African American women playwrights in the early part of the twentieth century used live theater to protect and promote Black lives. Through performance, they aimed to educate audiences about pressing social issues and move them to act. Antilynching plays were intended to move audiences to end the widespread practice of lynching, the extralegal murder of African Americans by white mobs. One of the genre's most prolific playwrights, Georgia Douglas Johnson, confronted the logics and practices of lynching by upending popular derogatory images of Black men as brutal savage rapists and of Black women as uncaring, bad mothers. Her short scripts strengthened Black communities by undermining white knowledge claims about African Americans and undercutting the tales they told to justify the murders.

At the end of the Civil War, whites across the country embraced private and public acts of violence to (re)affirm white domination. White mobs used arson, ropes, knives, bullets, and branding irons to stop African Americans from exercising their freedoms and to prevent them from pressing for more rights, more economic autonomy, more safety and security. Erecting lynching posts on trees, over bridges, on utility poles, and at other public locales imbued with symbolic meaning, they murdered nearly 6,500 Black men, women, and children between 1865 and 1950, the period marked by the most heightened incidence of violence.[19] Koritha Mitchell finds that these acts of

---

18. DeFrantz, "Black Beat," 4.

19. Bryan Stevenson, *Reconstruction in America: Racial Justice after the Civil War* (Montgomery, AL: Equal Justice Initiative, 2012), https://eji.org/reports/reconstruction-in-america-overview/.

white *know-your-place aggression* were designed to curtail Black striving, even when Black success did not directly affect or injure whites. Accusations of sexual violence against white women covered up underlying economic motivations for the lynchings. Rather than pay Black people their due or allow them to live or work independently, whites used lynchings to steal Black land and to compel Black subordination to white rule.

African Americans viewed public lynchings as a deadly *theater of mastery* in which "whites seeking (not assuming) racial supremacy used the black body as muse, antagonist, and stage prop" to inscribe their authority and enforce racial boundaries.[20] To escape the violence, tens of thousands of African Americans joined the Great Migration and left some of the most dangerous parts of the country behind. Local and national leaders such as Ida B. Wells-Barnett called for law enforcers to put a stop to the practice, describing lynching as "our country's national crime."[21] Black media carried stories of the violence across the country to inform readers and incite them to act. As part of their efforts to raise awareness and encourage activism, the National Association for the Advancement of Colored People (NAACP) published antilynching plays in *The Crisis* magazine.

Antilynching plays sought to protect Black lives by creating spaces for African Americans to come together to learn about the violence and strategize preventative measures. The short scripts—often roughly ten-to-fifteen-minutes long—emerged just as the leaders of the Negro Little Theatre Movement called for African American artists to invent a new Negro culture of freedom.[22] The scripts were meant to be read, not publicly performed, reflecting the danger posed by white mobs who certainly would have objected to their content. Circulating instead as scripts for readers among the news articles published in *The Crisis,* they invited subscribers to gather in their own homes to read the scripts aloud with friends and family. As pedagogical tools, the scripts informed readers about how and why lynchings occurred. Many subscribers were likely familiar with the choreography of a lynching, as these acts of domestic terror were widespread and directly targeted Black families. The play reading invited and encouraged participants to socialize, reflect upon the past, tell their stories, and use their wisdom to strategize new approaches to better protect Black lives, homes, communities, and cultures. As such, the scripts not only directed readers to take on specific characters

20. Koritha Mitchell, "Love in Action: Noting Similarities between Lynching Then and Anti-LGBT Violence Now," *Callaloo* 36, no. 3 (2013): 700.

21. Ida B. Wells-Barnett, "Lynch Law in America," *Arena* 23, no.1 (1900): 15.

22. Jonathan Shandell, "The Negro Little Theatre Movement," in *The Cambridge Companion to African American Theatre,* ed. Harvey Young (Cambridge: Cambridge University Press, 2012), 103–17.

within the scenes to be read, they also modeled how to fight white mob violence by educating readers about the issue and making it available for individual and collective analysis through the intimate performances of the plays by Black families at home. The plays scripted readers to literally and figuratively act to protect Black lives.

Two short works by Georgia Douglas Johnson exemplify how playwrights represented white power in operation and how Black people might respond. In *A Sunday Morning in the South* (1925), lead character Sue Jones's grandson, Tom, is accused of jostling a white woman on the street one night. The following Sunday morning, a white police officer brings the "white girl" to Jones's house to identify him. Over the objections of the family, she names Tom as the perpetrator. Despite the family's repeated assertions that Tom had been at home when the "injury" occurred, they, like thousands of other Black families, are unable to stop his arrest and subsequent lynching. *A Sunday Morning in the South* teaches readers that white lynch mobs used the pretext of protecting white women from Black male rapists to justify their actions. In *Sunday Morning,* we see the power of the myth of the Black male rapist in full effect. The script literally and figuratively restages the role of white femininity in these killings and of white male law enforcers in facilitating murder. The white woman appears not as the victim of a crime, but rather as the instigator of violence against a Black family. She, like her counterpart the white police officer, are fully invested in perpetuating and enforcing white supremacy.[23]

In *Blue-Eyed Black Boy* (1930) Johnson stages a more favorable, some might say idealistic, outcome. When the main character Pauline's son, Jack, is accused of "brushing up" against a white woman in town, she begs a visiting Black family doctor to ride to the governor's nearby home and deliver a message from her. The ring she entrusts to him to give to the governor and the words she instructs him to repeat exactly—"Pauline says they going to lynch her son born 21 years ago"—ultimately do save Jack's life. The governor calls up the military to stop the mob and rescues him. Here, Johnson again broaches the subject of interracial relationships between whites and African Americans, and does so without directly stating whether or not Jack was the child of a consensual relationship between Pauline and the white governor or the result of a rape. Regardless of how Jack came to be, Pauline is able to use her intimate knowledge of and connection to the governor and propel his

---

23. Georgia Douglas Johnson, "A Sunday Morning in the South," in *Black Female Playwrights: An Anthology of Plays before 1950,* ed. Kathy Perkins (Bloomington; Indianapolis: Indiana University Press, 1990), 31–37.

swift action. He wields the full power of the state on her behalf to save the(ir) blue-eyed Black boy's life.[24]

Taken together, *A Sunday Morning in the South* and *Blue-Eyed Black Boy* demonstrate how power operates along racial and gender lines and how Black women in particular can wield influence as women and mothers to stop violent racist practices. The results are mixed, reflecting the reality of the time. Sue Jones is unable to save Tom, and even though Pauline's message reaches the governor in time, she saves only one life, her son Jack's. The governor does not use the enormous power of his office to end lynching outright. That much-desired outcome was beyond the scope of the play. In Black homes and other meeting places where these scripts were read, however, they did fuel readers' political imaginations. Antilynching plays educated readers about how white power operates and provided a space for them to embody and rehearse oppositional, Black-life-affirming practices in the safety of the Black home. Coupled with the efforts of other cultural workers, they would build a powerful social and political movement to end Jim Crow and impact the practice of law and punishment.

ART AND SURVIVAL

In the mid-twentieth century, civil rights organizers mounted nonviolent, direct action campaigns nationwide to expose the injustices of the legal system and encourage political and economic change. One of the most effective was the 1961 Jail-No-Bail initiative led by volunteers with the Student Non-violent Coordinating Committee (SNCC) to pack Southern jails rather than post bail or pay fines.[25] Posting bail and paying fines impoverished already cash-strapped civil rights organizations and put money in the pockets of law enforcers who relied on fees and fines to run their jails and pay police salaries. When they were arrested, SNCC activists refused to pay, declaring that the payments "indicate[d] acceptance of an immoral system and validate[d] their . . . arrests." By serving their sentences organizers took money out of the system. Packing the jails also helped to "dramatize the injustice, intensify the struggle, and gain additional media coverage." The approach worked. The

---

24. Georgia Douglas Johnson, "Blue-Eyed Black Boy," in *Black Female Playwrights: An Anthology of Plays before 1950*, ed. Kathy Perkins (Bloomington; Indianapolis: Indiana University Press, 1990), 47–51.

25. See Zoe A. Colley, *I Ain't Scared of Your Jail: Arrest, Imprisonment and the Civil Rights Movement* (Gainesville: University Press of Florida, 2012).

Jail-No-Bail campaign energized people throughout the South, garnering local and national attention for SNCC's work.[26]

Jail-No-Bail campaigns also had an unanticipated effect, bringing SNCC volunteers closer to one another and connecting them with other people serving time. Spirituals such as "Oh Freedom," with its rousing chorus, "Before I'd be a slave, I'd be buried in my grave / And go home to my lord and be free," were widely sung behind bars, becoming movement anthems. Singing together helped to bolster their spirits, reaffirm their commitment to the cause and to each other, and educate listeners (including other prisoners and guards) about the Black freedom struggle. In her liner notes for *Jailhouse Blues,* Berniece Johnson Reagon reminisced about singing with other women while locked up in Georgia jails for crossing the color line: "There was the most powerful and prolonged singing I had ever done in my life. The singing I did in jail was a celebration of a stance. We were in battle, we were right, jail was not going to stop us."[27]

Singing behind bars connected the SNCC political prisoners with "disreputable" low-income Black people who were serving time for crimes such as shoplifting. The SNCC volunteers soon realized that people incarcerated for common crimes, even for violent offenses, had much to teach them about the justice system. For the struggle for liberation to be truly effective, it had to reach and include every Black person.

BLACK ARTS MOVEMENT

In the 1960s and '70s, in conjunction with direct-action political campaigns to end Jim Crow segregation, a confederation of "poets, theorists, playwrights, artists, dancers, and musicians who advocated a black aesthetic as a means to promote racial solidarity and incite community activism against racist social and institutional practices in the United States and abroad" rose up to fight for Black freedom and self-determination.[28] The Black Arts Movement (or BAM, approx. 1965–75) began following the death of jazz musician John Coltrane and in the wake of the assassination of Rev. Malcolm X, and declined following the closure of *Black World* magazine. Coltrane and X were "twin pillars

---

26. "Feb. 6, 1961: Jail, No Bail in Rock Hill, South Carolina Sit Ins," Zinn Education Project, accessed August 24, 2021, https://www.zinnedproject.org/news/tdih/jail-no-bail/; see also Orlando Blackwell, dir., "Ain't Scared of Your Jails: 1960–1961," *Eyes on the Prize,* episode 3 (New York: Public Broadcasting Service, 1986).

27. Reagon and Reitz, "Liner Notes."

28. La Donna L. Forsgren, *In Search of Our Warrior Mothers: Women Dramatists of the Black Arts Movement* (Evanston, IL: Northwestern University Press, 2018), 4.

of the new outlook," which emerged as African Americans worked to "determine their own political and cultural destiny" alongside global movements to end anti-Blackness and white colonization. John Bracey Jr., Sonia Sanchez, and James Smethurst write that Coltrane's "dismantling the foundations of western music while simultaneously producing beautiful and moving works outside its constraints demonstrated that a new world was possible." [29] Rev. Malcolm X's example of a formerly incarcerated Black man with a history of substance abuse who transformed himself into a well-respected Black spiritual and political leader inspired BAM artists and others to commit to personal and community development. Their examples demonstrated the importance of education, culture, and community organizing in the liberation struggle.

BAM artists believed that a liberated Black people required a strong cultural foundation. Culture and politics are not separate spheres. Culture is a site for political struggle, and they were all in. Black artists, both amateurs and professionals, were expected to produce work that was relevant to the struggle for Black freedom and equality, and Black audiences were expected to support them. By (re)working existing Black performance forms such as storytelling, poetry, music, song, theater, and dance, and suturing aspects of the old to birth the new through complex, emerging, idiomatic stylings, BAM artists built on the past while insisting on more. [30]

For some, arts in corrections initiatives were a way to contribute to the struggle and to directly respond to the growing number of young Black men behind bars. African American theater director Elma Lewis expanded her performing arts school for Black children in Roxbury, Massachusetts, into the Elma Lewis Technical Theatre Training Program at the Massachusetts Correctional Institute-Norfolk prison, so men there could also develop as artists, write poetry and plays, and perform. [31] Celes Tisdale, a Black poet, English professor, and member of the Buffalo Black Drama Workshop based in upstate New York, taught a poetry writing class at the Attica men's prison soon after the September 1971 uprising there. Out of the workshop came one of the most enduring first-hand accounts of the standoff, "The 13th and Genocide," by Isaiah Hawkins. [32] Even popular artists like Aretha Franklin found ways of sup-

29. John H. Bracey Jr., Sonia Sanchez, and James Smethurst, eds. *SOS—Calling All Black People: A Black Arts Movement Reader* (Amherst: University of Massachusetts Press, 2014), 1–2, 201.

30. Emily Lordi, *The Meaning of Soul: Black Music and Resilience Since the 1960s* (Durham, NC: Duke University Press, 2020), 57–58.

31. Errol G. Hill and James V. Hatch, *A History of African American Theatre* (Cambridge: Cambridge University Press, 2003), 16–17; see also Elma Lewis, *Took the Weight?: Black Voices from Norfolk Prison* (New York: Little, Brown and Company, 1972).

32. Lisa Biggs interview with Celes Tisdale (July 2016).

porting the movement such as by giving concerts behind bars and offering financial support where needed.[33]

The decision to extend the performing arts into carceral settings as part of the struggle for Black liberation indicated a sea change in popular thinking, including within African American communities. The political work of civil rights, Black Power, and other organizers in this era made new connections between so-called common criminals, those incarcerated for crimes of accommodation such as shoplifting, sex work, or drug sales, and political prisoners, those confined for their political beliefs.[34] Civil rights organizers and other Black political leaders realized that the same legal system that criminalized people for what they did to survive Jim Crow also criminalized people like themselves who were working to bring the system down. The so-called common criminals and political prisoners were fighting the same enemy.

BAM-era artists used their creative work to further the struggle for Black liberation and built inroads between and among incarcerated and free Black people. For many African American women, however, Black liberation meant eliminating racism and sexism. In the 1970s, the very public trials of Angela Davis and Joan Little raised public awareness of how racism and sexism target women, and catalyzed many artists to work with women behind bars.

FOR THE WOMEN'S HOUSE

Angela Y. Davis was thrust into the international spotlight when on August 7, 1970, guns that she had purchased for personal protection were used in a misguided attempt to free George Jackson, a Black political leader serving an indefinite sentence for stealing $70, from California's Soledad Prison. Jackson's younger brother, Jonathan, staged an armed takeover of the San Marino County Courthouse. Outmaneuvered and overpowered, he fled the scene but was shot and killed in the courthouse parking lot alongside the judge he had taken hostage and two imprisoned Black men whom he had armed in the takeover. Investigators connected Davis to the Jacksons through her organizing work with the Che-Lumumba Club, a California-based African American communist organization. Letters found in George Jackson's cell revealed that he and Davis also had a close personal relationship. The authorities charged Davis with murder, kidnapping, and criminal conspiracy. She fled. The Federal Bureau of Investigation placed her on its Ten Most Wanted fugitives list days

---

33. Lordi, *Meaning of Soul*, 57–58.

34. See Gloria J. Browne-Marshall, *Race, Law, and American Society: 1607–Present*, 2nd ed. (New York; London: Routledge, 2013).

later, igniting a nationwide manhunt. After two months underground, hidden and protected by a network of Black Power and other radical movement allies, police arrested Davis in a midtown New York motel on October 13, 1970. New York state authorities held her at the Women's House of Detention in downtown Manhattan for two months before transferring her to California to await trial.

To get Davis out of jail and prepare for trial, Che-Lumumba organizers Franklin Alexander and Charlene Mitchell, along with Davis's younger sister, Fania Davis Jordan, immediately formed the National United Committee to Free Angela Davis and All Political Prisoners (NUCFAD). Knowing that state and federal prosecutors would do everything in their power to convict Davis, they planned and executed an unrelenting nationwide defense campaign to enforce her right to be presumed innocent before proven guilty at trial and win her release on bail. NUCFAD and the Communist Party (CP) took the lead in printing and handing out tens of thousands of flyers, coordinating public meetings and press conferences, organizing demonstrations, building partnerships with labor and student organizations, and raising money for the defense at home and abroad.[35]

Black artists also played a significant role in the Free Angela campaign. Aretha Franklin offered to pay Davis's bail, set then at some $250,000 (almost two million 2022 dollars). In an interview in the December 3, 1970, issue of *Jet Magazine,* she explained why:

> I've been locked up (for disturbing the peace in Detroit) and I know you got to disturb the peace when you can't get no peace. Jail is hell to be in. I'm going to see [Angela Davis] free if there is any justice in our courts, not because I believe in communism, but because she's a Black woman and she wants freedom for Black people. I have the money; I got it from Black people—they've made me financially able to have it—and I want to use it in ways that will help our people.

Voicing her support of the Free Angela campaign, Franklin paved the way for others who were, as Davis put it, "reluctant to associate themselves with me because of my communist affiliations."[36] It worked. Within six months,

---

35. Bettina Aptheker, *The Morning Breaks: The Trial of Angela Davis* (Ithaca, NY: Cornell University Press, 2014), 29.

36. "Aretha Says She'll Go Angela's Bond If Permitted," *Jet Magazine,* December 3, 1970, 54; Angela Davis interview with Amy Goodman, "Angela Davis: Aretha Franklin Offered to Post Bail for Me, Saying 'Black People Will Be Free,'" *Democracy Now!,* August 18, 2018, https://www.democracynow.org/2018/8/17/angela_davis_remembers_aretha_franklin_who.

"two hundred local committees in the United States, and sixty-seven ones in foreign countries" were working in conjunction with NUCFAD.[37] By February 1971, Che-Lumumba Club codirector Charlene Mitchell could report to the CP National Convention in New York City that folks could "go to a horse farm in socialist Mongolia and enter the dwelling of any family and find a poster on the wall with a picture of Angela and the slogan 'Free Angela.'"[38] The campaign to Free Angela Davis had, because of their combined efforts, taken on global dimensions.

Like Franklin, in response to Davis's arrest the visual artist Faith Ringgold wanted to help. After having been repeatedly admonished by male community organizers that Black women did not need to be "liberated" from Black men and accused of trying to "divide" people for insisting that women's visual art work be exhibited prominently, she had recently struck out on her own. She staged "America Black," her second solo show, in Harlem and was in demand as a teacher. Further, she played critical organizing roles in several important political actions to challenge American imperialism abroad and diversify museum exhibition practices at home.

In March 1970, the New York–based Creative Artists Public Service program (CAPS) awarded Ringgold a three-thousand-dollar grant to develop, paint, and install a new mural, her first public commission. Their only stipulation was that she had to find an institution that would display it publicly. The first institution she approached, her alma mater, City College of New York, turned her away—stating she was too Black, too female, and not "prominent enough." Undeterred, Ringgold asked herself where her work might be really needed, and her thoughts soon turned to Davis and the New York Women's House of Detention. For two months in late 1970, Davis was confined to the Women's House, a towering but crumbling jail in Greenwich Village, an epicenter of 1960s counterculture activity. With CAPS staff member Isabelle Fernandez at her side, Ringgold approached the New York Department of Corrections with a proposal to design and install a new mural for women in the Women's House of Detention. It took some time to convince the corrections administrators, who initially encouraged Ringgold to work with the more easily accessible men, but she prevailed.

In an interview with her daughter, Michelle Wallace, for the first issue of the *Feminist Art Journal*, Ringgold reflected on why the Department of Corrections resisted her initial proposal: "The stigma attached to having been in jail for a woman [was] a still very threatening one. . . . How dare [a woman]

---

37. Apetheker, *Morning Breaks*, 29.

38. Charlene Mitchell, *The Fight to Free Angela: Its Importance for the Working Class* (New York: New Outlook Publishers, 1972), 4–5.

not be a good wife and mother" or refuse to "play her traditional role?"[39] Because the State of New York had plans to demolish the deteriorating Women's House in late 1971 and move all the women to a repurposed cell block on Riker's Island, Ringgold agreed to develop the project with the new space in mind. To do so, she asked for permission to interview women at Riker's about what they would like to see. As Ringgold remembered the conversation, "Many of [the women] voiced the opinion that they wanted to be able to see women being things in the world other than some of the things they had gotten arrested for" and in roles that were more "important other than being somebody's girlfriend."[40] They wanted to see women like themselves in the future, but succeeding at work and in their personal lives and embedded in a more equitable world. She recalled, "They wanted to see justice, freedom, a groovy mural on peace, a long road leading out of here, the rehabilitation of all prisoners, all races of people holding hands with god in the middle. Eighty-five percent Black and Puerto Rican, but they didn't want whites excluded. There was a kind of universality expressed by their feelings."[41]

The resulting mural, entitled *For the Women's House*, is an 8'-by-8' oil-on-canvas work divided into eight equal triangular quadrants in a style that echoes Central African BaKuba painting. Each quadrant portrays women actively working at jobs that were not widely held by women in the 1970s. In the upper left corner of the painting, a Black woman with a large afro and a white doctor's coat instructs a Black woman student who is reading a book. To its right is a white woman driving a bus. At top center right, a handful of women of color are all gathered around a microphone as if at a political rally. Moving clockwise, the next quadrants depict women playing professional basketball and as police and construction workers. The lower three sections include a blond-haired woman holding a dark-skinned child on her lap, a Black woman artist sculpting a mound of clay on a potter's wheel, and finally a religious scene in which a young woman wearing a veil stands before two older women at a wedding, confirmation, or other sacred rite.

For the Women's House gathers a diverse assemblage of women and diverse images of women's futures on a single, unified canvass. Taken together, they represent "all the things life could bring [the imprisoned women] if they had freedom."[42] Ringgold considers the mural to be her first explicitly feminist

39. Michele Wallace, "For the Women's House," *Feminist Art Journal* 1, no. 1 (1972): 14–15.

40. Rebecca Mead, "Behind Bars," *New Yorker* (Oct. 25, 2010), accessed October 7, 2017, https://www.newyorker.com/magazine/2010/10/25/behind-bars-rebecca-mead

41. Ringgold, qtd in Wallace, "For the Women's House," 14–15.

42. Bob Morris, "Faith Ringgold Will Keep Fighting Back," *New York Times*, June 11, 2020, accessed June 11, 2020, https://www.nytimes.com/2020/06/11/arts/design/faith-ringgold-art.html?action=click.

work. The piece relates the shared recognition among the project participants that they were all criminalized as Black and Brown women in America. Further, the piece aligns the challenges faced by women confined at Riker's with Davis's struggle and the larger struggle for Black liberation in the United States. One of the mural's strongest contributions lies in its critique of the systemic factors that built the "long road" women behind bars have to navigate to find themselves in jail and the equally long way out, both of which were paved with repressive notions about women's roles in society.[43] *For the Women's House* expressed the women's struggle for a way out of the facility and the racist and sexist paradigms that bound their lives. Ringgold's mural articulated a collective vision of a more fair, just, and inclusive world. From its place on the Women's House walls, it interjected their expansive, collective, and liberating vision into one of the least free places in the world.[44] Ringgold continued for a number of years to return to Riker's with a small cohort of other artists whom she recruited to offer art-making workshops to women.

For Davis's part, her time behind bars changed the trajectory of her scholarship and her activism. Since her acquittal on all charges related to the takeover of the San Marino County Courthouse, she has dedicated much of her career to advocacy for incarcerated women. When Joan Little went on trial for killing the corrections officer who raped her in 1974, Davis lent her voice, her intellect, and her celebrity to save Little's life. Little's murder trial became a rallying cry for a broad coalition of artists, prison reformers, death penalty abolitionists, and advocates working to end violence against women well into the 1980s, as the War on Drugs transformed the landscape of the US prison system.

A LESSON FROM JOAN LITTLE

Although its role is often overlooked in histories of antiprison organizing, the song about Joan Little played a powerful role in educating the public about her case. As noted in chapter 1, "Joan Little," written by Berniece Johnson Reagon

---

43. Diana Wilkinson, "Faith Ringgold Captures the 'Long Road' Ahead for Women," National Museum of Women in the Arts, accessed January 17, 2018, https://nmwa.org/blog/2013/09/26/faith-ringgold-captures-the-long-road-ahead-for-women/.

44. In 1971, Ringgold continued to create art works to advocate for imprisoned women and men. She specifically designed and printed three posters to raise awareness and funds on behalf of Black political prisoners—*The United States of Attica, Angela Free Women Free Angela* and *America Free Angela Free America*. See Ringgold, *We Flew Over the Bridge: The Memoirs of Faith Ringgold* (Durham, NC: Duke University Press, 2005).

and sung by the acapella women's group Sweet Honey in the Rock, played a pivotal role in mobilizing supporters far and near.

When she heard Little's story, Reagon, then a single mother living in 1970s Washington, DC, was in the throes of her own feminist awakening. Like many people, she had grown up believing that disreputable women who became pregnant out of wedlock or were sent to jail were to blame for their circumstances. However, the story of Little's rape behind bars set her on edge. She was mulling the case over one afternoon while visiting a local, Black-owned barbershop. There she overheard several Black men discussing the case. They discounted the possibility of the rape and exchanged crass jokes about Little's sexual prowess. Outraged, Reagon was soon humming the chorus to the new song, "Joan Little."

"Joan Little" tells the story of a woman like Reagon who was raised with mainstream African American values and who experiences a personal and political awakening when she hears "the news" of Little's case. Although Little and the singer have lived very different lives, Little's experiences illuminate how American society positions them both as "fair game," deserving targets of racialized, gender-based abuse and exploitation. This unanticipated sororal relationship commits the singer to stand with Little in her fight for justice. The song not only retells Little's story, it communicates the larger message that women can exercise sovereignty over their lives and their bodies, and that they have the right to defend themselves with lethal force. As Reagon put it, when faced with "the greatest danger and at your lowest point, you can fight back with the life you have. And sometimes, rapists die."[45] Its rousing refrain became the rallying cry for the Free Joan Little Movement:

Joan Little, she's my sister,
Joan Little, she's our mama,
Joan Little, she's your lover,
Joan's the woman who's going to carry your child . . .
Joan is you, Joan is me,
Our prison is this whole society.[46]

"Joan Little" was not as widely sung as other Black liberation anthems such as "Lift Every Voice and Sing" and "We Shall Overcome" or South Africa's "Nkosi Sikelel'iAfrica." But, like them, it carried and communicated a recognizable, shared experience, as Shana Redmond writes, of "misrecognition,

45. Bernice Johnson Reagon and Sweet Honey in the Rock, *We Who Believe in Freedom: Sweet Honey in the Rock . . . Still on the Journey* (New York: Anchor Books, 1993), 29.

46. Reagon and Sweet Honey in the Rock, *We Who Believe*, 30–31.

false histories, violence and radical exclusion" while offering up life-affirming "alternative theorizations and performances of blackness" to singers and listeners.[47] Unlike the more recognizable anthems, "Joan Little" spoke specifically to Black women's subjugation in American society and reinforced the messages Little's legal team wanted to share about the racism and sexism of the North Carolina judicial system to change US discourses about rape. As a performative utterance, singing "Joan Little" was a protest against and an interruption of rape culture's enduring scripts, which trivialize, dismiss, and seek to silence survivors. The song educated listeners about Little's case and made her relatable, empathetic. Claiming Little as an intimate relation or family member—"sister," "mama," "lover"—the song refused law enforcers' efforts to cast her as a "loose" woman unworthy of support. By singing "Joan is you / Joan is me / Our prison is the whole society," supporters refused the privatization of rape and the isolation of victims. Little was not alone as a sufferer, a survivor, or a stakeholder in this case. The act of collective singing sonically suspended otherwise rigid social divisions between Little's supporters in a moment of collective action. Through performance, the song prepared, rehearsed, fortified, and encouraged Little's supporters to literally and figuratively act en masse to defend her and, by extension, to protect other "disreputable" women and girls whenever and wherever they might be.

The support for Little did not translate into an end to sexual violence, but some changes did occur. Little was found not guilty, a decision that for the first time in US history affirmed that Black women had the right to use lethal force to defend themselves against rape, even by a white male attacker in uniform. The verdict made her eligible for work-release programs and allowed her to participate in the drama club at the North Carolina prison for women, where she served the remainder of her sentence for breaking and entering.[48] There was a wellspring of women's organizing to address everything from economic equality and welfare rights to fair housing, reproductive justice, LGBTQ rights, domestic violence, policing, and rape culture. More broadly, the publicity surrounding her case and Angela Davis's spurred women theater and dance teachers across the country to start offering courses behind bars.

Women needed the help. The 1980s–2000s ushered in the era of the War on Drugs. Unfounded narratives about Black "crack hos" birthing super-predators flooded the airways as neoliberal and neoconservative economic and political leaders sought to mitigate the successes of the Black freedom movement, women's liberation, and the war on poverty. It was in the mean and unforgiv-

---

47. Redmond, *Anthem,* 2.
48. "Joan Little Gets Job Outside Jail," *New York Times,* March 13, 1977, 26.

ing climate of the War on Drugs that one of the best-known theater programs for incarcerated women was born—the Medea Project: Theatre for Incarcerated Women, led by the actress, playwright, and director Rhodessa Jones.

MAKING THEATER FOR INCARCERATED WOMEN

Joan Little's case was on Rhodessa Jones's mind when an opportunity to teach aerobics at the San Francisco County Jail landed in her lap in the mid-1980s. Born in Florida as the daughter of migrant African American farm workers and raised largely in Upstate New York, Jones had made her way west to San Francisco in the 1960s. She had built a name for herself as an innovative and experimental theater/dance performance artist and teaching artist when the War on Drugs began sending unprecedented numbers of women to prison and jail. Changes in law and sentencing compounded by the introduction of "gender-neutral" policing strategies criminalized the survival behaviors of low-income women, primarily women of color, across the country. In the forty-year period between 1970 and 2010, the number of women behind bars rose at nearly double the rate of men.

Jail administrators scrambled to house women and provide programming to keep the peace and improve opportunities for early release. Unfortunately, the changing tone of the national discourse around prisons brought the rehabilitative model that historically characterized women's facilities to an end. Overcrowding forced administrators to reallocate what limited space they had for programming to beds as the country heeded increasing calls for every convicted person to be locked away forever. Draconian federal "three-strikes" laws coupled with anti-vice policing mandates and new state-level protections such as the Law Enforcement Officers' Bill of Rights granted police almost complete impunity to stop, frisk, abuse, and arrest poor Black and Brown people. Prisons and jails across the country were soon overcrowded. California led the way. As the number of prisoners grew, however, funding for programming at women's facilities largely did not. One exception to this rule, however, could be found in San Francisco.

The sheriff at the San Francisco County Jail partnered with the California Arts Council to bring in artists to teach the growing number of incarcerated women. Jones was an actress and dancer, but she agreed to teach aerobics because it was considered by corrections staff to be an appropriate and accessible exercise for the women. Jones accepted the assignment because she was curious about whom she might meet behind bars. One of her older brothers had served time at the Attica state prison and had been there in September

1971 during the uprising so she knew something of the struggles that families faced when loved ones went away. She too was inspired by Joan Little's story and was curious about the life journeys of women behind bars. Once inside, it quickly became clear, however, that the women were not interested in V-steps or knee repeaters so Jones began talking about her own life. Some women asked her why she was telling them "her business." To which she replied, "I'm an artist." The answer that came back, "What's that?," initiated what has evolved into a more than thirty-year creative conversation with imprisoned women about their lives and the possibilities that art, theater in particular, open up for personal and community transformation.[49]

Stories, Jones believes, can be "exits" out of jail and back to our homes, back to ourselves, if we are willing to tell the truth and claim everything that we have experienced. Since 1989, she has been exploring with incarcerated women ways in which to "create words as a highway" out of jail, by which she means both the physical lockups that hold women's bodies and the psychological, emotional, and spiritual confines into which our society puts women to convince them that they do not own their lives.[50] The ensemble took its name from the myth of Medea, the fierce mother-sorcerer who kills her own children rather than allow them to be raised by her treacherous ex-husband and his new bride. Jones introduced Medea when she learned that the women in her class would not allow another woman to participate because she had allegedly chosen her man over her child. He had laid down an ultimatum. He wanted her but not the baby. The baby died. The other women at the jail were outraged and so sought to isolate and hurt the accused mother. When Jones learned what was going on, she confronted the women in her workshop. In a difficult conversation she reminded them that they too were mothers who were not taking care of their kids. In the eyes of many of their family members and of mainstream American society, it appeared that many of them had chosen their men or some other entity over their kids. They might not have killed their children like Medea did, but their babies were suffering too. The point was that one ought not judge based on rumors and appearances. Dig deeper. Get some information. Stand in the other person's shoes. Learn the real story. After all, as Jones often says, "We aren't born bitches, a lot of stuff happens to us." Rena Fraden, who has written extensively about Medea, states that this kind of frank talk has become a hallmark of Jones's work because she understands that the stories we tell ourselves and one another shape who we

---

49. See Fraden, *Imagining Medea: Rhodessa Jones and Theater for Incarcerated Women* (Chapel Hill: University of North Carolina Press, 2001); Zoom conversation with the author, September 2021.

50. Quotes and insights gained from a phone conversation with Rhodessa Jones on August 18, 2021. Brown University, Churchill House, Providence, RI.

are, how we see ourselves, and how we know our place in the world.[51] Stories instruct.

By encouraging women to tell the truths about their lives, by witnessing and affirming the tellers and the tales collectively and individually, the Medea Project *stages healing*. Working together, Jones and the ensemble established the conditions for self-repair by encouraging participants to *name the real*. Naming the real encompasses sharing life experiences as well as naming the causes of women's suffering, specifically those social and political factors that produce Black/incarcerated/women's abjection. Medea participants name the real as a first step in a larger process of imagining alternative ways of organizing society, including new ways of redressing harm and mitigating human conflicts. Sara Warner calls this process "re-story-a-tive justice," a way "of rereading and retelling life stories" to restore women's value to themselves, and it is fundamental to their work.[52] The Medea Project responds to the judicial system's "grand narrative" of "an impartial and objective truth" with myth-making at a "messianic" scale. This approach helps participants and audiences become aware of the constructed nature of the truth and the criminal legal system, encouraging spectators to reconsider their perceptions of justice. Warner surmises that, while this approach offers no ready or easy answers to interpersonal dramas or social conflicts, it does present a "productive way" to think about the "breaches" that occur in daily life and "their solutions" as well as "crime and its consequences" in ways that avoid the reductive "true/false binary." It creates possibilities to develop other responses to wrongdoing than the narrow crime and punishment scripts that mainstream American society advances.[53]

Through creative writing, movement, and sound work, participants in the Medea Project figure out how individual stories link up with the bigger story of women's lives, meaning how women are narrated and scripted to act and how stereotypes and reductive expectations conscribe their choices. In rehearsal, participants in the Medea Project talk frankly about their experiences as women. Gender, sex, sexuality, family, work, race, class—all of it is on the table. As they talk, Jones encourages them to physicalize their experiences. Fraden writes that connecting to the breath and the body is important because women are shaped by their bodies and by the ways in which society treats those bodies. Reconnecting with the body is required to get

---

51. Fraden, *Imagining Medea*, 17.

52. Sara Warner, "Restoryative Justice: Theatre as Redressive Mechanism for Incarcerated Women," in *Razor Wire Women: Prisoners, Activists, Scholars and Artists,* ed. Jodie Michelle Lawston and Ashley E. Lucas (Albany: State University of New York Press, 2011), 239–40.

53. Warner, "Restoryative," 239–40.

real. Moreover, it is important, Sean Reynolds, a social worker with whom Jones partnered for many years reminds us, because "self-esteem, drug abuse, dysfunctional families, battered [women's] syndrome—these are all standard topics for American women in the late twentieth century, crossing class and race lines. . . . [But] the *remedies* for such ills have not crossed class and race lines."[54] For women locked out of other means of regaining a sense of wholeness, well-being, belonging, and equilibrium, the theater work invites them to heal in part by getting real, by (re)engaging with the past through word, sound, song, poetry, breath, movement, and more. Getting to the real together, incarcerated performers find ways to acknowledge, confront, and even shed the narrow social scripts that define and confine them, including those they hold as true in their own minds. Opportunities to put women's experiences into song, writing, scenes, monologues, and movement exercises through the Medea Project move the personal work into "the real, material world."[55] Nina Billone argues that, pedagogically, the work strives to uncover and critique the connections between individuals and "the systems of power that conspire both to produce and to police those who are caught simultaneously within and beyond the boundaries of the nation," as criminalized women are.[56] Over time, participants realize that the real is not "somewhere outside of the theatre, it is in the lives the women have led, waiting to be accessed, brought forth on stage."[57] Further, through drama workshops, a new category of "realness" is established, even if it may only be temporary. That a performance is ephemeral does not mean it is not impactful. Embedded within each scene or moment of choreography is the opportunity and invitation to, as my mentor Rebecca Rice used to say, "Allow this moment to change you."

Medea thus encourages women to reclaim their time behind bars to do what they need to do to heal themselves and each other by confronting head-on the death-dealing systems that animate society and the reductive gender-based expectations they have learned growing up. Further, in so doing, the Medea Project also places performances *of* prison—of civil death, erasure, and processes of women's cancellation that occur on both sides of the prison door—center stage. Audiences walk away from productions more knowledgeable about who is behind bars and for what, and better understand how our society cancels women's and girls' lives under the heavy intersecting weight of patriarchy, racism, and classism long before they actually go to jail.

54. Fraden, *Imagining Medea*, 82.

55. Fraden, *Imagining Medea*, 68.

56. Nina Billone, "Performing Civil Death: The Medea Project and Theater for Incarcerated Women," *Text and Performance Quarterly* 29, no. 3 (2009): 262.

57. Fraden, *Imagining Medea*, 70.

While she is perhaps today the most well-known practitioner of theater for incarcerated women, Jones was not the only artist devising new work with women behind bars in the wake of Joan Little's case. The rise in women's incarceration rates forced municipalities across the country to offer more programming, and although most opted to stay within the familiar bounds of religious services, parenting classes, and GED courses for those without high school diplomas, at a few scattered sites theater and dance were also offered. In Indiana, Laura Bates taught Shakespeare to men and women, including people locked in solitary.[58] On the East Coast, Jean Trounstine ran a Shakespeare theater program in Framingham, Massachusetts, while Eve Ensler worked in New York's Bedford Hills Correctional Facility and Ashley Lucas directed women imprisoned in North Carolina.[59] Among the longest-running of such programs was the modern dancer/choreographer Pat Graney's Keeping the Faith—The Prison Project (KTF), a "non-religious" dance program that began in 1995 at the Washington State Corrections Center for Women. KTF conducts intensive, three-month-long writing and dance residencies that culminate in performances at the prison for an audience consisting of other incarcerated women and selected guests. Graney situated her program within the discourse of self-help and rehabilitation that was popular when KTF was founded, in association with goals that involved "re-patterning" prisoners' bodies by interrupting old thought processes that contributed to their incarcerations. Jessica Berson, however, observed that prohibitions against touch, moving quickly, and expressing an explicitly political viewpoint curtailed women's explorations and therefore their discoveries.[60] Considering these limitations, Berson questioned how Graney, and arts-in-correctional-settings practitioners in general, measured and assessed the outcomes.

The research that I conducted from 2008 to 2018 sought to answer these questions about art and healing. My time in the field dramatically changed how I think about crime, safety, justice, accountability, and performance, and how I define hurt and healing. In the next chapter I share the first steps on my journey to understand how theater for incarcerated women can *stage healing*. I record how sororal, sisterly, relationships form between theater instructors

58. Laura Bates, *Shakespeare Saved My Life: Ten Years in Solitary with the Bard* (Chicago: Sourcebooks, 2013).

59. Jean Trounstine, *Shakespeare Behind Bars: One Teacher's Story of the Power of Drama in a Women's Prison* (Ann Arbor: University of Michigan Press, 2004); Eve Ensler, "What I Want My Words to Do to You" (Arlington, VA: PBS Public Broadcasting Service, 2003); Ashley Lucas, "When I Run in My Bare Feet: Music, Writing, and Theater in a North Carolina Women's Prison," *American Music* 31, no. 2 (2013): 134–62.

60. Jessica Berson, "Baring and Bearing Life behind Bars: Pat Graney's 'Keeping the Faith' Prison Project," *TDR: The Drama Review* 52, no. 3 (2008): 85, 81.

and workshop participants through the use of humor and storytelling. These techniques also helped the ensemble at Midwestern Jail identify the causes of their pain, their shame, and their rage, and push through them. They later drew upon this sense of collective belonging to develop their final performance, *Well-Behaved Woman,* a theater work that staged healing by telling the truth about women behind bars and inviting others into their circle of belonging.

CHAPTER 3

Bad Bad Bad Bad Bad Bad Woman

Making Theater in a Midwestern Jail

The first time I visited Midwestern, a small county jail in the Midwest, the Inmate Program Coordinator, Mr. Bertram, reviewed the basic procedures for volunteers from his office in the library.[1] The training manual I had been provided earlier by email listed a number of dos and don'ts. Mr. Bertram, a trim white man in his sixties with salt-and-pepper hair who approached his work with a combination of evangelical faith and military-like precision, emphasized the following:

1. Do not touch the inmates.
2. Do not give them anything. No gifts of any kind, no money, no candy— that's an infraction. They can have paper and pencil for class, but you must collect all of the pencils at the end. Count the pencils before you hand them out. Make sure you have all the pencils when you leave. This is very important. *Do not forget any of the pencils.*
3. Do not accept anything from the inmates. They may try to pass you a note or ask you do something for them, like contact someone on the outside with a message. That's a serious infraction and something we would need to know about so we could handle it.

---

1. To protect the identities of the incarcerated women at the center of this study, I use pseudonyms to identify all of the people, organizations, penal institutions, and settings where this research occurred.

4. Do not share any personal information with them—home address, where you work, your phone number, your mother's phone number, your cell phone number. *Nothing.* Do not tell them where you live.
5. The officer is in charge. That is their pod. If there are any problems, the officer will handle it.

In spite of these warnings, by the end of this project I had broken almost every one of these rules. I did not set out to do so, but as the days went by, I could not watch women break down in tears while sharing their creative writing and not reach out to them. I could not refrain from offering—giving—them pencils, tissues, or words of support when needed. Women in jails are often overlooked in scholarship and discourses about incarceration, crime, safety, and prison reform, resulting in abuse and neglect, even though they have been the fastest-growing segment of the prison population for more than fifty years. The number of women in jail daily in the United States grew fourteen-fold, from just under 8,000 in 1970 to 110,000 in 2014. Annually, American jails hold over 2 million women, 80 percent of whom are mothers, including many single parents to small children and some 150,000 pregnant women.[2]

Most women, like their male counterparts, have been charged but not convicted of any crime. Many have been arrested for actions taken to cope with the serious life challenges they face, including deep poverty, unemployment, housing insecurity, and domestic violence as well as physical and mental health issues. Most are detained on charges such as shoplifting, sex work, and substance use, which could mean driving under the influence or possession of an illegal substance. They have not been convicted of any wrongdoing and are awaiting release on bail or, in many instances, for the case against them to fall apart. As they wait, they are subjected to the jail's regular punishment regime. Because jails are built primarily to regulate and punish men, they are ill-equipped to meet women's needs. As a result, many women leave jail worse off than when they entered. They walk out mentally and physically diminished with greater stress, less money, no job, no place to live, and much work to do to reunite with and stabilize their families. Recognizing that Demeter's Daughters offers their drama class as a means of supporting women in jail, I found it impossible ethically to withhold support when needed even as I

2. Wendy Sawyer and Wanda Bertram, "Jail Will Separate 2.3 Million Mothers from Their Children This Year," Prison Policy Initiative, May 13, 2018, accessed September 21, 2021, https://www.prisonpolicy.org/blog/2018/05/13/mothers-day-2018/; Elizabeth Swavola, Kristi Riley, and Ram Subramanian, "Overlooked: Women in Jails in an Era of Reform," Vera Institute of Justice, 2016, accessed January 21, 2022, https://www.vera.org/publications/overlooked-women-and-jails-report.

conducted research at the site. This meant at times sharing parts of myself, my past, my skills as a writer (serving as a scribe for some women who were confident speaking their ideas but not writing them down), and my expertise as a teaching artist and performer.

In this chapter, I chronicle moments illustrating the pedagogy and practice of teaching theater to incarcerated women, focusing on the work of Demeter's Daughters at Midwestern county jail. The workshop leader, Aaron, a white, twenty-something young gay man, staged critical conversations eliciting what the women knew about the relationship between gender and justice in the United States. Humor and mythological stories about bad women as well as the participants' own tales anchored our collective inquiries into what it meant to be a "bad woman." The women often used Aaron's prompts to share deeply personal stories about surviving domestic violence, sexual assaults, and problematic substance abuse. The sharing of these stories in workshop bound the participants together as a community that belonged to each other and to the drama program. As the workshop transitioned from creative writing exercises and into theater production mode, I considered how the participants built upon their stories and sense of community to tell the larger story about "bad women" when the jail's chief administrator instructed us to create a show, and in so doing, staged healing. I conclude that one moment toward the end of the show of Black expressive culture that evoked Black Arts and Black Power motifs was critical in linking the written play script to the participants' deep desire for healing. With it, they issued a poignant call for personal healing and structural transformation that was impossible to miss.

METHODOLOGY

How does one teach drama in jail? How do you build trust in a space designed to cause pain, isolation, and fear? What do the participants derive from drama club? How do you glean participants' authentic experiences? What can ethnography possibly offer that other approaches do not?

To help me answer these and other research questions, the Demeter's Daughters staff and Midwestern jail administrators granted me permission to observe and participate in a weekly drama class for sixteen months (December 2009–April 2011). I found Demeter's Daughters through a Google search and, after reading through their website, I emailed and called, spoke with someone on staff, and then later visited their office on the upper floors of an expansive yet aged pale-yellow stone brick church to meet Dorothy, the passionate, middle-aged white woman who was the founding artistic director, and later

Aaron. As Dorothy welcomed me into their modest offices, I noticed awards, pictures, and posters of past productions on every wall, which gave evidence of the group's independence, vision, and entrepreneurial spirit. Dorothy developed new work—both solo and ensemble performances—that told the stories of some of the most marginalized people in our society, including the disabled and incarcerated. She taught at local correctional facilities and in homes and centers for people with disabilities, training participants in the work of the artist—playwright, actor—so that they might be able to tell their own stories. Her labor supported a small cadre of other professional artists who directed and acted in the shows and taught alongside her. They too believed that art is for everybody and everyone can be an artist. It soon became clear to me that Dorothy and I shared many of the same values and experiences. When she introduced me to Aaron, I also saw in him a like-minded, generous, caring, and compassionate spirit, teacher, and artist.

As I was working to obtain permission to conduct this research, going through both the Institutional Review Board (IRB) process and the jail's evaluation system, Demeter's Daughters added me to the visitors' list to witness another show they had developed at a federal prison. That cold November day was my first time in a prison, my first time seeing a prison drama-club production, my first time meeting people who were locked up, and my first time meeting most of the Demeter's Daughters' staff. I left the venue moved by the show, which was performed in the prison library, and with so many questions about their process, how they built trust with the women, how they navigated the demands and limitations of the space. It was clear that this site held rich potential and I very much hoped it would work out.

So that Dorothy and Aaron could learn more about me and come to know me, I was invited to join the company at a nearby bar for karaoke and a post-show celebration. The bar looked like it had been around since Prohibition, and it had been. Beyond the long, velvety-smooth bar, however, there was a small black platform with a speaker and a microphone for karaoke. Aaron and other members of the ensemble quickly made their selections and lined up to perform. As someone who can carry a tune but would never call myself a singer, I opted to sip my drink and flip through the voluminous song catalogue as I listened in awe to the others on stage. Aaron received hearty applause before he even stepped to the mic. As the opening chords of Tina Turner's rendition of "Proud Mary"—Aaron's signature piece—rang out, he glanced at me and at Dorothy and invited us both to join him as spontaneous karaoke backup singers. I took a chance. As I climbed on stage I felt the stakes were high. They knew I was a performer and that I was interested in their work, but until then they did not know whether I was any good. Could I play? Could I hang? This was my shot. I deferred to Aaron as he sang the hell out of "Proud Mary," but proceeded to make a total fool of myself with a sorry rendition of Turner's iconic choreography, including a now legendary logroll. As I dusted myself off at the end of the song, Dorothy, Aaron, and I laughed and laughed and laughed, and the rest of the ensemble laughed with and at us, and I was in. Successful audition![3]

Such serious play in which the stakes are high despite the playful context became a central feature of my working relationship with Aaron throughout our time together. Prison drama clubs invite participants to tap into their imaginations and to share their ideas and experiences through scenes and monologues. Because the content of the incarcerated women's work is often autobiographical, sharing their writings can be difficult, raw, and it can make people feel vulnerable. Women take these risks because the stories are killing them and they must be told. Truth will out, and she is looking for justice. Knowing how powerful the work could be, Dorothy and Aaron took big risks when they allowed me to research their practice—especially Aaron, whom I accompanied for almost two years.

In addition to my ethnographic fieldwork at the jail, I interviewed Aaron, Dorothy, and other members of Demeter's Daughters several times to understand how they came to the work, what their goals were, how they assessed their efficacy, and how their practice had changed over time. Because of their generosity I was able to witness Demeter's Daughters' powerful, creative work again and again in multiple prison and jail settings and in schools and daycare centers for the disabled. Their work was deeply moving every single day. Researching their work was never, ever easy.

Almost every Friday morning for those sixteen months, Aaron and I met and rode a local commuter train to Midwestern jail. During our hour-long ride, we would catch up and then talk about his plan for the day. Once inside, at the start of every class, I introduced myself as a Northwestern University graduate student conducting research on theater for incarcerated women, a disclosure required by the IRB but which violated Mr. Bertram's rule about not sharing personal information, including any indications of where you worked. I explained that I was there primarily to learn what the class facilitator, Aaron, was doing, but if they wanted to learn more about the project, I would be happy to tell them. If they wanted to participate in a small-group interview they would be most welcome. I did, however, commit to not write about them

---

3. Author fieldnotes, September 17, 2009.

without their permission and vowed that I would do my best to protect their identities in whatever I wrote. This framing eased everyone's concerns about my purpose and allowed me to observe and participate in class. I completed the same writing and acting assignments as the women did. When the workshop moved toward production and finally to performance, I transitioned into a new role as Aaron's assistant director.

Throughout the study I made jottings in and around my drama-class writing assignments and later in the margins of the script. In the close confines of the drama-club room, taking more extensive notes with my head down felt disrespectful. I also worried that my notes might one day be confiscated by officers should an issue associated with my presence ever arise. As such, I focused not so much on documenting everything that happened, but instead scrawled what I felt were keywords, phrases, and images in a roughly poetic form that would trigger my memories. Because I did this every week, people became accustomed to my jotting and with time it felt less awkward. My notes were deepened and expanded every day immediately after class when Aaron and I grabbed a bite to eat at a local Chinese restaurant before boarding the train back home. As we scarfed down hot noodle dishes, we rehashed the day's events and I expanded my jottings in a notebook. At the restaurant, I could pose questions to him about his process, reflect with him on what went well in class and what he thought the next steps would be. This process would continue until we boarded the train for home. Once I was back in my apartment, I transcribed my jottings from class and the restaurant into more detailed, typed journal entries.

Recognizing that my jottings and transcriptions were based solely on my personal recollections, I obtained permission from Mr. Bertram and the jail warden, Chief J., to conduct one small-group interview with Aaron and several women at the jail who attended class regularly over the course of the study. Aaron and I both made jottings during that session rather than record it because, again, we feared that, should any of the women reveal something related to their cases, the records might be used against them. Also, anything that I recorded had to be screened by Mr. Bertram, who had the right to withhold the tape. To address these concerns, I interviewed Mr. Bertram, the jail's head administrator Chief J., and other members of the jail's programming staff. I also interviewed and spent extensive time with Aaron, Dorothy, and other drama-program facilitators outside of class. Finally, I shared this chapter with Aaron and Dorothy to solicit their feedback. Taken together, their insights have been invaluable in helping me clarify and analyze how the drama club operated.

TIME FOR DRAMA CLASS

The lights are always on at Midwestern, an accredited, five-story combined adult court and carceral complex that allocates one crescent-shaped, two-tiered cellblock (the pod) to the twenty to sixty women it holds each day. Narrow cell windows allow a measure of daylight or the night sky to creep in, but the monotony of the days is interrupted only by routines orchestrated by officers. A prisoner's time, use of space, mobility, basic needs, and social interactions are structured by a local power hierarchy that flows from the County Sheriff to Chief J. down to the rank-and-file officers and other support staff. The intense labor involved in surveillance and monitoring that comprises officers' days is not meant to transform prisoners into "productive" or "law-abiding" citizens; it teaches them to comply with orders. Jail administrators and corrections officers point out that the routines ensure that people's basic needs are met and provide for everyone's safety, meaning the imprisoned people, officers, and staff. The timetable inducts and acclimates the incarcerated into the habitus of the facility and instructs or scripts them into daily life as prisoners. Willingness to participate in the routine—eating, showering, sleeping, cleaning one's cell, count, and lockdown—demonstrates acceptance of one's status as a prisoner. Compliance rehabilitates.

As self-identified Christians, Chief J. and the Inmate Programming Coordinator Mr. Bertram considered it their responsibility to offer prisoners "a way out," in this case by encouraging the women to take advantage of the courses the facility offered them. Volunteering to participate in additional programing there signaled a prisoner's acceptance of their status and determination to improve, to grow, in ways deemed acceptable, appropriate, and effective to jail staff. Of course, prisoners' freedom depended upon their willingness to comply and participate. Contemporary scholars of the prison system agree that "the monotony and regimentation of everyday life [behind bars] by themselves foster participation even when the activities being offered are not to the imprisoned women's liking and do not actually contribute to their resocialization."[4] Demeter's Daughters was one strategic initiative that met what the officers and staff understand to be the women's need for emotional release. Attending class Friday mornings, I learned why the incarcerated women also valued it.

In promotional materials, Demeter's Daughters describes their theater program, first introduced in 2007, as providing "space and resources for incar-

---

4. Wilma Santiago-Irizarry, *Medicalizing Ethnicity: The Construction of Latino Identity in a Psychiatric Setting* (Ithaca, NY: Cornell University Press, 2001), 131.

cerated women to engage the humanities" using "literature . . . reflections on life . . . writing and the discussion of ethics and philosophy."[5] Months of creative writing workshops culminate in a performance of the women's writings on the pod for an audience of other women prisoners, staff, and invited guests.

While Aaron and I threaded our way to the women's unit, accompanied sometimes by Chrissy, a petite, twenty-something blond woman interning with the theater, the women who signed up for drama club climbed the interior stairs of their pod to the second tier and waited in line outside of a small program room for class to begin. After we were buzzed into the pod, the officer on duty (usually a woman in her late twenties or early thirties) escorted us up the stairs and unlocked the program-room door. The women filed in behind us and took seats around two long, thin folding tables pushed into a room not much bigger than a family bathroom. As soon as the officer was confident that her count of the participants was accurate and that their cell doors were secured, she shut the door behind her with a rush of air and a solid click.

Then the tension quickly broke. Smiles rounded eager cheeks and eyes awakened with a mixture of anticipation and trepidation. Each week, this was for some participants their first time behind bars, and for many more it was their first drama class. Veterans take newcomers under their wings and talk up the class in the days and hours before we arrive. As soon as the door shut, one veteran, Mattie, an African American woman in her mid-twenties with long, rumpled hair, announced what was on many people's minds: "I wait all week for drama class. When I'm not feeling it, I say to myself, just hold on, here come Thursday, and then, hoo hoo! Friday morning! I know Aaron is on his way."

"Hello, ladies!" Aaron chirps, pulling up a chair. As noted, Aaron is a twenty-something, openly gay white man. He grew up in the Midwest in a small, predominantly white town. His journey to the jail began when he heard Dorothy, who founded Demeter's Daughters, give a talk at his college, where he was a Women's Studies and Theater double major. Their friendship was instantaneous. Months later, he was interning in her office, directing two shows, and leading workshops with adults with disabilities. After graduation, he became their office manager and a regular instructor at two women's facilities. Aaron divided our class into three phrases—first, a women's studies/theater course in which the participants read, discuss, and respond (in writing and on their feet) to materials that he brings in; second, the women devise and rehearse a performance developed from their writings; and third, the shows

---

5. Demeter's Daughters company brochure.

themselves, which are performed within the women's pod by the drama-class participants for an audience consisting of other imprisoned women, jail staff, volunteers, local legislators, and invited guests. At the start of every session, Aaron engaged the women in a much-anticipated ritual—"the check-in." During the check-in, everyone said their name or what they wanted to be called that day, and shared how they were feeling if they wanted to. Aaron set the tone by going first.

"Hello, ladies!" Aaron repeated to get their attention.

"Hello, Aaron!" they giggled in reply.

"Let's get started"—then Aaron launched into a story about his week, often one that highlighted his many adventures looking for love in a nearby city. One example:

A couple nights ago Aaron was making a sandwich in the kitchen of his studio apartment and got interrupted by Tobias, his new boyfriend. Something about sex on the countertop having to do with condiments. . . . I was laughing too hard! Basically, now when they're doing it, they call it "making a sandwich."

He brought the drama of his personal life to class every week with a campy sense of humor marked by verbal dexterity, an embrace of incongruity, and open celebration of his own sexuality, much to the women's delight. They *loved* it. They ate up his stories about trying to meet a decent man, have great sex, and develop a loving relationship. Aaron began class every week with raunchy and deeply intimate tales, a tactic that set the tone for our time together. The scandalous content, made more so by the jail's explicit regulations prohibiting homosexuality, dispelled any potential confusion about his sexuality and jokingly disarmed anyone who may have been inclined to ridicule him or the class based on his identity as a young white gay man. Aaron's sexcapades served as his "check-ins" but further demonstrated that the drama program could serve as an alternative public space within the jail in which one might share personal stories as well as constructed fictions without fear of being attacked or shamed. In fact, the women greatly appreciated Aaron's style of teaching because he brought his full authentic self to class. As one participant put it, Aaron was "himself . . . a lady 100% of the time." He was never "shamed to be himself," they said, but rather "live[d] in his skin," and from that place "genuinely care[d]" about "everyone." Homophobia did deter some, but one regular participant summarized the feelings of most attendees: "Aaron does not prevent people from coming to class, he draws people in."[6]

Little has been written about prisoners' use of jest behind bars, but Charles M. Terry, a scholar who was once incarcerated, suggests that male prison-

---

6. Lisa Biggs interview with women imprisoned at Midwestern County Jail (September 2010).

ers use humor to express how they really feel. Because prisons for men are spaces where "any exhibition of emotion relative to pain of any sort is seen as weakness and is unacceptable," humor offers a critical means of voicing the otherwise inexpressible.[7] Men use humor to express dissatisfaction with prison rules and practices. Some actions like vocal mocking of officers or acts of "insubordinate farting" may not be "dignified," but Terry argues that they interrupt prison routines and help to constitute a community of "convicts," instruct newcomers in how to behave, and "help inmates maintain their dignity," individually and collectively, in the face of the demeaning practices of the state.[8] Such jokes get their "punch" by revealing the shared, devalued perspectives and experiences of the tellers and their listeners.[9] Laughter creates "solidarity" among the incarcerated by enabling them to challenge dominant norms and reframe past "inappropriate behavior(s) as acceptable, even admirable."[10]

One example of incarcerated women's humor can be found in the African American stand-up comedienne Mo'Nique's special, *I Could Have Been Your Cellmate* (2007), filmed at the Ohio Reformatory for Women, a maximum-security facility, before a majority audience of Black women. Early on in the show, Mo'Nique shares her surprise at the prison's prohibitions against touch, including masturbation. She offers a mischievous workaround, demonstrating how one might substitute the side of the neck for the clitoris to achieve orgasm. Katelyn Woods argues that here Mo'Nique uses her position as a Black feminist performer to "reveal the shams, hypocrisies, and incongruities of the dominant culture" and to "confront and subvert the very power that keeps women powerless," in this case, powerless to control their own bodies and pleasure for themselves. In this moment of autoeroticism on the prison grounds, she leads the crowd in confronting "the mythology that sexual pleasure is a privilege granted to some, not an inherently human endeavor."[11] The incarcerated women laugh in collective recognition of both the desire for sexual touch that she performs and the critique she stages of the prohibition. They agree: the rule is ridiculous.

---

7. Charles M. Terry, "The Function of Humor for Prison Inmates," *Journal of Contemporary Criminal Justice* 13, no. 1 (1997): 24.

8. Terry, "Humor," 32.

9. Donna Goldstein, *Laughter out of Place: Race, Class, Violence and Sexuality in a Rio Shanty Town* (Oakland: University of California Press, 2013), 129

10. Terry, "Humor," 30.

11. Nancy Walker, *A Very Serious Thing: Women's Humor and American Culture* (Minneapolis: University of Minnesota Press, 1988), 9, quoted in Katelyn Woods, *Cracking Up: Black Feminist Comedy in the Twentieth and Twenty-First Century United States* (Iowa City: University of Iowa Press, 2021), 68.

Mo'Nique loses her audience later in the show, however, when she compliments several on-duty officers. The women will not clap for their captors. A cacophony of jeers stops the show. This moment of unscripted laughter further reveals the women's intimate knowledge of how prison actually works and critiques both the officers and Mo'Nique for trying to manipulate them into approving of how prison is performed. To avoid losing them altogether, Mo'Nique must quickly pivot her stand-up routine before they fully unleash their laughter at her. Taken together, these moments of incarcerated Black women/women's laughter communicate that this special event, orchestrated by the prison and featuring a celebrity performer, will not erase the day-to-day abuses the prisoners endure. Through laughter, incarcerated women communicate that they will not be compelled to "respect the state" or "concede to humanizing the guards in an institution that refuses to humanize the[m]."[12]

Aaron's virtuosity as a humorous, femme, and campy storyteller drew women to the drama program. Through his practice of strategic joking, Aaron entertained, but also used performance to cast the programming room as a sanctuary. For women with the greatest needs, jails offer limited, temporary sanctuary from their daily struggles to secure reliable, safer shelter, including a place to sleep, shower, eat regular meals, and access minimal health care. Midwestern helped such women meet some of their most basic needs but did not fulfill many other needs such as the need for membership in a supportive, caring community. In drama class, however, some women who rarely, if ever, talked on the pod would speak. They even laughed. People who did not know each other and may have even judged one another harshly as "real criminals" at first glance discovered they had interests and experiences in common and could learn from one another. Drama class constituted an alternative community in the jail. In the opening moments of class, Aaron's bawdy humor and the squeals of our collective laughter bound us together:

What can M&Ms do that you can't? Come in different colors.

For many weeks when first I accompanied Aaron, I did not realize how important this opening ludic moment was to setting the tone and scope of the classes. I was overwhelmed by the heavy weight of despair blanketing every surface of the jail and the profound sense of loss slapping up against the hard, white concrete walls. I felt dislocated by the incongruous juxtaposition of multiple sets of outdoor lawn furniture set up as if for a party strewn across its wide, white linoleum floor in the middle of the pod, and I was intimidated by the officers. I was alarmed that the women were overwhelmingly African Americans, round-bodied, with hair scattered around their heads, teeth in all

---

12. Woods, *Cracking Up*, 75.

kinds of shambles, and faces that looked far too familiar—like my family and neighbors. "What did she do?" resounded in my mind, unspoken, whenever I introduced myself to the drama class in the early weeks of the research. How could I treat these women who looked like my family, friends, and neighbors like prisoners? I was also often frightened, unsure of how to move or interact, especially regarding how to interact with the officers, who had enormous sway over both how class was conducted (or not) and my own research. Laughter felt disrespectful; it was a reminder that I had something to laugh about in a place where there was a lot of sorrow, anger, and loss.

Over time, I learned how to comport myself because the stories helped me to forget I was in a jail and bridged a connection between life on the inside and that on the outside. I even found myself laughing at Aaron's use of dark humor, jokes or funny stories that revealed suffering and articulated "a perspective that would otherwise be inexpressible"[13]: *Why does Smokey the Bear have no kids? Whenever his wife gets hot, he covers her with a blanket and beats her with a shovel.* Over the weeks and months to come, Aaron's bawdy, dark, at times disturbing—even offensive—humor, laid the groundwork for the women to tell their own stories in the styles that felt most right and appropriate for them. His humor gave them permission to be impolite, un-lady-like, and raw, but never pressured them to speak.

Community-corrections poetry and performance programs have come under scrutiny for coercing women into telling stories of personal victimization using psycho-criminological modalities that represent them as traumatized figures lacking agency. These initiatives end up discouraging women from critically engaging dominant narratives about "bad" women, especially if their analysis complicates or outright contradicts law enforcement perspectives about why crime happens and women's culpability. Megan Sweeney writes, "Given that many women prisoners feel intensely isolated in their victimization, lack knowledge about the dynamics of abuse, and blame themselves for their experiences, it seems crucial—on a political level—for them to learn that they are not alone and that their experiences reflect wider structural patterns."[14] Uncritical, sensationalist accounts of women's exploitation perpetuate their subordination and degradation. Sweeney concludes, however, that "complex engagements with narratives of victimization," in which women are allowed to represent themselves as embodying complex personhood, may offer "avenues for thinking and talking about victimization and agency in

---

13. Goldstein, *Laughter,* 264–65, 124.

14. Megan Sweeney, *Reading Is My Window: Books and the Art of Reading in Women's Prisons* (Chapel Hill: University of North Carolina Press, 2010), 89.

more nuanced, grounded, and productive terms."[15] As time goes on, I realize that this is the work Aaron wants to do.

Following the ritual check-in, Aaron divides class into three sections—a physical warm-up that includes a series of stretches in place and sometimes an on-your-feet group improvisational theater game; second, the sharing of a piece of writing (short fiction, play, poem, picture) that he reads aloud; and, finally, a written or physical response time. Class was short—only two hours on the best days—and every second felt precious. It was often interrupted by corrections officers, the commissary and medical staff, the plumber, or a sergeant whose need to address the entire group stopped everyone in their tracks. Whether these interruptions were intentional—a means of maintaining control over the space—or accidental, I did not know. The threat of these interruptions and the possibility of spontaneous lockdown loomed over every session. In the time allotted, women used our sessions to articulate their needs, get some of them met, and, eventually, as the workshop moved toward production, to *stage healing*.

I CHOSE TO LIVE

One grey February morning about three months into my fieldwork, Jeannette, a petite white woman with long greying hair in her forties, who had been awaiting trial now for nearly two years, brought before the group an urgent issue for collective analysis. A few weeks after we met her, she revealed that, in the six months before we came, she rarely spoke, rarely interacted with the other women on the pod. As her case moved to trial, court officers insisted that she sit for an intelligence test to assess her mental state and to screen her for disabilities. Jeanette came to drama class because she was curious and stayed because she liked Aaron. With time she began talking more often and connecting with others.

During her check-in Jeanette complained that her privacy had been violated and that she was being negatively "labeled." Jeannette was extremely angry that she was being tried in the media before her case could be heard in court. Concern over how being labeled might affect the proceedings and how that information would circulate inside the jail prompted her to bring this issue to class. She told us, "The officers are required to scan the newspapers for articles about people in here and cut them out. That's to protect our privacy, you know? Nobody needs to know why I am in here. It is none of

---

15. Sweeney, *Reading*, 88.

their business." Aaron facilitated a short discussion about how the labeling impacted them all. Other women around the small brown folding table agreed that labeling was an issue they wanted to delve into so Aaron pledged to find a way to address it.

The next week, Aaron opens the dialogue by reading aloud a passage from *The Scarlet Letter* (1850) by Nathaniel Hawthorne, a classic work of American literature. Set in the mid-1600s, the novel tells the story of Hester Prynne, a white settler colonist, who is abandoned by her husband and left to fend for herself in a small Puritan community. After years of what appears to be complete solitude, local townspeople discover she is pregnant. Her refusal to reveal the father's name results in a public hearing, during which she is convicted of adultery and condemned to wear an embroidered scarlet letter "A" on all of her clothing. The A signifies not only her past wrongdoing but within the political sign system of clothing instructs those she encounters to treat her like a criminal, a "bad woman." The daughter she bears, Pearl, becomes the only positive link between Hester and their world.[16]

Aaron asks the women to respond with a timed free write. For seven minutes, they write continuously, first about what they think or feel about the core ideas in the passage, and, when they have nothing more to say about it, about whatever else comes to mind. Spelling and grammar will not be checked, he reminds them. Aaron wants to know what they think and feel. A few minutes later, we go around the circle to hear their passages read aloud. Three people share. One remarks on how differently Pearl sees her mother from how everyone else sees her and from how Hester sees herself. The second notices that Pearl sees the "essence" and "truth" of Hester, "who she really is" when "nobody else could see it." Another agrees and hopes her own children will see her in a similar light, as "the good parts." As discussion of the story unfolds, the women around the table consistently connect with this concern about being a good mother. As they talk, I notice myself wondering, "What kind of mother have you really been?" and "Who is taking care of your children now?" This kind of labeling is what they want to confront, the assumption that they are bad mothers because they are in jail. Aaron picks up on their observation that, in Pearl's eyes, her mother looms larger than the label, but Hester thinks the "A" has all but consumed her. The women draw parallels between their own experiences and Hester's, remarking that they have been—are—treated like "animals," "dehumanized," and "defeminized."[17] Like her, most of the participants are single mothers with young children at home.

---

16. Nathaniel Hawthorne, *The Scarlet Letter*, ed. Ross C. Murfin (Boston: Bedford Books of St. Martin's Press, 1991), 93.

17. Fieldnotes taken February 19, 2010.

They had limited support systems outside of the jail and inside are in search of community to feel safe, valued, and whole. Labeling, more specifically the process by which women are collectively devalued and labeled criminal, becomes the major theme of the work for the next six months. Aaron describes it as an investigation into "the grand narrative of the Modern American Woman . . . especially of the women we forget."[18] The stories we read next invite them to consider what constitutes appropriate female behavior and the consequences and possibilities of failing to perform.

About a month later, in March, when our little group assembled in the program room with Jeannette, January, Frida, Nettie, and Rocky as well as Aaron and I around the table, they would elevate the question of women's ostracization to the next level. January had been at Midwestern almost as long as Jeanette and was also awaiting her court date. January was a twenty-something white woman with shoulder-length brown hair and a history of substance abuse. Frida was a tall Latina with long dark tresses and a bold laugh who grew up around the Great Lakes. We first encountered her while she was on lockdown. Red-shirted and isolated in her cell for twenty-three hours a day, we walked past her every day for weeks to get to the program room. From her adjacent cell she was able to overhear what we were doing. Often, she laughed with us from the other side of the wall, resisting the isolation and dehumanization that this punishment was designed to impose. When she was finally able to fully join in, she revealed that being able to overhear our improvisations and discussions about women and their position in society kept her from "going crazy." Nettie, a petite Latina in her late twenties with long dark brown hair and sad, soft eyes, and Rocky, an angular, twitchy, white woman also in her thirties with extensive track marks on both arms, completed the circle.

After check-in, Aaron read aloud passages of a short story from *Glamour Magazine* written by Maia Morgan entitled "I Chose to Live." In this poetic nonfiction piece, Morgan (an associate of Aaron's) narrates her journey to get a tattoo as a reminder that she survived being repeatedly molested by her mother's father, an outwardly loving and highly respected member of his community. Unlike Hester's "A," Morgan's self-inflicted labels—scars—are intended to be guardians against grief. The passage we read begins minutes after Morgan leaves the tattoo parlor. Staring down at her arms, she realizes that the bandages make her look more wounded than powerful and doubt begins to creep in. A chance encounter with an Emily Dickinson poem posted on an ad inside a public bus shifts her perspective. The ad reads, "Hope is the

---

18. Aaron, "Well-Behaved Women," program director's note.

thing with feathers that perches in the soul, and sings the tune without the words, and never stops at all." The story concludes:

> I can't tell you that I got off the bus and strode blissfully into my future. But I did get off the bus and buy groceries and go home and cook dinner and wake up the next day and the next one after that. I kept on making friends and falling in love and working and writing and dreaming. People used to think that when a child died, swallows carried its soul to heaven. That is what made me decide on the swallow tattoo. It would serve as both a remembrance of the parts of me that didn't survive and an acknowledgement of my capacity to rise above, away from the painful past. . . . It's a bold mark. But I suppose it is beautiful. And it's mine now: remembrance of pain, acknowledgment of strength. With the swallow tattoo, I wanted to mourn my losses, bury my dead and then move on. But here's the thing: I don't think you move on, really, from the past. You do, but you don't. You carry it with you. You make it as light as you can. As light as feathers.[19]

Aaron wipes tears from his eyes as he puts down the page. The sound of his sniffles fills the room. No one can speak. No one moves. Even the pod below is quiet. I stare down at the table, sorrow heavy in my chest. I want to say something, but what? What does one say after hearing this? What words can possibly honor the story, the speaker, the moment?

After a long pause, Frida breaks the silence. She, quite surprisingly, playfully teases Aaron, saying, "You're crying?"

Shocked and embarrassed, he protests, "Stop looking at me. I hate crying in front of people."

"But you know me!" she babies him back.

January, Jeannette, Nettie, Rocky and I feel something shift. Aaron wiggles uncomfortably in his chair trying to signal outrage at her teasing, but his movement just makes us giggle. Frida's playful banter has opened up the space for the rest of us to speak, to move, to return to the now where our bodies are. Instead of being isolated in our grief for Morgan, feeling shamed and powerless to respond, Frida's comment activates a moment of shared laughter that pulls us together. We attach, attune, and sync. This is a community of vulnerable "bad girls" wearing scarlet letters of various shapes and sizes. Knowing some of each other's shame and vulnerabilities, we chose to be together.

---

19. Maia Morgan, "I Chose to Live: One Woman's Story of Surviving Sexual Abuse," *Glamour Magazine,* March 4, 2010, accessed September 18, 2021, https://www.glamour.com/story/i-chose-to-live-one-womans-story-of-surviving-sexual-abuse.

Morgan's story educates readers about how molestation happens in families and how healing can occur. The swallow tattoos are part of her healing process. They are meant to publicly mark the molestation, help her "mourn" and "bury" the trauma, and thus enable her to privately "move on." This example demonstrates how healing is a process of self-repair, one that can happen even where no cure can be found, where justice never comes, and the harm itself cannot be forgotten, forgiven, or taken back. Morgan can never recover those parts of herself that were lost in the violence, such as the little girl she was before the rapes occurred and the abiding trust that she had in her closest family members, but she realizes her healing is not predicated upon their return. Healing means processing the trauma and finding ways to manage the memories so that she no longer relives the events in flashbacks that shut her down. As an adult now, the swallows serve as visual reminders that the molestation happened in the past and that it is over. Knowing that she is not in immediate danger helps Morgan live life in the present. Her short story teaches us that just as we are individuals and our traumas are our own, so our healing is our own. Over time, as Aaron continues to put the drama club participants' stories in conversation with both contemporary and classic women's literature, what emerges are stories of women, really girls, surviving violence, coping with loss, and forging lives for themselves despite the harms done.

The story and its example of healing as an ongoing process of self-repair invite women in the workshop to engage in their own reparative storytelling. Once the laughter over Aaron's tears subsides, January and Rocky immediately reveal that Morgan's story is their own. Both have survived sexual violence. They echo the anger Morgan felt that the people to whom they turned for protection betrayed their trust, trivialized their concerns, or flat-out called them liars. In the last moments of class, Rocky lands a deep punch in our collective gut that sums up her analysis when she proclaims: "Disposable, that's what I am, disposable. It's what I been my whole life. And now I'm a bad, bad, bad, bad, bad, bad woman." Just then, the officer arrives, early, to unlock the door and end class. We have no time to respond to Rocky's words, but Morgan's story opens a new space in the coming weeks in which to talk about how women are rendered disposable, and how they can use drama class to heal.

WRITING AND STAGING HEALING

When we return the following Friday, January brings an original story she has worked on all week to share. It contributes to the class's understanding of the multiple overlapping forces that have contributed to women's degraded social status. It reads:

"Are you angry?" the therapist beckons.

But I'm not sure if I've ever felt that kind of anger . . . the kind where blood boils like sweltering lava embedded in a Hawaiian volcano; the kind that fuels a person in rampage-laden quest for revenge. I don't know what that feels like. Sometimes I'm not sure I know how to feel. But I do know what it's like to be underneath a man twice my size, to be pinned to a putrid smelling mattress, to resist with every ounce of strength in my body, to flounder like a catfish pulled from murky waters—knowing that I cannot escape.

As he dehumanizes me, I am aware he seeks only power, not sex. So rather than flail and scream, I take direct, calculated punches—to the cheekbone, the ribcage, the kidneys. All the while taunting him, "You're not a man! I can't even feel your small dick! I hope you enjoy this, you pathetic fuck!" My punches don't faze his imposing 6-foot, 5-inch statue, but I want him to remember my words.

I'm on the third floor—windows are of no avail. I'm in the Ida B. Wells Homes—screaming will yield nothing. I barricaded and fortified the door myself—imposing steel, plywood 2 x 4s roped in an intricate maze around the door's frame. I had thought I was clever with my arrangement to keep both the narcotics unit and the warring Gangster Disciples from storming my once-abandoned apartment. I hadn't fathomed that I would barricade myself in with a demon. . . . After reassuring him that I won't file a report, he helps me with the door. I walk between two junkies on the stairwell, exchanging clean works. I step over a puddle of urine, avoid the handrails, bypass the gym-shoe boys who sling rocks and blows at both ends of the corridor. A line of fiends weaves through the first and second floors under the enticement of sample dope, but no one seems to notice me. Yesterday I valued the way they ignored me, the way that my white skin no longer stood out to them, the way that they never called me Snow White anymore. But today, I actually feel separate from them—and no one notices.

I walk onto 35th street, head north for Mercy Hospital. The rape kit is performed painlessly for I am not this body. I will report the assault because that's what I have learned to do. Unlike the last time, or the time before that, I vow to follow society's procedure. It's a shame no one taught me how I'm supposed to feel.

Police officers, doctors—all with milky white skin—ask me how I'm coping. What they can get for me. Detectives, nurses, patrolmen—all with skins of various shades of brown—ask me if I'm a drug addict, a prostitute—ask me what I'm doing in the projects. They escort me to 51st and Wentworth, where my attacker is being detained in a holding cell awaiting charges.

After twelve hours of questioning, I'm told that no one believes my story. The Black female middle-aged detective delivers the consensus of the police department; when a white girl ventures into the projects, she deserves what she gets. If I continue with formal charges, I'm told I will be arrested for the crime of criminal trespass to state-supported land.

This isn't what I learned in school. White people don't face discrimination. We follow a protocol and people believe us when we file complaints. But I'm logical. I don't want to cry. I want to protest. I want to appeal. I want to find fucking Jesse Jackson. But at 3 a.m., with no money for a bus that isn't running, petrified of looming withdrawal symptoms, I walk back to 3535 S. Vincennes, and life goes on.[20]

When she puts the paper down, I am sick to my stomach and can hardly breathe. Several people around the table have broken down into tears. Aaron is a mess. Feeling paralyzed, I slip my hands into my front pants pockets and discover I have several pieces of crumpled tissue in my jeans. They are contraband and, hearing Mr. Bertram's entreaties to never give the prisoners anything echo in my mind, I hand them around anyway. Sometimes you just cannot abide by the rules. As I pass the tissue, I touch January's arm lightly. She is crying too and while Aaron looks like he would like to do it, better it be me, another woman, so no one can accuse him of impropriety. Folks need human contact. If the study gets cancelled, so be it.

Mine is a small gesture of support in a place where real care, kindness, and support are rarely on offer. Giving women tissue is a violation of the rules, and touching them even lightly on the arm is a violation as well. Jail is designed to break people's bodies, spirits, and connections to other people. I take January's story as a call to action to resist the no-help norm that passes for social services in this country, the inadequacies of which are detailed in her story. The public-housing apartment she occupied because she had no other place to live was substandard and in disrepair. Other nearby people struggling with substance abuse cannot help her because, in the throes of their own addictions, they need help themselves. There is no help to be found at the hospital, nor from the police, who ultimately declare her a liar. Even the therapist whose question opens the tale is suspect.

---

20. January, "Are You Angry?," unpublished manuscript shared with the author.

This assault, and the series of events that led up to it, should never have happened. January did not deserve to be violated in these ways; no one ever does. Unfortunately, stories about sexual violence, poverty, homelessness, addiction, and the nonresponsiveness of people entrusted and employed to help and to heal us are far too common. People who engage in prison work know that the overwhelming majority of women behind bars are survivors of domestic violence and sexual assault; between 5 and 10 percent are subjected to further sexual abuse while incarcerated, most at the hands of guards.[21] Officers, prison staff, counselors, desk workers, volunteers, and chaplains—we all hear these stories. The only people who do not know that the overwhelming majority of women behind bars are survivors are the survivors themselves. Yet, despite the prevalence of such stories, many prison workers do not believe they are true, and those that do believe are often unequipped to stop the violence or to help people heal. Midwestern's drama class became a site, a refuge, for survivors to gather and tell their stories and, in the telling, to find some support from others—me, Aaron, their classmates—who saw them, heard them, understood, and believed what they said. In casting and holding a space for incarcerated women to tell these and other stories about what they endured, drama club staged healing.

Aaron did not design drama class to elicit survivors' stories; they came out because they needed to be told and because the participants made drama class a site where their stories could be told. In Zora Neale Hurston's autobiography, *Dust Tracks on the Road,* she writes, "There is no agony like bearing an untold story inside you."[22] Women brought these stories forward as fictions, nonfictions, parables, myths, poetry, and as simple conversation pieces around the table because they needed to share and realized that drama class was a place where they would be seen, heard, understood, believed, and held in the telling. Naming what happened to them was an important step in the healing process, one that would have been incomplete without the communal support offered by the group and directed by Aaron. In every class the participants learned that Aaron (and I) valued them and what they had to say. What led up to these moments of personal narrative storytelling was just as, if not more, important than the stories themselves. The check-in ritual, including Aaron's comedic monologues, followed by the physical warm ups, the stories he read aloud, the writing prompts he assigned, and the ongoing group discussions

21. Kim Shayo Buchanan, "Impunity: Sexual Abuse in Women's Prisons," *Harvard Civil Rights—Civil Liberties Law Review* 42, no.1 (2007): 45–87; *National Prison Rape Elimination Commission Report* (2009), accessed Jan. 17, 2022, https://www.ojp.gov/pdffiles1/226680.pdf; Gina Fedock, with Cristy Cummings and Sheryl Kubiak, "Incarcerated Women's Experiences of Staff-Perpetrated Rape: Racial Disparities and Justice Gaps in Institutional Responses," *Journal of Interpersonal Violence* 36, no. 17–18 (2021), 8668–92.

22. Zora Neale Hurston, *Dust on the Tracks* (Philadelphia: B. Lippincott Co., 1942), 220–21.

all set the stage for women to tell their own stories and for healing to occur. The acting, writing, and storytelling activities in drama club were not going to relieve all of their suffering. They did however communicate to participants that they were not alone, and that many of the experiences they had prior to their time at Midwestern other women had also gone through. Unless a problem is named it cannot be addressed. The exchange of intergenerational human experience, what Stephanie Mitchem defines as wisdom, is foundational to the process of healing. Drama club encouraged women to build new relationships and connections between group members and to deepen them beyond the classroom so that they could exchange knowledge. Aaron communicated and demonstrated through these activities that he was willing and prepared to hold drama club as a space for them to step outside of the familiar and the everyday, get in touch with their bodies and their breath in new ways, test the boundaries of their capabilities through play, and to share their experiences, including some of the most difficult events of their lives.

The reading of their stories, however, was not the end of the process. Afterward we always took time to comment and reflect individually and collectively on what was shared. That time, and at every other step of the process, Aaron's pedagogy showed the women that when they revealed traumatic events, or even funny, incomplete writings about whatever else was on their minds, they would not be abandoned, ignored, ridiculed, or dismissed. They mattered. They belonged. They were capable of doing this creative work and so much more. Did everything they shared happen exactly as they told it? I can never know, and that was not the point. Drama club was not a jury trial, and class was not designed to elicit confessions as part of some faux rehabilitative ritual. I know that there was no pressure for them to tell us anything. We were excited that they came to class, and we did not report to anyone whether or how they participated. They earned "good time" toward their release the moment they walked in the door. I believe some women took advantage of the opportunity drama club presented to earn "good time" or to end the isolation and boredom of being locked in the pod. It was something to do. Once inside, however, the communal experiences of joking, checking in, listening, moving, playing, and writing together laid the foundation for storytelling, a narrative and performative form that did not require exact recall of past events to reach a larger truth. As Imani Perry explains, "Stories are neither fact nor fiction. They're greater than that—they are allegories, philosophical treatises, and fables that hold the potential to entertain, reveal and instruct."[23] Drawing on personal narrative, myth, poetry, fiction, and nonfiction, these stories got

---

23. Imani Perry, "She Changed Black Literature Forever. Then She Disappeared," *New York Times,* September 19, 2021, accessed September 19, 2021, https://www.nytimes.com/2021/09/17/magazine/gayl-jones-novel-palmares.html.

to a larger truth about women's lives. Aaron always affirmed the women's value and their capabilities. He always saw things in them that they did not see in themselves, and he told them that he cared.

It was never easy.

In the weeks that followed, as the stories about sexual violence accumulated, Aaron gently prodded the participants to consider the implications of so many stories about violence against women and girls. He turned to mythical women as resources—Eve, Lilith, Pandora, Medusa—to invite an examination of how patriarchy constructs and uses women and girls. By late April, we have arrived at the story of Medusa.

We are an unusually large group the day Aaron reads the story of Medusa, and so we hold class in the middle of the pod in full view of everyone, including the officer on duty. Medusa, the prized servant of the goddess Athena, is raped by Poseidon, god of the sea. Athena responds by disfiguring and then banishing Medusa. Shalondra, a late-forties African American woman with a clipped Southern drawl and close-cut hair, begins the responses, saying that something similar happened to her with her family when she was molested. She expresses great anger at her own mother for not believing her. Many heads begin nodding around the room, and again, some tears begin to be shed. Aaron looks like he is at a loss; we have arrived at this heavy and sad place again. The group feels stuck.

I step outside of my normal role to venture a question to the group that I hope will help. I ask, "What kind of goddess is Athena? I mean . . . here's a trusted servant who gets sexually assaulted and Athena punishes Medusa, her girl? Is that justice? What has all her faith brought her?"

There is a pause; then January opens up with, "Beauty is a curse. To be beautiful as a woman is to lose your power, to have no power."

Nods around the room and a chorus of "hmms" agree.

Jeannette interjects, "To be beautiful means that you have to concede any power that you might have to conform to men's expectations about how a woman is supposed to act."

"To be beautiful means you have to stop acting like Medusa, demanding space and time and autonomy and respect for who you are. It means shrinking and twisting yourself into another shape," Louise, in her fifties, a greying white woman, a professional educator, breaks in. Then I lose track of who says what exactly, it all comes so fast:

"It means Eve was wrong for eating the apple, even if she wasn't happy in the Garden."

"The garden was supposed to be paradise."

"For both of them."

"Was it paradise for her being there with him?"

"Pandora too, how wonderful could the world have been if opening the box seemed like the right thing to do?"

From Aaron: "What's so wrong with being a woman who wreaks havoc in the world when it [the world] ain't right?"

January says, "It means taking responsibility in the sense that you know you're being blamed for things that are actually not your fault."

Queen, a lanky African American woman in her late teens, responds, "How can you not want to be beautiful or loved? I don't understand. That don't make no sense."

To move the discussion forward, Aaron asks them each to write about something beautiful they know. Mimi, a heavyset forty-something white woman, reads hers aloud off a crumpled, trembling white paper:

> I remember when I met you. My God, you were gorgeous, I held you and in your eyes was a symphony, ours all alone. I remember your first word, your laugh. When you took your first step. I was there in your world a shadow. No longer just mine. I've watched you grow and when I had to let go, I cried. Today you're a young adult, and going through your thing. I've tried to tell you, "Turn back, don't take that way." Looking at you, so much like me, the fear takes my breath away, just like when I held you the first time. You were a beautiful symphony all your own.[24]

When asked, Mimi reveals that her daughter is now thirty-one years old. "You're too young to have a thirty-one-year-old," I said, trying to kid her. For the last couple of weeks, I have been trying to let myself laugh at what I hear and witness behind bars, to find ways to joke with the women like Aaron does. I quickly realize it is a swing and a miss when Mimi replies, "That's because I got pregnant when I was eleven and gave birth a few days before my twelfth birthday. By my older sister's husband, my brother-in-law." I feel like an asshole, but out of my failed jest she generously shares more. Blamed for the rape and for the pregnancy, her family banished Mimi until her daughter was born. Her older sister then adopted the child and raised it with her husband, Mimi's brother-in-law and rapist, as her own. No one has ever told the daughter who her real mother is. Mimi connects these traumatic events and the betrayals that ensued to her persistent substance abuse, a problem which

---

24. Fieldnotes, April 30, 2010.

also has had serious ramifications in her younger children's lives. At the end she sighs heavily: "When you have a baby, when you become a mother, everything changes."[25]

As the months went by the realization slowly dawned on me that even a prompt about beauty might elicit a story about sexual violence and child abuse. This was the story that the women wanted us to know. Working in jail means confronting the worst things that people do to each other in surprising ways. People often assume that those who are confined are the bad guys and they deserve to be punished. In drama club, we met people every day who had done harm to themselves and in some cases to other people. Every one of them also had a story to tell about the disrespect and violence they had also endured. This is the story that women at Midwestern wanted, needed, to tell, and they told it again, and again, and again. As new women cycled through the jail, class time arrived and with it their stories about surviving gender-based sexual violence. It was always there, ready and waiting to be told. The protagonists changed as did the locations and the exact circumstances of the events, but the larger truth that sexual violence against women and girls is a pervasive, unaddressed threat to our individual, familial, and societal well-being did not. That story had to be told.

Aaron, the other participants, and I together cast drama class as a space where women could name sexual violence and in so doing engage in the process of self-repair. Naming is a first step in the process of staging healing. In drama class, the women learned that they mattered to us, to the group. They might not have all liked or agreed with each other, but their thoughts, their words, their insights, and their dreams mattered in there. In drama class, they could share their worst nightmares, and we would not cast judgment on them. That may seem like a small gesture, but for women in crisis and in jail—jail itself being another crisis—it made a difference. It helped ease feelings of isolation and shame in some, and affirmed in others their value even if their past behavior was problematic or criminal. Our support did not excuse the harm that some of them had visited upon themselves or others. But, arbitrating right and wrong was not our business. Casting judgment was beyond the scope of the project. Like most people, Aaron, the workshop participants, and I did not like stealing, problematic drug or alcohol use, survival sex, or physical violence. We wanted people to do well and be well. Drama club was designed to support the women in a place where there were few, if any, other supports available. That abiding commitment was instrumental when Chief J. asked us to share what we had been working on in class.

---

25. Fieldnotes, May 27, 2010.

WELL-BEHAVED WOMEN?

Eight months into the project, Chief J. asked when there was going to be a show. In response, Aaron combed through all the writings that he had collected and compiled a lyrical, poetic, spoken-word style piece called *Well-Behaved Women*. Looking around the room at the first read-through, I realize that most of the women whose writing was to be included are no longer there. The grapevine told us Mimi has been transferred to court-mandated rehab. The charges against Frida had been dropped and she was released. We have no idea what happened to Mattie, Queen, Shalondra, or Rocky, but they are also gone. Louise got out on probation having completed her court-mandated drug course. January, under the advice of her lawyers, pled guilty to aggravated DUI. She was sentenced to six-and-a-half years and transferred to one of the women's prisons downstate. Nettie was also sentenced and transferred to one of the women's prisons to serve her time before being deported. At least a hundred Black women have passed through the class along with a handful of Latinas and white women doing short time. From our original group only Jeannette, who is still awaiting trial, continues to attend class. Aaron and I consider her our best student. We have gotten to know her and she has taken ownership of the class and of us. Much of the script is her writing, so it is good having her there. She provides useful, clear directions to the group as we read it aloud.

Reading the script brings up anxiety in class. Some of it reflects the disparate levels of literacy that make the pace of the reading laborious at times. Some of it also reflects the assembly of collected voices as an abstract poem. It does not make sense without the months of context created through the drama class. Therefore, newcomers require some additional translation because, like other materials that archive human experiences, the writing here provides insights into the ideas, experiences, and intentions of the authors, but cannot catalog everything. To translate the ideas on the page to the stage, the women need some concrete and compelling staging, which they are impatient to master. Squabbles arise. Tension mounts at the prospect of standing up and performing the words—even as a stage reading—and people begin freaking out and then shutting down. Aaron repeatedly has to tell the cast to allow each other to stumble through; that they are not expected to be perfect the first time they read it aloud, or the last time; that we are here to work it through. It will take practice, and practice, he says, is "just fine."

Rather than reenact the normative discourse that insists perpetrators of crime are to blame for their own incarceration and for any abuse they have endured, in "Well-Behaved Women" the cast exposes and critiques the reductive processes of law enforcement that require their containment behind bars. They further challenge the patriarchal ideologies that fuel women's degradation in the nation as a whole, taking particular aim at the family as a site of women's oppression. Individual writers' complex past experiences, dislocated from the particular locations where they were enacted and written down, are recast and extended through performance for "public viewing and awareness."[26] This shift forces a reconstruction of what we know about criminalized women—the myths and the facts—in response to their multilayered storytelling.

For four weeks in a row, Aaron works to stage the show in an engaging and accessible manner that the women feel confident about presenting, but each Friday we return, we realize we have lost another reader. Jeanette along with Cookie and Monica, both Black women, anchor the show throughout, but two other women who thought they were going to be here for the rest of the month are transferred out. We are not sure whether they are home, in rehab, or at another facility, but Aaron has to replace one and then another, and finally, in the final week, a third and fourth disappear for reasons that remain unclear. In that third week of rehearsal, Bob, a lanky African American woman whom Jeannette is helping to improve "her pronunciation" so she can pass the GED, steps in along with Pink, a chunky Black woman, even though neither has ever been to drama class before. They are confident and it works. That same week, Coco, a pregnant young African American woman in her mid-twenties, with a forceful, direct manner, officially becomes the assistant director/stage manager. Unbeknownst to us, she had already begun gathering the cast members around the white plastic lawn chairs and tables downstairs to conduct read-throughs and discuss the material whenever they had free time out of their cells. In class, Coco takes meticulous notes regarding where all the actors are supposed to stand, their gestures, and any bits of action they are supposed to perform each time. We tease her that when she is released she has a future in the theater if she wants it.

The Friday before the performance the cast is finally set, we hope. They are five—Jeannette, Cookie, Bob, Monica, and Pink—with Coco as the stage manager. We squeeze in one full run-through before opening, and leave hoping that no one gets locked down for an infraction or transferred out before show day on Tuesday. Coco promises that she will have everyone run through their lines over the weekend.

---

26. D. Soyini Madison, *Acts of Activism: Human Rights as Radical Performance* (Cambridge: Cambridge University Press, 2010), 166, https://doi.org/10.1017/cbo9780511675973.001.

THE PERFORMANCE

Performance day arrives and, when I reach the pod, the cast has rearranged it for the show. An audience has been built by moving the white lawn chairs into neat rows on one side. Fifty of them are oriented toward the front of the room, creating a distinct performance space that is still within full view of the officer on duty at her station near the exit. With this small adjustment, a new sense of formality has been introduced. There is some hopeful excitement in the air! Most of the chairs are already occupied when I arrive carrying the show programs. A quick scan of the pod reveals that a handful of women have been prohibited from attending. They are segregated into closed cells on upper and lower tiers, but we make eye contact when I walk in and I suspect they were able to watch, if not hear, everything. A thin white woman with stringy dark hair paces frantically back and forth in a darkened lower-level cell adjacent to the performance space, her cell door open so she can hear and see if not come any closer. Whatever has her walking the linoleum in this way will not allow her to sit and watch with the others. Several invited guests fill out the audience at the back—Chief J., Mr. Bertram, and two other Inmate Programming Coordinators; a pair of regular volunteers from a local Christian ministry; a few public officials concerned with crime and recidivism; and a handful of teaching artists and other Demeter's Daughters supporters. I take a seat toward the back of the room near the other guests so I can enjoy the show and observe audience reactions.

The performance begins with the cast standing shoulder to shoulder in their brown and blue medical-scrub-style uniforms, grey socks, and open-toe puke-pink shower shoes. Like a Greek chorus they compose a loose half-circle facing the audience, scripts in hand. Behind them are the doors to the showers. Coco is stationed in front, script with stage directions in hand. Chief J. and Mr. Bertram both offer short introductions, followed by Aaron, who tells the assembly we have been investigating the "grand narrative of American women." The lyrical work weaves fiction and nonfiction stories, poetry, and prose around simple staging. Although the words were written by different women, the cast speaks as one persona, in one voice.

As Aaron steps aside, the piece begins with a poem that Jeanette penned, written from the perspective of someone standing in a cell staring out her window toward the lights of another city in the distance. The cast reads:

ONE (COOKIE): Rising in the distance from the depth of the Great Lake, the
    familiar jagged outline etched against the endless sky evoking feelings

of desperate longing . . . close enough to touch, impossible to reach, another lifetime away.

THREE (JEANETTE): Simultaneously beckoning and taunting me, a sign of hope, a symbol of all that has been taken, of all that I have lost . . .

In delivering these lines and later speeches, the cast stands or sits in chairs placed close to the shower stalls. They talk to one other but do not touch. I recognize that these staging choices are in part a function of the restrictions placed on their movement and respond to the real challenge of working with a highly transient population. The simplicity of the staging and the unified tone of the script make the women appear to speak as one. The sense of cohesion is heightened by the visual homogeneity of their baggy uniforms. Because the uniforms are repeated on the bodies of the other incarcerated women seated in the audience, there is a sense of borderlessness between performer and spectator. These stories could belong to any one of them. From the perspective of a woman who is reflecting on the distant city, the piece quickly transitions into the speaker's reflecting on her own face in an imaginary mirror.

TWO (BOB): I stare at my face in the mirror. At the scar, the lines, the wrinkles. All the chapters of my life are written there—a story to be read by people I meet. Expressions that have become etched over time into my skin.

The self-reflective look in the "mirror" initiates a process of charting the past. Imprisoned people are expected to reflect on the past and express remorse for wrongdoing to fulfill the jail's rehabilitative script. Here, instead of mentioning past crimes, they trace the molestation, sexual abuse, and other betrayals I had heard recounted in class. The portrait is not one solely of innocent victims who have been harmed. From the opening moment they appear as people with pasts that exceed the moment of their arrest and the labels that Jeannette and others were so concerned about in the beginning of the process. They were children who played, laughed, hurt, grew, and were loved. Their bodies tell these tales:

FIVE (PINK): The fall I took on the playground in third grade is there—a small white line just above my right temple.

THREE (JEANETTE): And the almost invisible circle of smooth skin near my chin is there too, representing a week of chicken pox, and my mother's constant warning not to scratch them. I'm not sure which was worse, the itching or her nagging.

FOUR (MONICA): A faded rough spot forged along my jawbone celebrates the milestone of learning to ride without training wheels.

THREE (JEANETTE): Right next to the small jagged irregularity left behind by the gold ring, worn by that guy who seemed so caring at first.

ONE (COOKIE): Ages of laughter shared with family and friends have dug deep trenches into the sides of my mouth, and the freckles sprinkled across my nose like sugar crystals betray a lifetime spent outdoors under the sun.

The early glimpses in the mirror expose faded chicken pox marks and other "almost invisible" scars. The marks evidence illnesses, physical injuries, heartbreak, and betrayal as well as family connections worth celebrating. Special attention is given to how the accidents that formed the scars mark more than trauma to the body. The chicken pox becomes a reminder of a mother's attention while "a faded rough spot" signifies a personal milestone. The bad times are not overlooked, as the line referencing the "small jagged irregularity left behind by . . . that guy who seemed so caring at first" indicates. Much of the piece will contend with the betrayals, violations, and losses that the speaker has endured. In this opening moment, however, the cast insists that the collective body cannot be reduced to either an innocent victim or an unredeemable perpetrator, despite the uniform. Their bodies bear a multitude of experiences, evidence of their full and complex personhood.

From this catalog of both joyful and rough-and-tumble childhoods, their inventory of the skin offers up evidence of less secure adulthoods. This turn hinges on Mimi's story of giving birth to her daughter, which Aaron transcribed word for word:

FOUR (MONICA): I remember when I met you. My God, you were gorgeous. I held you and your eyes were a symphony, ours all alone. I remember your first word, your laugh. When you took your first steps. I was there in your world, a shadow. No longer just mine. I've watched you grow and when I had to let you go, I cried. Today, you're a young adult, and going through your own thing. I've tried to tell you "Turn back, don't go that way." Looking at you, so much like me, the fear takes my breath away, just like when I heard you the first time. You were a beautiful symphony all your own.

Monica, who delivers this monologue, is an African American in her late twenties with glasses who is behind bars for the first time and very different from Mimi. Monica never met Mimi and listeners who knew Mimi felt the absence of Mimi's context in Monica's early delivery in rehearsals. The written script, like other archives, offered up only traces of the author's lived experience. They tried to give her directions but the suggestions were punctuated by complaints such as, "You're not reading it right." Frustrated, Monica asked Aaron, "What is this about?" He filled her in and, when Monica picked up the script again, she understood she needed to communicate a critique of violence against women and girls through the character of a young girl who had been injured, ostracized, and shamed, but who somehow found a moment of joy and amazement in her own daughter's birth.

In the performance, she holds Mimi's imagined baby in the crook of her arms and tells the child—tells us all—what happened and how much Mimi loves her. The room becomes very quiet as people lean in to hear this pivotal story. Aaron chooses not to stage more of the context out of which it emerged, but allows Monica to communicate the underlying ideas with her voice and body. The gestural vocabulary she performs communicates that she is a mother and the lilting tone of her voice aurally signifies that she is now disconnected from the child and experiencing her loss as the haunting "shadow" that her family has forced her to become. In the performance, the details of Mimi's tragedy are lost, but the sense of being relegated to the margins and devalued pervades Monica's delivery. We are left with the impression that the speaker yearns to reunite with the child, but it is unclear exactly where the speaker is and why the child is not with her. That sense of loss and of disconnection undergirds the next section of the script, "Single/Black/Mother," a poem written weeks earlier by a woman who, like so many others, has come and gone. Each cast member takes a line:

Single
Black
Mother
Raising boys with no job
No one to talk to
No one to call for help
Not easy
Single
Black
Mother
Make sure we have some place to stay
Something to sleep on
Something to eat
Something to call your own

Like no other, this short work, written in a style reminiscent of the Black Arts Movement, encapsulated the life struggles facing most women at Midwestern. It is jarring to hear our integrated cast of Black and white women conjure this being into existence, but the sense of disjuncture and uneasiness mirrors the speaker's ungroundedness. In rehearsal, there was some discussion about whether this staging choice of having everyone in the cast take a line made any sense. The experience of being a single parent was not unique to African American women. Some white women argued that the repeated use of the phrase "single Black mother" collapsed their experience, erasing the possibility that white women might also have to contend with chronic financial and social insecurity. Aaron recognized their concern, but insisted they keep to the script, stating, "That is how the author wrote it." Just as Black women had been asked to tell the stories of white women like Mimi and Jeanette, women whose bodies were not raced Black would articulate the experience of those who were African Americans or Latinas. In performance, the incantation divided across the bodies unites them visually and sonically as a single constituency making these claims in solidarity.

The "Single/Black/Mother" section builds to a story about a mother who fails to reunite with her children, also written by Mimi. Ambiguity haunts the encounter between mother and children, leaving the separation unexplained but the devastating impact clear. Jeanette and Monica deliver it in alternating lines. Cookie interjects with an inner, self-reflective tone expressing trepidation and urging caution:

THREE (JEANETTE): I walk to the door nervous. I'm trembling in fear and excitement. My mind is wandering a million miles a second. I'm going to see them this time.

FOUR (MONICA): I'm going to see them this time. Will they know who I am? I have missed them so much and this is all that I could think about.

THREE (JEANETTE): Will they know who I am? Will they forgive me? So my mind wanders. I knock on the door . . .

ONE (COOKIE): Be like water. Transparent clear and run away.

THREE (JEANETTE): This little guy opens the door. I instantly burst into tears. He called out for his mom, but he wasn't calling for me. This lady is crying!

FOUR (MONICA): As my mom walked to the door I was infuriated. So many emotions going through my head I'm going to break.

ONE (COOKIE): Look into my mirror but not halfway. Allow tranquility to consume your soul. Feel free inside and out. Not hold the worry of the day through to tomorrow.

THREE (JEANETTE): A girl who is all grown up comes down the stairs to see where the commotion is coming from.

FOUR (MONICA): She recognized me instantly and ran back up the stairs, I feel like a puddle of—

THREE (JEANETTE): While my mother asks me to leave, I reach for my son and I can see he's scared. This is the worst day of my life.

FOUR (MONICA): How could I let this happen? Could I have changed this? I walk away falling down the stairs in torment. I pick myself up and stumble to my car.

This is the only moment in the performance where the speaker acknowledges responsibility for any kind of harm to others. Her offense remains ambiguous, but the effect is undeniable. Her tripping exit confirms what we already know: the speaker has let people down and fallen, fallen apart. Incarcerated women have historically been labeled "fallen women." According to Andrew Hewitt, the label of a "fallen" person reflects bourgeois concerns about what slips or errors in proper speech or behavior might reveal about an individual's unconscious interior mind.[27] But stumbling also reveals the "constructedness of the social order."[28] In the play, the stumble or trip that lays the speaker low initiates a process of unveiling both the intimate familial concerns and the external, systemic factors that have tripped her up. In African American English, to "trip" means to "act unconventionally." The unspoken question in the script about what has happened, what has made the speaker "trip" on her responsibilities as a mother and a daughter to her family, are answered in the performance through another kind of "trip." The cast responds by taking the audience on an imaginary voyage through the speaker's memory using an urban landscape as inspiration.

In addition to revealing the speakers' intimate knowledge of this world beyond the walls of the jail that their recounting unveils, from the bottom-up perspective of the tripper, the multiple interlocking factors—familial, systemic, personal, spatial—have contributed, each in its own way, to the fall. What is initially established as an individual's fault or failings is reconstituted as an opportunity for the collective—cast and audience—to "trip" with her and to inhabit the perspective of the one who falls. Her lowly position enables her to see things others may not see and in performance to speak what others cannot speak. The foundation of this examination and her testimony is laid through an aural mapping of the physical territories that the speaker has

27. Andrew Hewitt, *Social Choreography: Ideology as Performance in Dance and Everyday Movement* (Durham, NC: Duke University Press, 2005), 87.

28. Hewitt, *Social Choreography*, 89, 95.

known. Relayed from both a bird's-eye and a ground-floor view of the world, the images reveal the speaker's extensive knowledge of the landscape where she stood, both the built architecture and the invisible and hidden sociocultural community ties. It becomes clear she is narrating a life located literally in Chicago. It begins with an entreaty:

ONE (JEANETTE): Just fly.
  The hushed silence of the Art Institute
  Its stone lions guarding the entrance
  A Mecca of international history and culture
  While outside on the sidewalk, the Bucket Boys beat a fiery rhythm
  On their plastic drums
  The live music of a street fair on Halsted
  A boiling stew of human emotion and life . . .
  The Friendly Confines . . . Wrigleyville . . . Goose Island . . . Division
    Street . . .
  Farris the Fry Cook tirelessly turns out countless pounds of breaded
    shrimp
  In the shadow of the towering giant of Cabrini's broken and boarded
    windows across the street

The images shift the listener across varying terrains known for "high art" and "high culture" such as the "Art Institute" and the profoundly disadvantaged world of "Farris" and "Cabrini," one of the most infamous public-housing projects in the world. The references are both personal and easily recognizable. Throughout the text, the mantra "fly" will be repeated again and again to articulate the women's desire to leave the most distressing circumstances of their lives behind. Knowing that so many of the writers and the current cast have histories of substance abuse, for me the entreaty to fly resounds on multiple levels as a call for physical movement, for pharmaceutically induced escapes, and as an appeal to enact new modalities wherever you may be.

Listening, I am reminded of Morgan's story about the power of birds as talismans, of the legend of the Flying Africans, those mythical figures who, when confronted by the driver or the lash, suddenly cast a spell with magical words they had long held beneath their tongues and then rose into the sky to fly home to Africa.[29] This classic tale circulates in the African diaspora, tak-

29. Wendy W. Walters, "'One of Dese Mornings, Bright and Fair / Take My Wings and Cleave De Air': The Legend of the Flying Africans and Diasporic Consciousness," *MELUS* 22, no. 3 (1997): 12–16.

ing on distinct nuances in the Caribbean, and in Central, South, and North America, but in each telling there are several unifying themes. The captive body has latent potential to transform its circumstances and to return to a distant homeland, but only if it has maintained a connection to the other enslaved people in the community and a commitment to the cultural or discursive practices of the faraway African homeland. The "magic words" are framed as an African retention, something passed orally among members of a community who share a commitment to each other and to one day returning home. "Climatized" or assimilated Africans, Creoles, and whites are regularly left behind because they are unfamiliar with the community's cultural practices. These critical cultural retentions are maintained by individuals, but rarely, only rarely, do they fly alone. The legend is a story not only about individual achievement, self-reliance, and self-care but also about interconnectivity and interdependence within a community. As they have collectively endured oppression, so they must together partake of the ritual incantation to break free and rise in flight as one.[30]

The juxtaposition between the imposed stillness of the performers on the jail stage and the soaring flight of the speaker/mover across the remembered terrain reconceptualized for me the performers' stillness as held-movement potential. By remaining motionless, the cast physically conforms to the discursive demands of the jail to act like immobilized prisoners, but their words challenge the notion that stillness means acquiescence. In the next moment of the piece, the tone shifts, affirming that women's stillness contains potential and power. Out of the stumble, she comes to stand and testify to the mistreatment by others that she has endured. She names the state as well as individual actors, especially men, as the cause of her shame and hardship:

> TWO (BOB): Even though they have stared, gawked, and gazed in wonder. Even though her outer trappings have been brutally stripped away. Even though her loins have been maliciously violated, her body defiled. Even though the foul sons of Man have trampled upon her, in her, around her—pacing, prodding and probing, bleeding her dry.
> ONE (COOKIE): Still she stands.
> TWO (BOB): From the beginning of time, she has defied reason while civilizations have crawled, stood, fallen and decayed.
> ONE (COOKIE): She stands.
> TWO (BOB): With grace and dignity, she endures
> With strength and beauty, a majestic splendor

---

30. Walters, "One," 12–16.

ONE (COOKIE): She stands. She is called Mother. She is called Earth. She is called Life.

THREE (JEANETTE): I am a woman because I have a child.

FOUR (MONICA): Because I have a vagina.

ONE (COOKIE): And I have periods every month.

FIVE (PINK): And mood swings.

FOUR (MONICA): I have kids as well.

FIVE (PINK): I have a menstrual cycle.

THREE (JEANETTE): Women go through a lot of things in life.

ONE: I am in the female division of the institutional center.

TWO: I am doing more time than a man would do for the same crime.

THREE: I'm disposable.

FOUR: Disposable.

ONE: Disposable.

THREE: Disposable to the people who brought me into this world.

ONE: All the people I know in this world,

TWO: And the judges,

FOUR: And the prosecutors of this country

ONE: As well as a source of income for this state.

With the last words of this section, the piece exposes the undergirding repressive patriarchal logic of the penal state and indicts it. There is a moment of collective hush around the room. I find myself scanning the place for the officers and Chief J. to gauge their reactions even though I know that Aaron sent the script to them for prior approval so this should not come as a shock. Standing in the back of the audience, I noticed that, as these lines were spoken, the Chief, chaplains, and the Inmate Program Coordinators all shifted uncomfortably in their chairs. From where I stood I could not harbor a guess as to why specifically, other than that acts of direct criticism of the institution are considered threatening and therefore strictly monitored if not completely prohibited. To their credit, they allowed the production to continue. I suspect this is in part because, after this line, the script turns away from further indictments of the state and instead offers a mythical, even metaphysical, escape from its precepts.

FIVE (PINK): I am a bad

THREE (JEANETTE): Bad Bad

ONE (COOKIE): Bad Bad

FOUR (MONICA): Bad Bad

FIVE (PINK): Bad woman.

TWO (BOB): How dare you!?

FIVE (PINK): How dare you think for yourself, stand up for yourself?

ONE (COOKIE): Set boundaries?

FIVE (PINK): How dare you have feelings and opinions that you don't keep to yourself?

TWO (BOB): How dare you step out of the kitchen and into the board room?

FIVE (PINK): We will stone you, crush you, control your bodies.

ONE (COOKIE): Force you to wear a scarlet label.

TWO (BOB): Turn your head and look longingly to the horizon.

ONE (COOKIE): But never,

FIVE (PINK): Never,

ONE (COOKIE): Dare to call yourself a victim.

THREE (JEANETTE): Victim? We are women. They are threatened by us. By our power, our capabilities. The strength that we are born with. They know what we can do. Civilizations have risen and fallen over the "weaker" sex. . . . We nurture, we support. We suffer in silence. We give life. They don't have that power, so they seek to take it from us, to control it. To own it.

These lines reveal the cast's understanding that prison is not a given, but a societal choice. "Bad, bad, bad, bad, bad, bad" women who defy social expectations must be regulated. The prison system is designed to punish and control them. In the final scene, as the piece returns to the perspective of a woman staring out a window at Midwestern, it launches a poignant entreaty to the audience to move.

THREE (JEANETTE): I reach out with my fingertips to touch the cold window
Dissolving the images
And I am reminded that I am only an observer now
Deep in exile
Like a lonely old woman, existing only on memories

TWO (BOB): The space that I used to occupy
Closed up like a long-healed wound
With nothing but a faint scar to mark my former presence
. . . I must have missed a scene somewhere . . .

FIVE (PINK): Look into my glass

THREE (JEANETTE): But not halfway

TWO (BOB): Feel free

ONE (COOKIE): Inside

FIVE (PINK): And out.

ONE (COOKIE): Just flow.

FOUR (MONICA): Just fly.

THREE (JEANETTE): Because I am soft

    Because of my strength

    Because I love and nurture

    Because I give birth to children, and then I let them go.

    I bleed. I suffer in silence. I carry the burdens of the world.

    I am a woman because I rise above.

ALL: Just fly "bad woman." Fly.

"Well-Behaved Women" ends with a call to action for spectators to look beyond the labels and see the speaker for what she really is, a person imbued with a complex personhood that has been criminalized by multiple over-lapping social forces. This appeal is directed most pointedly at the imprisoned women in attendance. They are the objects to which the speaker directs her indicatives to mobilize or, in their words, to "flow" and later to "fly, bad woman, fly." The urgency of this spoken entreaty is reinforced in the final moment as the cast repeats the last line of the script, one after another.

Cookie, a heavyset African American woman in her thirties with glasses, who has some experience behind bars, gives the final iteration of the last line her own flavor. She connects the gesture of a swirling Black Power fist with her delivery. It is the last symbol enacted in the performance. Cookie's fist animates the images, emotions, and histories of the long Black Liberation struggle, specifically the efforts of Black Power militants to end anti-Black oppression and establish an alternative world where Black people in the US and across the Global South were no longer exploited by white capitalist colonial elites. Often performed with a single outstretched arm that reaches toward the sky like a lightning rod or a rifle, it symbolically linked the status of African Americans under Jim Crow at the mid-twentieth century as "bad" people unworthy of full citizenship to the legacy of slavery in the United States and colonialism abroad. Cookie's decision to activate the Black Power fist as she enunciated the final "Fly, bad woman, fly" linked the women's stories to the historic struggle for Black liberation and more contemporary work to transform the prison system and to nullify patriarchy and sexism. In Cookie's hand, Rocky's long ago scripted "bad bad bad bad bad bad woman" now declares that they are "bad(ass)" women. Cookie's gesture is met with delight and surprise. Heads nod around the room and smiles grace many audience members' faces.

The collaboration between writers and performers, drawing on their diverse experiences and repertoires of cultural knowledge, brought *Well-Behaved Women* to life, but the visual and physical linking of the Midwestern women's stories with the long struggle for Black liberation through the Black Power fist makes it accessible and relevant to audience members in ways the spoken word alone could not. The Black Power fist reveals the stakes of the work as well as the critical perspective on interpersonal and structural violence against women that the drama class over the last nine months has formulated. It expresses their concerns about women's gendered roles in society and the impact of racism and misogyny on both sides of the prison door. The gesture enables them to critique the reductive logic of law enforcement with its simplistic concepts of innocent/guilty and victim/perpetrator. It interrupts the social and political processes that marginalize "bad" women and asserts that they have a role to play in coalition-building efforts to address public health, crime, and safety issues. The fist stages these interventions from the expert perspectives of those who have been cast out of the center, journeyed to the underworld, and lived to tell the tale.

LIKE A HUMAN BEING

As the audience members return to their cells to prepare for the mid-afternoon shift change, there are moments before lockdown in which is it possible to interact personally with the cast. I extend an arm to Bob for a light hug of congratulations. Standing a good distance away, she responds, stretching her arms in my direction with an "inmate air hug." Her arms reach out toward me but she stands three feet away and just barely inclines her upper body toward me, never touching. Then she says, "I don't wanna get locked down for this." Her words remind me that I have to treat these women like prisoners. In the glow of the moment, I have not forgotten where we are, but perhaps I have invested too much faith in the possibility that this particular performance seems to offer. The institution is the same. In the time/space of the performance, the regular corrections protocols and constraints seemed to lift, but they never fully disappeared.

Looking across the room, I see Mr. Bertram offering hearty handshakes. The woman who serves as the jail chaplain is lightly hugging another woman and asking, "Do you feel as wonderful as we do seeing it? Do you feel as wonderful?" In her enthusiasm, however, it seems she is not letting the other woman get a word in. Another guest is warmly shaking Jeanette's hand. My impulse to reach out is not isolated. The regular prohibition against contact with the women, except in the case of a death in someone's family, has been momentarily suspended. "Bob, I think it's okay, look," I say gesturing around the room, "but only if you want . . . " In the end, we do share a light hug.

The performance does not end for me until I have shaken the hands of or returned waves from all the women involved in the show, including the audience members.[31]

Later, in a post-show interview with a half dozen members of the cast, Jeanette encapsulates the sentiment of the group. She recalls more than a week later how empowering it felt to shake the hands of the visitors after months of isolation and to hear their appreciation for the group's performance.

"They treated me like I'm a human being," she states, "Like a human being."[32]

In separate interviews in the weeks that follow, Mr. Bertram and Chief J. intimate to me that the women's show taught them several things, which they cannot fully disclose to me. The show was more powerful for both of them because they have insight into women's personal stories we do not have. That additional layer makes the accomplishment even more potent. Chief J., an African American woman and lifelong corrections officer who grew up in public housing herself, expresses a heartfelt desire that all the women realize there is not much difference between them. She repeats and affirms, "We are all just women."[33]

By reclaiming the power to name, to represent, and to interpret their own lives, Demeter's Daughters challenges the disciplinary boundaries designated by law enforcement, criminology, penology, psychology, and mainstream arts organizations to represent who they are, explain why crime happens, and express what justice feels like. Through the performance, the idea that law enforcement officials can and ought to be the sole arbiters of justice, that justice has been enacted by law, or truth evidenced through forensics alone, are themselves interrogated, folded back upon themselves, through the writing and performance praxis of the drama program at Midwestern. The classes provide incarcerated women with an opportunity to double the past upon itself, to disidentify with their present status as "disposable," and trace the paths they have trod to arrive where they are. By dedicating their time to critical analysis, art-making, and collective consciousness-raising in drama club, the women surfaced new understandings of their life experiences and the overlapping processes of oppression that confined them. Their explicit use of the Black Power fist in the final performance linked them to the long history of antiracist, life-affirming activism led by other Black captives. The potent combination of humor, creative writing, poetry, and Black expressive culture that Aaron facilitated in drama class prepared them to do this work because

---

31. Fieldnotes, August 31, 2010.
32. Group interview with the author, fieldnotes September 4, 2010.
33. Fieldnotes, August 31, 2010.

his classes staged healing. They created the conditions for the women to forge new ties that enabled them to craft and tell these stories about the past and prepared the ensemble to speak in a defiant, critical voice that could be seen, heard, and understood. In performance, they mattered.

WHAT LIES AHEAD

In the next chapter, I build on this exploration of theater as a site of community building and storytelling to stage individual healing and consider how drama clubs can also use performance to ignite institutional change in a women's prison.

CHAPTER 4

The Pink Dress

In 2010, Big Water, a maximum-security prison for women on the US Gulf Coast, imposed a new sartorial punishment to isolate and control women who did not conform to the new warden's expectations of appropriate female behavior.[1] He ordered that prisoners who violated the facility's uniform dress code by sagging and bagging their clothes be identified, stripped of their clothing, and forced to wear "the pink dress." The pink dress was a large, flowing pink caftan, reminiscent of a muumuu or bed sheet with a hole cut out for the head. Its wearers stood out on a compound of over one thousand other imprisoned people dressed in the decidedly "un-masculine" regular uniform—baggy jeans, long- and short-sleeved white shirts, and chambray, denim jackets.

The pink dress punishment did not redress any wrongdoing committed outside of the prison. During the two years I spent conducting ethnographic and historiographic research into Big Water, I was repeatedly told that the pink dress was designed exclusively to discipline the "too masculine" Black prisoners, especially "the homosexuals," who purposefully sagged their pants, wearing them low on the waist, threatening to reveal their underwear. At Big Water,

---

1. To protect the identities of the incarcerated women at the center of this study, I use pseudonyms to identify all of the people, organizations, penal institutions, and settings where this research occurred.

Black lesbians, transmen, queer/quare folks, and gender-nonconforming people who violated the dress code were targeted for discipline.

When members of the Big Water Drama Club learned about the pink
dress punishment, they sprang into action. They quickly realized that the pink
dress would not only punish "the homosexuals" targeted by prison officials.
It could leave many women open to harm. The public shaming threatened to
interrupt the vital social networks on which they all relied to survive behind
bars. The artistic/activist coalition they formed in response to the pink dress
policy exemplifies the Black feminist political scientist Cathy Cohen's vision of
a new political coalition committed "to promoting an understanding of sexuality that rejects the idea of static, monolithic, bounded categories" of "straight
and queer" in favor of "a more intersectional analysis of who and what the
enemy is, and where . . . potential allies can be found."[2] In this chapter, I argue
that the Drama Club's original production of *Beauty Coming 'n Going* pro-
moted such understanding by staging healing. Their comedic performance
revealed the twisted logic behind the pink dress policy and then used the stage
to restore the much-maligned figure of the masculine-identified Black lesbian
to a valued place within the community.[3]

METHODOLOGY

Conducting research in carceral settings is always difficult, but Big Water
presented unique challenges. I met Jodie, a white forty-something-year-old
actress and playwright, through a mutual friend and mentor who thought
highly of her and her work. After a quick Google search, I realized that her
project might fit my criteria. She and a small team of other women artists had
for more than a decade been volunteering to teach theater and devise new
work with women at Big Water. I called her and we immediately connected.
Multiple research visits between 2008 and 2013 followed, enabling me to meet
her and the Drama Club codirector Ngozi, an African American woman
dancer and choreographer, as well as the other volunteers who work with
them at Big Water and, finally, the entire ensemble. During those trips Jodie
and Ngozi connected me to several formerly incarcerated women with whom

2. Cathy Cohen, "Punks, Bulldaggers and Welfare Queens: The Radical Potential of Queer
Politics?," in *Black Queer Studies: A Critical Anthology*, ed. E. Patrick Johnson and Mae Henderson
(Durham, NC: Duke University Press, 2005), 441, 457.

3. A version of this chapter was previously published in *Applied Theatre: Women and the
Criminal Justice System*, ed. Coaimhe McAvinchey (London; New York: Bloomsbury Publishing/
Metheun Drama, 2020), 57–76. Reprinted with permission.

they continued to work. I interviewed them and other members of the team. Unfortunately, despite repeated requests, the prison denied my application to observe regular Drama Club workshops or to interview the participants. I did eventually obtain permission to attend the one and only performance of the show they produced in response to the pink dress issue, which I call *Beauty Coming 'n Going*. Gaining entry to see it was a trial. Twice Big Water postponed the performance, citing staff shortages. At another time a hurricane shut down operations, and then a scabies outbreak at a nearby men's facility closed everything down. When I finally received the call in early September 2011 that the performance was on, I had just hours to book a flight. Arriving at midnight, I spent the day with Jodie and Ngozi before heading out to the facility for the early evening performance.

Because the prison banned me from taking notes, photographs, or videos and prohibited me from interviewing Drama Club members or anyone in the audience, Jodie and Ngozi concocted workarounds so I could develop some sense of the incarcerated artists' perspectives. In the weeks leading up to the show, I emailed them questions to ask during rehearsal and they reported the women's answers back to me via email or when we next met in person. On the day of the show, they made sure I had a front row seat and figured out how to circumvent the prohibition against my talking to members of the ensemble afterward. To celebrate the performance, they had obtained permission to present a beautiful sheet cake to the cast. They asked me to cut the cake and hand out generous slices. As I passed each Drama Club member a slice, we chitchatted about the show, their experiences making the work, how they felt about the audience's reaction, and the like. They knew who I was and were delighted to conspire with me to help me complete my research. Later in Ngozi's car, as we headed back to the city, I jotted down as much as I could remember in a notebook along with her immediate impressions and those of the other volunteers who rode with us. Finally, the opportunity to review the script and a videotape of the performance (shot by another volunteer with Department of Corrections approval) helped me reconstruct the events and analyze their intervention. The live performance, jottings from my field site visits, interviews, the script, and the video form the basis of this chapter that highlights the work of the Drama Club at Big Water.

INVENTING THE PRISON LESBIAN

The Drama Club learned about the "pink dress" as most people did. Jovita, an African American woman in her forties and longtime ensemble member, came dragging into rehearsal one Saturday morning wearing what looked like a bedsheet. The pink "dress" was so thin you could see her body and her undergarments beneath it, and it was so long it trailed on the floor at her feet, making it difficult to walk. Jovita had to decide where to put her hands; should she cover herself up or not trip? The twenty-five to thirty other members of the Drama Club who saw Jovita stumble in that morning were shocked. They let out a loud, collective gasp, then busted up laughing. Visibly upset, Jovita dove into a chair on the edge of the room. Jodie and Ngozi laughed, too, at first. It was just so unlike Jovita, who normally styled her uniform in a more masculine fashion, to be wearing a dress. The group soon realized that she was hurt and angry and that she wanted to do something about it. Subsequent dialogue within Drama Club revealed that the pink dress was a problem for Jovita and for everyone on the compound. That it was used to humiliate individuals who violated the dress code was bad enough. It had the potential to threaten the wellbeing of every person on the compound.

Popular perceptions of lesbian, gay, bisexual, transgender, queer, non-binary, and gender-nonconforming people impact how they are treated by police, prosecutors and defense attorneys, the courts, and corrections officers. Since the early 1900s, law enforcers have aggressively policed spaces where LBGTQ folks socialize. These policing decisions combine with laws that criminalize heteronormative gender nonconformance and same-sex sex, resulting in disproportionately high rates of LGBTQ incarceration. Reformatory advocates responded to the growing number of women prisoners and insisted that their disciplinary practices would restore white women to their proper social roles. By the mid-twentieth century, however, sociological research into reformatory life concluded that the "institutionally sanctioned model of [the] rehabilitative family" that structured everyday life had been appropriated by the prisoners to establish "transgressive kinship" networks.[4] Regina Kunzel found that same-sex couples, whose queer gender expression and sexuality often included identifying themselves as "husband and wife," claimed generations of female and male descendants in extensive, long-lasting kinship networks that impacted every aspect of Northern reformatory life.[5] Incarcerated women of all races took their relationships, their roles, and their responsibilities within their chosen families seriously. Prisoners who performed men's traditional familial roles fashioned their hair and clothing to visibly express their masculinity, even if that meant running afoul of administrators. Everywhere breasts were bound down and male names and pronouns were deployed. Men's hats

---

4. Regina Kunzel, *Criminal Intimacy: Prison and the Uneven History of Modern American Sexuality* (Chicago: University of Chicago Press, 2008), 118–19.

5. Kunzel, *Criminal Intimacy*, 118–19.

were mail-ordered and worn until the practice was disallowed. State-issued pants (where allowed) and shirts were altered to approximate popular men's fashions and ties were even devised out of prison-issued handkerchiefs to complete the look. In institutions where skirts were required, more femme prisoners lifted their hemlines in accordance with national fashion trends while masculine-identified prisoners adopted longer lengths and drew down their side-zipper pockets to approximate a man slipping his hands into a pants pocket. Masculine identities were "established through gesture, behavior, and affect as well as outward appearance and dress" in particular, Kunzel notes, by (re)iterating or citing well-known performances of working-class African American masculinity.[6]

By the 1960s, these observations finally forced sociologists to acknowledge that some incarcerated women may have dressed in masculine attire and pursued same-sex relationships in their preprison lives. These facts did nothing, however, to shake researchers' belief that white women behaved in these ways only if they had been exposed to African Americans. The prospect that white women would "reject heterosexuality . . . and their racial duty to reproduce," even temporarily, was unacceptable.[7] Prison administrators insisted that white women were not "real lesbians." They dismissed white women's same-sex relationships as harmless school girl crushes or situational responses to the enormous stress of being incarcerated. When interracial couples were discovered, administrators insisted that the white women did not truly desire the Black women. They argued that the white women had sex with the Black women only because they had no access to white men—a preposterous assertion that erases how white men have historically dominated the corrections profession and used their positions of power. Nonetheless, to return imprisoned white women to their proper heteronormative roles as wives and mothers and restore order both behind bars and in American society at large, strict segregation policies were imposed to isolate and contain all of the Black women.

---

6. Kunzel, *Criminal Intimacy*, 122–23; Kunzel does not elaborate on how researchers' interpretations of Black working-class masculinity impacted the knowledge they produced about incarcerated women's sexual cultures, except to note that a limited number of feminist scholars and activists began to express concern for the more femme partners in same-sex relationships. Their writings obscure the danger of miscegenation, instead critiquing butch/femme prisoner relationships for reproducing the most limiting aspects of heteronormative sexuality. Relegating feminine lesbians to the status of "nonliberated housewives, worrying about their appearances as they were forced to do all the couple's domestic labor (cleaning the cell, mending or making clothes, cooking snacks, etc.)," they argued in the heat of the women's liberation movement, did nothing to promote equality (125–26, 210).

7. Estelle Freedman, "The Prison Lesbian: Race, Class, and the Construction of the Aggressive Female Homosexual, 1915–1965," *Feminist Studies* 22, no. 2 (1996): 400.

Today, prison administrators condemn all same-sex couplings on the pretext that they disrupt prison discipline and regularly attribute other problems that arise at facilities to these practices.[8] Bans on altering uniforms and on touching, ranging from handshakes and platonic hugs to masturbation, hinder, but do not foreclose, the development of same-sex relationships, including those that cross the color line. Unsurprisingly, these policies do continue to authorize officers to monitor, control, and punish Black woman on the presumption of predacious sexuality.

Sexual identities and sexual-expressive practices are not fixed. Individual sexual expression changes over time as desires, experiences, and sexual partners change. Despite this, heteronormativity works in conjunction with "institutional racism, patriarchy, and class exploitation" to marginalize and render some people "expendable."[9] Cathy Cohen argues that the history of the invention of the homosexual as a sexual identity demonstrates that whole new social identities can emerge over time and that social categories such as race and class can "enhance or mute" both the "marginalization of queers . . . and the power of heterosexuals."[10] So too a quick overview of slavery, lynching, and rape history confirms that dominant definitions of heterosexuality have marginalized many, including by forcing "presumably heterosexual men and women to endure physical and mental terrorism" to maintain patriarchy and the color line.[11] Because so many people exist outside the boundaries of dominant, white, upper-class heterosexuality, Cohen believes, queerness (if untethered from whiteness) has the "radical potential . . . to challenge and bring together all those deemed marginal and all those committed to liberatory politics." Yet simply having a "marginal identity" does not automatically produce consensus. Acts of mutual support are required to build unity and lay a foundation for "transformational politics."[12]

(UN)DRESSING THE PRISON LESBIAN

Little has been written about the importance of attire or dress to women behind bars, but officers continue to rely on prisoner uniforms to categorize, distinguish, and control. For example, in the 1980s Big Water introduced color-coded medical-style scrubs to distinguish prisoners by their work assignments and to better manage the *keep-aways*. Keep-aways include any people who

---

8. Freedman, "Prison Lesbian," 397–400.
9. Cohen, "Punks," 448.
10. Cohen, "Punks," 448.
11. Cohen, "Punks," 454.
12. Cohen, "Punks," 440–62.

argue with each other and disrupt operations when they are together or who encourage others to defy orders. Of course, folks who attempted to establish and maintain same-sex intimate relationships were the number-one targets on Big Water's keep-away list. Assigning specific uniforms to each work detail to some extent limited keep-aways' ability to disrupt operations. The new uniforms were met with stiff resistance, especially given the state's insistence that underneath they wear diaperesque "granny panties."

According to Celeste, a formerly incarcerated member of the Drama Club, women read these regulations as another attempt to dehumanize them by stripping them of their femininity. Big Water already prohibited many practices that were integral to their identities, restricting the use of make-up and banning certain methods of styling hair. The facility banned many of the basic tools any home esthetician would need—mirrors, nail polish, tweezers—on which people had relied to care for and style their own bodies. Concerns about intimate relationships within a segment of the population had led to a direct assault on everybody. In response to the growing outcry, Celeste went to work. An industrious woman, skilled at knitting and using crochet needles and a self-described serial "rule violator," she began to design custom thong- and bikini-style underwear to sell. A select clientele who understood the risks and could be trusted not to snitch began patronizing her handicrafts.[13]

Big Water introduced the pink dress policy at a time when the United States was embroiled in heated arguments over the meaning and permissibility of oversized, saggy pants, especially when worn by young Black and Latino men. Fashion is often dismissed as frivolity, but dress operates as a powerful social sign system. We read clothing for clues about the person wearing them, recognizing that dress can be used to costume, embellish, or display the body as well as to conceal.[14] In human society, dress is implicated in "the nature of social interaction and the meanings that evolve from it."[15] Dress signals and produces belonging among group members. It does so by representing the experiences of the participants who have lived and grown up within a social, economic, and political community.[16] Jeff Ferrell writes that stylized clothing

---

13. Phone interview with Celeste, 2011.

14. Mimi Thi Nguyen, "The Hoodie as Sign, Screen, Expectation, and Force," *Signs: Journal of Women in Culture and Society* 40, no. 4 (2015): 791–816.

15. Jeff Ferrell and Clinton R. Sanders, *Cultural Criminology* (Boston: Northeastern University Press, 1995), 179.

16. Whenever I visit a prison arts program, I double-check the visitor guidelines to ensure that officers cannot turn me away based on my attire. I have developed a wardrobe of "Christian conservative" clothing for field research. I pull my hair back into a clip away from my face, pull on closed-toe, low-, or no-heeled shoes, slip on loose, dark slacks (never leggings or jeans) and bulky long-sleeved shirts or sweaters that show no cleavage. To wear other clothes marks me as someone the officers need to watch for acts of defiance, rule-breaking, or interference. My clothes signal a willingness to conform to dictates inside penal facilities.

can "ritually celebrate" a collective past and affirm current connectivity by sig-naling, reiterating, and even lauding temporally bounded and geographically specific conventions, "neighborhood ties," and shared histories.[17] As Karen Tranberg observes, the dressed body "mediates between the self and society" but styles evolve across space, time, context, class, and generations.[18] Where clothing style can make a person visible within a group as a member, accord-ing to D. Soyini Madison, in new arenas style increases the visibility of the wearer to others outside of their original sign system, prompting any number of emotional responses ranging from pleasure to outrage. Out of place, dress can still play a performative role, but it need not always (re)produce existing hierarchies. Attire can instead be understood and used to stage the wearer's discontent, dissent, or alienation from the norm as it expresses their aspira-tions for and efforts to establish alternative social modalities.[19]

As Big Water imposed the pink dress punishment, parts of Louisiana, Georgia, and other Gulf Coast states passed ordinances prohibiting sagging one's pants. State and local governments imposed fines and brought charges of indecent exposure against those who defied the ban. Defenders of the fash-ion choice countered that young people had a right to freedom of expression and that most wearers were simply emulating hip-hop fashion. They insisted that low pants ought not be equated with low moral values or criminal intent. But officials in school districts and other state-operated and privately owned institutions across the nation tried to outlaw the practice.

Just as graffiti reveals and disrupts dominant aesthetics by undermining the "hegemonic hold" of political elites and economic developers on built landscapes, behind bars the act of modifying or defacing a prison uniform reveals and disrupts the flow of power.[20] At Big Water, authorities harbored unfounded fears that masculine-identified African American lesbians were disrupting operations by having same-sex sex, sagging and bagging their uni-forms, and violating other policies. Administrators and staff members used these concerns to justify the pink dress policy. Once Drama Club members understood the implications of the pink dress, they knew they had to act.

---

17. Jeff Ferrell, *Crimes of Style: Urban Graffiti and the Politics of Criminality* (New York: Gar-land Press, 1993), 176.

18. Karen Tranberg Hansen, "Introduction," in *African Dress: Fashion, Agency, Performance*, ed. Karen Tranberg Hansen and D. Soyini Madison (London: Bloomsbury Academic Press, 2013), 2.

19. D. Soyini Madison, "Dressing Out-of-Place: From Ghana to Obama Commemorative Cloth on the US American Red Carpet," in *African Dress: Fashion, Agency, Performance*, ed. Karen Tran-berg Hansen and D. Soyini Madison (London: Bloomsbury Academic Press, 2013), 217–30.

20. Ferrell, *Crimes of Style*, 176.

DRAMA CLUB HERSTORY

Since 1995, people imprisoned at Big Water have brought their most pressing issues to the Drama Club for creative, collective analysis. A small cohort of lifers (people serving life sentences) anchor the ensemble, complemented by another fifteen to twenty folks serving shorter sentences. They are led by two women volunteers—Jodie and Ngozi—each of whom directs their own professional performing arts company in a nearby metropolitan area. Drama Club's roots lie in a solo performance piece Jodie composed and performed at Big Water soon after she graduated from college. *Fury* drew on interviews Jodie conducted with six domestic violence survivors she met while volunteering at the Illinois Clemency Project for Battered Women. Public performances of *Fury* in Chicago led to an opportunity to perform the work at the Dixon Correctional Institute, a medium-security prison for women in downstate Illinois. It was "the most powerful performance" of Jodie's life:

> I was terrified. I felt like I was performing their stories and in my heart I did not know if I had earned that right. But I was young and didn't stop myself when those fears and questions came up. . . . After the performance, they lined up to thank me and shake my hand. I had an interview with one of the inmates afterward and she asked me why I had come there. I don't remember my answer now, but she asked me when I was coming back, and if I would teach them to do what I did. . . . I told her I was leaving Illinois and moving back home to [the Gulf Coast] . . . [but] I would try to teach and she told me I should definitely do that. . . . [That] conversation bound me to her, and to incarcerated women all over the world, especially in [Big Water] where I fulfilled my promise to her two years later.[21]

Back home, without consulting the prison administration, Jodie wrote a grant proposal to support the offering of a drama class once a week for six months to a small group at Big Water. When she learned the proposal had been funded, a sympathetic social worker found a way for her to proceed. They began by having Jodie perform *Fury* to a gym full of prisoners and, a week later, Drama Club was on.

The incarcerated women traveled a different path to Drama Club but share Jodie's deep love of performing. Celeste, one of the founding members, heard her name called from a list created by prison staff. She and about twelve or

---

21. Jodie, "How the Drama Club Was Born," unpublished manuscript.

fifteen other women assembled as required in the gym. A woman from the prison's social services department introduced Jodie and explained that the idea was "to explore the effects of drama on people who are incarcerated." Celeste, like many others who stayed with the program, quickly understood Drama Club as a way to "do better time" as well as an opportunity to momentarily shift "our mentality." She recalled:

> The word *drama* instantly sparked my interest because I've always enjoyed drama. . . . I've always been interested in doing things. In church, in school, in the community, I was always involved in plays, in giving talks and debates and speeches. . . . [The] actual drama wasn't new to me, but [it was] so real. . . . Drama is different as an adult. . . . As children and young adults we act. But as adults, and then as a mature adult, we *perform*, and I think there's a vast difference in just acting and performing. In performing you're really putting yourself into it. That person becomes you and you become that person but as a child you're acting—I read this, I need to do this, and I'm gonna do this, so it's none of you but it's all the paper, black and white. And one of the things I love about Drama [Club]—and I didn't think I would because when I thought of drama, I thought of plays, performances, but it's not that. . . . We do bring ourselves, and we chip off pieces of ourselves, and then the pieces we're chipping off are replaced with newer pieces.[22]

Ava, another original member of the Drama Club, an African American woman and a lifer who serves as club president, also had early, powerful experiences with drama:

> I did a lot of drama when I was in elementary school and high school. . . . It was a new door opening for me in the drama that we do now. It was a different door. Because then it was a kid doing things without really understanding what she's doing, she's following instruction. And in Drama [Club] if you ask us to write a piece, I put a lot of myself in that piece. And to me that's a healing and that's a difference because then I was a child and now I'm a woman.[23]

Drama Club invites women to "bring their [full] selves" to the work and encourages them to explore old and new social roles in both theatrical and real-life settings. That means going beyond acting, the process Celeste and Ava

---

22. Jodie, Interview with Celeste and Ava, June 16, 2007.
23. Jodie, Interview with Celeste and Ava.

described from their childhoods of embodying a role someone else dreamed up and following their directions. In Drama Club, participants can test what is possible. They do not have to just do what other people tell them to do. They do not have to play the role of the repentant prisoner that the state demands. They can write scripts, develop their own roles, and tell their own stories. Through performance, Drama Club members explore and expand what is possible for them in their own minds, on stage, and in everyday life. They take on roles that would never have been offered to them or that they may have doubted they could manage in other situations. In so doing, they access, animate, and cultivate a sense of inner freedom, self-worth, and agency under captivity.

With the support of the ensemble, Ngozi, and Jodie, the women of Drama Club grow through the roles that they choose in new and surprising ways. As Aimee Meredith Cox states, Black women and girls who have been marginalized use performance as "a way of speaking [themselves] into being in the way [they] choose, to become more than just the body that others allow to visually overwhelm and solely define [their] existence."[24] Through performance, they "chip away" at internalized racist, sexist propaganda and old, limiting beliefs and habits, including those that may have served them in the past but that are no longer needed or helpful. Opportunities to compose and perform the stories and characters they dream up for an audience of other incarcerated women affirm and reaffirm their self-worth, wisdom, and creativity. The effect can be transformative, healing. Performance offers the opportunity to mine and uncover the wealth of knowledge and creativity in them. Further, as D. Soyini Madison asserts, "a performance of possibility" like those staged at Big Water, "not only creates alliances while it names and marks injustice . . . it also enacts a force beyond ideology; it enacts and imagines the vast possibilities of collective hopes and dreams coming into fruition, of actually being lived."[25] It is this commitment to incarcerated artists' creativity, personal growth, and agency that grounds Drama Club's praxis and sustained Celeste, Ava, and the other long-term participants' interest.

In the first workshops, Jodie began by sharing acting techniques. Realizing that the women had some experience with performance and were willing to engage but did not know each other, Jodie began class with Viola Spolin–inspired theater trust exercises such as partnered blind walks. She required the women to partner with others with whom they were not familiar and encour-

24. Aimee Meredith Cox, *Shapeshifters: Black Girls and the Choreography of Citizenship* (Durham, NC: Duke University Press, 2015), 215.

25. D. Soyini Madison, *Acts of Activism: Human Rights as Radical Performance* (Cambridge: Cambridge University Press, 2010), 166.

aged them to explore and use their environments in nonnormative ways—ways that are usually not open to prisoners. These activities progressed to object work, improvisation, and writing exercises. Celeste recalled one time where Jodie asked them each to find an ordinary object and create a two-minute solo that used the object in both a "natural" and a "nontraditional" way. Opportunities to work together over a series of weeks and months, exploring the boundaries of the natural, normative, or everyday world, slowly drew the diverse group of women from "different races" and "different times" (i.e., sentences) into a close-knit performance ensemble that belonged to each other despite their differences.

In 1996 the Drama Club staged its first play, inspired by *The Oprah Winfrey Show*. Since then they have created adaptations of the Nativity that explored their own birth stories, devised original poetic choral pieces that put Maya Angelou's "Phenomenal Woman" and Marge Piercy's "For Strong Women" in conversation with the women's writings, reframed the prison wall into a Wailing Wall, and explored how incarcerated women mask and protect themselves behind bars. In 2001, the addition of professional performer and choreographer Ngozi as codirector enabled the ensemble to expand its repertoire, incorporating Afro-centric, Pan-Africanist, and Circum-Atlantic dance and movement-based approaches to investigate and stage issues about which they were concerned. The first production I attended in 2010, *Life Is,* expressed the lifers' perspectives on living behind bars. Its rousing chorus, "Life is what you make it / Life is happiness / Life is where you're going / Life is where you've been," has become a kind of anthem for the ensemble and for the Graduates, a small group of returned (i.e., formerly incarcerated) citizens from Big Water who perform with Ngozi and Jodie on the outside.

Jodie and Ngozi begin rehearsal each week with a check-in. Seated in chairs in a large circle in one of the prison's windowless program rooms, everyone shares how they are feeling and what is going on in their lives. Check-in is followed by a short physical warm-up. From there, the group members might transition into acting games inspired by Viola Spolin, or opportunities to tell stories, perform scenes, and write short stories or poetry in response to a prompt Jodie or Ngozi brings in. Depending on the mood and needs of the group, song and dance may be incorporated as well. These training sessions build every participant's artistic skill base and establish trust. Each week Ngozi and Jodie reflect upon what they learn during the ninety-minute drive back home and brainstorm next steps. Creative prompts encourage the women to delve deeper into emerging themes. In the past these themes have been introduced by questions such as "What's in your foot locker?" Because many of the women prefer to improvise rather than write down their responses, Jodie and Ngozi often facilitate what they call "Popcorns," a physical theater "brainstorming" exercise in which the women spontaneously share ideas in rapid succession on their feet. Performance pieces are developed over the course of a year and emerge out of the rich, imaginative mix of stories that the prisoners share.

What sustains Drama Club week after week, year after year, is the facilitators' refusal to impose limits on the women's creativity, actions, emotions, or desires. Ngozi and Jodie reject the popular agonistic models of prisoner correction and rehabilitation, which value the arts as a putatively therapeutic tool to induce particular lines of self-reflection and encourage confession, remorse, and of course compliance. They recognize that theater and dance can do far more than train prisoners to comply with orders, or more narrowly to confess, express remorse, and seek forgiveness in a convincing manner.[26] Prisoners and facilitators instead describe Drama Club as "freeing" and "healing," for the process of art-making allows the women to "leave" the facility "physically, mentally, emotionally, and spiritually."[27] Ngozi explains:

> When you lend yourself, your energy, your thoughts, your persona, your presence . . . when you allow that to be used in a more sincere and honest way, then the work becomes healing. . . . They know we are there because it is just love. It's none of these things other than love, and wanting to see them be better, grow better, even if they never leave [Big Water]. Still manifest your destiny. You are still obligated. Your destiny does not stop because you are incarcerated.[28]

Despite past misdeeds and harm done, criminalized women are not their mistakes; as human beings, they can—do—have lives of value and meaning. The Drama Club offered its members a network of supportive care and belonging when there was often no one else on whom to rely. When crises arise, they are there for each other. One way that they advocate for themselves and others at Big Water is through their art. Under the playful frame of doing drama, they could challenge institutional norms and impact the conditions of their confinement. Such was the case when they committed to addressing the pink dress in a new theatrical work, *Beauty Coming 'n Going*.

---

26. Ashley Lucas, "When I Run in My Bare Feet: Music, Writing and Theatre in a North Carolina Women's Prison," *American Music* 31, no. 2 (2013): 135.

27. Kalenda, personal interview with the author (December 2011).

28. Ngozi, personal interview with the author (December 2011).

BEAUTY COMING 'N GOING

Kalenda, one of the Drama Club cofacilitators, an African American lesbian known for her vibrant singing voice, related to me some of the steps taken to break down the impact of the pink dress policy and begin exploring it with the women:

> We talked about . . . dressing butch, dressing femme, transgender, and why certain women prefer to dress that way. . . . At the root of it for many women is having been abused or having been attacked. Wearing clothes that identify them as having a typically feminine shape or body [was uncomfortable]. . . . After that experience, they moved . . . on to clothes that don't accentuate their figure, because it makes them feel less vulnerable. . . . [The pink dress was] like adding to the trauma. . . . To say to a woman, "Oh you're trying to dress like a man, you're wearing your pants baggy so we're going to put you in a dress"—a *pink* dress no less?! This symbol of what you're supposed to be as a woman, or what a girl is supposed to dress like and look like.[29]

Legal systems around the world largely fail to protect women and girls from abuse. The overwhelming majority of incarcerated women (90%) survived domestic violence and at least one sexual assault prior to their incarceration.[30] For far too many, experiences of interpersonal violence continue behind bars. Knowing they were vulnerable at Big Water, the women dressed in oversized clothing for self-defense. Visibly fashioning their uniforms in a "masculine" style enabled some women to establish and preserve their bodily integrity and, I would argue, their identities. As Ruth Holliday has found, people use attire to communicate "externally" what is sensed "inside," thus fulfilling the human "desire to be self-present."[31] Yet individual identity is always constituted in relation to others. Comfort and belonging within LGBTQ communities (as in others) in part "derives from being recognizably queer," or out to oneself and to others.[32]

Beyond announcing the presence of individual Black lesbians, women at Big Water used loose-fitting uniforms to collectively constitute and signal the presence of active and engaged *quare* communities. E. Patrick Johnson coined the term *quare* to "foreground the ways in which lesbians, gays, bisexuals, and transgendered people of color come to sexual and racial knowledge." Quare

---

29. Kalenda interview.

30. Nancy Wolff, Jing Shi, and Jane A. Siegel, "Patterns of Victimization among Male and Female Inmates: Evidence of an Enduring Legacy," *Violence and Victims* 24, no. 4 (2009): 469–70.

31. Ruth Holliday, "The Comfort of Identity," *Sexualities* 2, no. 4 (1999): 481.

32. Holliday, "Comfort," 481.

studies, as a "theory of the flesh," is invested in exploring and "emphasizing the diversity within and among gays, bisexuals, lesbians, and transgendered people of color while simultaneously accounting for how racism and classism affect how we experience and theorize the world."[33] In addition, quare studies theorizes the previously ignored practices of community and coalition-building between and among Black LBGTQ folks and their Black cis-gender and heterosexual allies. Quare communities emerge from and value "Black culture and community"; as such, they are "committed to [struggling] against all forms of oppression—racial, sexual, gender, class, religious"—and more.[34] Social scientists working in the early 1900s noted that incarcerated women organized kinship networks to provide themselves with much needed social and economic support. According to Regina Kunzel, new arrivals learned proper decorum from their adopted family members, including how to navigate the hierarchies of guards and prisoners, what behavior was expected of them, and their responsibilities to their fellow prisoners. Today, quare kinship networks, like others behind bars, share information, help each other gain institutional privileges, enjoy in-prison social events, and access the essential, if illicit, underground economies that circulate goods and services (e.g., so many packages of ramen noodles in exchange for a book or laundry done in a certain way).[35] Without these invisible networks, the women would be more vulnerable to psychological and physical harm, including sexual violence by male officers, the most pervasive threat to women's safety and security.

To discuss violence, gender, and homosexuality in such a climate of racist, sexist, and homophobic hostility was to risk much. Nonetheless, Drama Club members set out to establish and hold a community space in which beauty, self-worth, violence against women, and homosexuality could be investigated. Ultimately, they chose to embed five short scenes into *Beauty Coming 'n Going*, a play about women's social value they had already begun developing. A four-phase creative process emerged that began with "Popcorn" sessions and in-depth discussions about Black women, beauty, and attire. This transitioned into the writing and devising process, followed by rehearsals, during which time the piece continued to be refined. The scenes they embedded in the work about a returned citizen's (i.e., formerly incarcerated woman's) efforts to land a job at a women's clothing boutique that exclusively sold pink dresses would *stage healing*, scripting alternative ways of being in the world that encouraged and affirmed more caring, just, and equitable human relations.

33. E. Patrick Johnson, "Quare Studies, or Almost Everything I Know About Queer Studies I Learned from My Grandmother," in *Black Queer Studies: A Critical Anthology*, ed. E. Patrick Johnson and Mae Henderson (Durham, NC: Duke University Press, 2005), 127.

34. Johnson, "Quare Studies," 125.

35. Kunzel, *Criminal Intimacies*, 119.

PINKY'S BOUTIQUE

I climbed into Ngozi's car on September 11, 2011, for the ninety-minute ride to Big Water. Tall oaks and magnolia trees lined the highways and sheltered squat, single-family homes embedded in verdant, green terrain. When we finally pulled off the highway, I did not realize that we had arrived at the prison until bright lights illuminated a tall, barbed-wire fence. After a brisk pat-down, we followed a round Black woman officer across the yard. The fresh flowers planted across the compound and the arrangement of the squat, two-story cellblocks in formations reminded me of a small women's college. After a brisk search and another pat-down, we were ushered into a large auditorium filled with a thunderous cacophony of voices, stomping feet, and metal folding chairs scraping the linoleum floor as some three hundred women prisoners and a handful of officers and invited guests like myself took our seats.

Almost as soon as we were ushered into the front row, Ngozi took the stage to welcome everyone. As she returned to the audience, two women pulled aside a makeshift front curtain of blue bed sheets strung on white clothesline. The ninety-minute performance interwove individual monologues with choral poems that challenged listeners to reflect on our society's preoccupation with outward physical appearance. Five short scenes in the middle of the piece—performed as structured improvisations—specifically addressed the pink dress policy.[36]

The blue bed sheet curtains pulled back to reveal Rae, a soft-spoken, middle-aged Black woman and longtime Drama Club member who was known on the compound as "The Mack." Rae was a smooth talker much admired for her ability to enact a confident, self-controlled style of working-class Black masculinity. On stage, she wore her Afro cut into a short fade and a baggy, white, long-sleeve shirt over loose-fitting white cargo pants and white tennis shoes. Rae's character—Starkey—was a serious uniform-code violator. Her clothing and hairstyle enlarged her body and made her appear masculine. Rae/Starkey's masculine appearance was heightened by the immediate arrival of a highly feminine Black woman who sat, ankles crossed, at a small desk down center stage, wearing a 1980s-style light grey women's suit with a knee-length skirt and expansive epaulettes. In this, the first of the five "pink dress" scenarios, they established the conflict. Starkey was a recently returned citizen looking for work.

---

36. The following is taken from the final script provided to me by Jodie and Ngozi. During rehearsals, Ngozi takes detailed notes on what the women say and compiles them into the script. In performance, though, they are allowed to improvise around the agreed-upon content. As such, this dialogue may not represent exactly what was said on stage, but it is close.

Scene 1

PAROLE OFFICER: Now what skills do you possess?

STARKEY: Well, I can do just about anything. I can lift, and stock shelves, what do you need?

PAROLE OFFICER: I do not have anything for stocking at this time. I do have something in sales—

STARKEY: Sales, what would I have to do?

PAROLE OFFICER: It is a lady's boutique and there is one stipulation. You have to wear a pink dress.

STARKEY: Pink dress?! . . .

PAROLE OFFICER: *(Aside to audience)* The nerve of her, coming in here, demanding assistance. I guess she doesn't realize that I am her Parole Officer and I hold the keys to her freedom. She can either accept this job or . . .

STARKEY: *(Interrupting)* At this point, I have to do what I have to do.

PAROLE OFFICER: Very good, here's the address to Pinky's Boutique. Good luck.

Having introduced Starkey and her search for employment the cast transitioned into the next scene at Pinky's Boutique by replacing the Parole Officer with a Receptionist at the desk. To establish a boutique as the setting, the Receptionist wore a loose-fitting 1980s-style business suit with enlarged shoulder pads in a bright shade of pink. Behind her, three women in elaborate pink ball gowns stood frozen as store mannequins. The Receptionist greeted Starkey:

Scene 2

RECEPTIONIST: Welcome to Pinky's Boutique!

STARKEY: Hello, mama! I came for the job, but I sure would like to work on you.

RECEPTIONIST: Let me get the manager. *(Exits)*

STARKEY: *(Looking closely at the mannequins)* Even the dummies look good up in here.

Starkey's bold flirtation with the Receptionist and open admiration of the mannequins produced an avalanche of audience laughter. The sound seemed to me to affirm a surprised, collective recognition that these scenes would address the prison's ban on baggy uniforms, masculine gender performance, and homoerotic desire. My quick glance around the room—repeated by many others—revealed that the corrections officers were also having a good laugh from their stations on the perimeter. This content had been approved.

Imprisoned people use humor to build solidarity among themselves and to "help maintain their dignity" in the face of the demeaning practices of the state.[37] In one of the only scholarly treatments of humor behind bars, Charles M. Terry finds that jokes interrupt and reveal everyday routines of confinement and punishment.[38] Humor is often the only available mechanism through which to voice otherwise inexpressible experiences and emotions. Ester Newton found that within LGBTQ and other marginalized groups, humor articulates the incongruous juxtapositions and challenges of life that result from being the object of hegemonic social contempt.[39] Donna Goldstein concurs that jokes between members of a marginalized group often get their "punch" by revealing the shared, devalued perspectives and experiences of the tellers and the told.[40] To communicate their point, the *Beauty Coming 'n Going* cast employs *signifyin'*, the African American practice of using a clever and funny turn of phrase to slyly point out incongruities or faults in another person, also known as the verbal art of the put down.[41]

Rae presents a familiar expression of urban, working-class, Black masculinity that invokes laughter for its bold, flirtatious style. Her portrayal of Starkey, however, resists the trap of equating this type of flirtation with predation, what Estelle Freedom, Don Sabo, and others have characterized as the most prevalent representation of "prison masculinity."[42] Instead of striking fear in the audience, Starkey's struggle to reintegrate into the free world and find work seemed realistic. The dilemma made her highly sympathetic and relatable.

In scene 3, the store Manager met Starkey:

MANAGER: May I help you?
STARKEY: They sent me here for the job and I can't wait to start working up in here.
(Starkey glances longingly at the sales women and mannequins)

---

37. Charles M. Terry, "The Function of Humor for Prison Inmates," *Journal of Contemporary Criminal Justice* 13, no. 1 (1997): 32.

38. Terry, "Humor," 30.

39. Esther Newton, *Mother Camp: Female Impersonators in America* (Chicago: University of Chicago Press, 1979).

40. Donna M. Goldstein, *Laughter Out of Place: Race, Class, Violence and Sexuality in a Rio Shantytown* (Oakland: University of California Press, 2003), 129.

41. Geneva Smitherman, *Talkin and Testifyin: The Language of Black America* (Detroit: Wayne State University Press, 1986), 118–19.

42. Donald F. Sabo, Terry A. Kuppers, and Willie James London, eds., *Prison Masculinities* (Philadelphia: Temple University Press, 2001).

MANAGER: First of all, here is a copy of our sexual harassment policy *(hands her the paper)*. Here is a copy of our rules and regulations *(hands her another piece of paper)*. And one other thing; you must wear a pink dress and stilettos. Here is the application, fill it out and meet me back here at 1:00 p.m.

Starkey's exaggerated ogling of the sales women and mannequins clarified for all her sexuality. But the Manager chose not to explicitly or directly repudiate her desire. Rather than reprimanding Starkey for her homosexuality, the Manager offered her their employee handbook and sexual harassment policy. This gesture demonstrated that she attributed Starkey's behavior to a lack of knowledge of proper workplace decorum, not to her sexuality, and sought to educate her. Most importantly, she demonstrated that she had faith that Starkey could master these skills. As audience members we realize Starkey may have a future that includes working at Pinky's if she can learn the rules and modulate her behavior accordingly. As Starkey stepped away, however, the other boutique employees challenged the Manager's decision:

Scene 3 Cont'd

WORKER ONE: *(Turning to the Manager)* You cannot possibly hire her!
WORKER TWO: She act like something is wrong with her, like she just came out of rehab! She look gay!
MANAGER: Some of y'all just came out of rehab. . . . Let's go to lunch.

In judging Starkey so harshly, the Workers restage the homophobic logic of the prison's pink dress policy. The Manager responds by using her knowledge of the Workers' own pasts to check their fears and express her distaste for their assumption that Starkey is a threat. Whether or not Starkey has actually "just come out of rehab" (i.e., prison) or is "gay," we learn that the Workers have been in treatment, "rehab," too. The Manager's critical comedic "dis" interrupts their speech by challenging the reliability of their interpretation of Starkey's "look." Instead of reading Starkey's clothes and mannerisms as evidence of perversion, the Manager undercuts the Worker's reliance on the visual as an arbitrator of human value. By implication, in critiquing the Workers, her words further rebuke the prison administration.

The challenge to the pink dress policy continues when the Workers and Manager exit and, through the magic of theater, the Mannequins come to life to discuss the employees' concerns until they too are interrupted by Starkey, who performs a short monologue.

Scene 4

MANNEQUIN ONE: *(Gesturing to one of the exiting sales women)* She needs a perm!

MANNEQUIN TWO: I cannot believe the other one is talking about how somebody look, she too old to be working anyway. Why do they have to judge people all the time?

MANNEQUIN THREE: Where do they get these clothes from? They are really horrible.

(They freeze as Starkey suddenly returns)

STARKEY: *(Entering)* Hello? Hello? I guess I'm early. . . . I really need this job. I'm tired of being what everyone else wants me to be. I am good just as I am.

Lord why can't they just accept me for who I am?

Just as I am cause I'm proud of who I be

Cause God created perfection, when He created me.

They say beauty's only skin deep, I say that's a lie—

I feel, Beauty is Love, and it comes from the inside.

So what my stomach isn't flat, I'm still a lady.

The reason for that is because I carried not one, not two, but three babies.

My hair is mine, it's natural and I like it like that.

Does that mean I'm not a woman, cause it's not down my back?

My breast used to be firm, it sags now, not a perfect pick,

That's alright with me, it's nothing a support bra can't fix.

I've put on a few pounds, so when I walk I wobble;

I guess I'll never be a contestant on *America's Next Top Model.*

Society tells me, I should look better, because I have cellulite.

When I walk my thighs rub together.

My eyes are not blue, hazel, green or gray,

[But] I don't need to buy contacts to see a mile away.

God made my nose the way he wanted it to be,

That's why I'm not self-conscious and can smell insecurities.

I am a Phenomenal Woman, God's work at his best—

Holding my head up high and wearing beauty around my neck.

When I look at myself in a mirror, I can't help but to grin

Because God made me perfect, He made me

Just as I am.

The Mannequins immediately voiced words of encouragement that Starkey was surprised to overhear:

MANNEQUINS: You can do it. . . . Believe in yourself!

This scene actualizes a deep-seated African American belief that the known world is not the sum total of our existence. Here the possibility of a magical, alternative world beyond the visible and familiar gives way to a personal reflection. Inanimate store mannequins come to life as experts not merely on fashion but on beauty as well, and they answer Starkey's plea to be accepted as she is. The scene accomplishes this by modeling itself on Maya Angelou's anthemic poem, "Phenomenal Woman," which Jodie introduced some years ago. Starkey's monologue mirrors Angelou's celebration of a woman who is "not cute or built to suit a fashion model's size" yet who nonetheless is desired and who moves with self-assurance, commanding respect.[43]

Starkey's desire to be accepted "just as I am" is answered in the final scene. After dealing with several disruptive customers, the Store Manager pulls her aside and says:

Scene 5

MANAGER: Fifteen year ago I was imprisoned. . . . And somebody gave me a chance. I know what it is like to be judged before you even open your mouth; folks stopping being your friend when you tell them that you've been incarcerated, and even having your family not trusting you because they still don't see you as a family member—they see you as a criminal, a convicted felon. My God is a god of second chances, and I am willing to give you a chance, but I expect great things from you!! Can you lift boxes and maybe stock the shipments when they come in?
STARKEY: Yes, I can do that.
MANAGER: I've been thinking about our dress code. Do you have a pink t-shirt and some pink pants?
STARKEY: Yes I do, thank you, thank you so much!
(They exit together)

In this final scene, the workplace itself has changed to welcome Starkey and to accommodate their needs. Rigidly gendered employment guidelines are revealed to be negotiable as long as the pink color requirement is met. This change is possible because the woman—Manager—in charge is able to access her own personal story, express empathy for Starkey, and apply knowl-

43. Maya Angelou, *And Still I Rise*, Kindle edition (New York: Random House, 2011), 12–13.

edge gained through her experience in the workplace. In this final moment the ensemble opens up space for the alternative world they desire to form. The transformation the audience sees in the Store Manager results in an institutional change that allows Starkey not only to find work but also to be themself and learn from the experience. The workplace becomes a fairer, more equitable, and inclusive site to the benefit of all.

THE RESPONSE AND THE TRAJECTORY

Moments later, as the curtain closed at the end of the show, an avalanche of applause erupted. The audience of three hundred spontaneously rose to their feet in a standing ovation, but before the celebration could draw down, we were surprised by the arrival of two final characters—a Mardi Gras Indian Queen (Ngozi) and her Chief, both resplendent in pink feathers and detailed beadwork. Entering from the back of the auditorium, their deliberate, stately parade to the stage respatialized the room, extending the performance to the ground where we audience members were standing. In response, the audience around me began to sing and dance the Indians' signature incantation: "Won't bow down, don't know how!"

At any other time, such a robust display would have been considered a riot, but in the afterglow of the show it was allowed. Singing and dancing, "Won't bow down, don't know how," the audience responded to the production with a collective rejection of the reductive notions of Black, queer identity and the repressive power relations that the prison, and the nation that created and sustained it, produced. In its embrace of the Drama Club's performance as well as its enthusiastic participation in the post-show celebration, the audience declared a collective desire and determination to disrupt and challenge homophobic, racialized, gender policing and to (re)occupy this prison/nation space previously marked for exclusion for the embodied expression of a Black and queer belonging. The masculine-attired African American lesbian catalyst who ignited this action by daring to fashion him/her/themselves in a flamboyant style of working-class Black masculinity (on stage and off) was met at the end of the night by a moving sea of white and blue denim uniforms dancing a welcome and affirmation of their presence now—and in the future.

Making theater that opposes penal administrators' policies and upsets social norms can be dangerous. Not because women use their skills to deceive or prey upon others. Rather, the work is threatening because participants can emerge from Drama Club with a stronger, clearer sense of who they are, how they got where they are, and who is to blame. The process of self-examination that undergirds the Drama Club's work does not produce more docile, obedient, or repentant inmates. As Ann Stanford reflects, art-making in this regard threatens because it "proclaims a making and remaking of selves despite state attempts to confine, fix, and stabilize identities as inmates." Moreover, Stanford concludes, this kind of theater "proclaims a 'we' within the confines of the razor wire [that] disrupts the individualistic discourse and practice on which any system of oppression is dependent."[44]

Unlike programs for incarcerated populations that seek to "rehabilitate" or "correct" the imprisoned and that measure their success only by their ability to induce prisoners to comply with orders or to adhere to impossible white, middle-class, heteropatriarchal ideals, the Big Water Drama Club strives to "correct" systemic injustices. By repositioning the women as the subjects and agents of their own stories rather than the objects of someone else's scripted agenda, Drama Club creates a space in which women can reconnect with themselves and with others. Their work ends isolation and redresses wrongs committed against them and that they may have done to others. The final product encourages feelings of connectivity and wholeness among ensemble members and among members of their audience alike.

In the act of reappropriating the sign of the pink dress, *Beauty Coming 'n Going* challenged prison policy and the prevailing societal myths associated with Black lesbians, trans, queer, and quare people behind bars. Through performance, the ensemble turned the stereotypes on their heads and placed their own stories, their experiences, their questions, and their fears at center stage. The pink dress in their hands encouraged us to look beyond the reductive representations. Women attire their bodies in various styles for a variety of reasons. Whether representing dress as a means of camouflage after a violation, as a method of self-defense, or as an indication of quare community belonging, the production emphasized that, far from being frivolous, dress helps us order, interpret, and navigate human social relations.[45] Rather than repeating the most repressive practices, however, in Pinky's Boutique the vernacular sign system of dress ultimately produced a larger community of belonging among the workers and, by extension, with the audience. In the Drama Club's hands, the pink dress uniform did not shame but rather recognized and affirmed valuable, shared community ties.

Misogyny authorizes violence against women and girls in the United States and abroad as but one of many attributes or privileges associated with

44. Ann Folwell Stanford, "More Than Just Words: Women's Poetry and Resistance at Cook County Jail," *Feminist Studies* 30, no. 2 (2004): 277–78.

45. Elin Diamond, ed. "Introduction," in *Performance and Cultural Politics* (New York: Routledge, 1996), 4–6.

masculinity. At Big Water, however, this performance of Black working-class masculinity upends the notion that gender expression is biologically determined and always already predicated on violence against women. The ensemble's detailed examination of the prison's assertion that "the homosexuals" are the source of all their troubles reveals the complaint to be an ill-conceived response to the women's determination to assert their self-worth and defend themselves from harm.

Kalenda perhaps summed it up best. In an interview a month or two after the production, I asked her about the show's impact:

> LB: Are they [the imprisoned women] wearing fewer baggy clothes?
> KALENDA: They pink dress ain't done shit.[46]

NEXT STEPS

Beauty Coming 'n Going did not single-handedly take down the pink dress. But it did contribute to an ecosystem of opposition at Big Water. Women continued to style their uniforms in "too masculine" a fashion despite the ban. Femmes made strategic decisions to violate the regulations, bagging and sagging their uniforms to get themselves put into pink dresses. They then activated their networks to connect with folks working in the mattress shop who agreed to tailor the pink dresses to flatter their figures. It had been so long since any of them had been in a dress, they relished the opportunity, no matter how it arrived or the potential consequences of defacing it. These quotidian acts of defiance along with the Drama Club's production demonstrated to prison officials that their energies were perhaps better spent elsewhere. If preventing sexual violence and operational disruptions was the order of the day, there were many other targets that deserved their attention. Using prisoner dress to shame, regulate, and punish may be accepted, but doing so does not produce the intended outcomes. Women who love women are not going to stop loving women if you put them in a dress. People are not going to submit to dominant gender norms and expectations that undermine their abilities, shortchange their possibilities, and threaten their lives. Incarcerated people, like members of other social groups, will not respect elected or appointed officials who refuse to see or treat them with respect and dignity. They will, however, act to express their dissent and to constitute more supportive social modalities behind bars and in the larger world.

---

46. Kalenda interview.

The impact of incarcerated women's theater beyond the prison wall is the focus of the next chapter. Most prison theater ensembles are limited to performances at their correctional facilities before audiences of other incarcerated women. These productions are invaluable for their pedagogical and political impacts, educating spectators about pressing issues on the compound and encouraging them to act collectively to address them. But there are rare instances in which incarcerated women are allowed to leave their facilities and perform their work before the general public. In the next chapter, I consider the implications of one such production in South Africa, a collaboration between Rhodessa Jones, a US-based African American director, and women at the Naturena prison in Johannesburg. The production, *Serious Fun at Sun City*, enjoined conversations between and among women at the prison and across the country to address gender-based sexual violence as a core cause of women's criminalization and incarceration.

CHAPTER 5

Bring Me My Machine Gun

The Medea Project in South Africa

Cued by the sound of a popular South African hip-hop track, the *Serious Fun at Sun City* cast of thirty, predominantly Black and Colored imprisoned women spread out across the wide black stage at the State Theatre of South Africa in downtown Pretoria for the finale.[1] Working in groups, they performed a series of popular social dances that brought the crowd of six hundred to their feet. As the song wound to its final chorus, they formed two lines downstage facing the audience, tits up, hands loose at their sides. With the beat of the music, they all took a wide step to the right and turned their heads to look right as well. Next, they took a wide step to the left and turned their heads to look left. Finally, now all facing the audience, they reached their hands forward, right then left, as if grabbing the barrel of a machine gun. Bending their legs simultaneously, they descended into low squats to spray the crowd with imaginary fire power.

As I watched rehearsals of this finale dance from my production assistant's perch on a narrow wooden bench in the prison courtyard in the weeks leading up to this moment in August 2010, I was surprised that the Department of Correctional Services (SADCS) allowed the cast to perform such a rou-

---

1. Colored people are a distinct linguistic and political group in South Africa. They include people of mixed African, Asian, and European descent as well as the indigenous Khoisan community. See Mohamed Adhikari, *Not White Enough, Not Black Enough: Racial Identity in the South African Coloured Community* (Athens: Ohio University Press, 2005).

tine.[2] The Johannesburg Female Correctional Centre, known locally as Sun City, an ironic and playful reference to a posh African resort, is one of a half dozen squat, red-brick, wagon-wheel-shaped prisons in an expansive carceral complex located in an area called Naturena on the border between Johannesburg, a sprawling city of 5.5 million, and Soweto, the largest township or suburb in the nation, with a population of nearly 1.3 million. During a break in rehearsal, the production choreographer Thandazila Sonia Radebe reassured me that, in South Africa, the Machine Gun choreography was popularly associated with Batista, an American professional wrestler who performed his own stylized Machine Gun every time he entered the ring.[3] Audiences at the State Theatre in Pretoria, she insisted, would read the bullet-spraying ending as a popular social dance, not as a threat of violence as I did, being an irregular wrestling fan and an American.

Standing at my post in the cacophonous wings of the State Theatre during the performances, however, I could not stop thinking about Black South Africans' often violent decades-long fight to end European settler colonization and *apartheid* (pronounced *apart-hate*), the system of institutionalized racial segregation and economic exploitation instituted in 1948 by the minority Afrikaner (Dutch-descended white) government. The struggle to end apartheid led by Black South Africans culminated in multiracial democratic elections in 1994, but the cast of incarcerated artists dancing the Machine Gun epitomized the gaps between the promises made and the tangible effects of the post(anti-) apartheid government's neoliberal policies.

In this chapter I argue that, under the cover of a rehabilitative prison theater project, members of the cast used performance to demand that South Africa rectify the political, social, and cultural practices that authorize systemic inequality. Monologues performed by three cast members anchor my analysis. They appropriate the form of the confession to smuggle onto the national stage pointed critiques of the structural inequalities that undergird the "new" nation. The monologues, in conjunction with ensemble performances of popular and customary dances and of sacred songs from the anti-apartheid Struggle, demand immediate action to stop racialized gender-based violence in the intimate spaces of South African society. Taken together, these moments called for radical political, economic, and cultural change now. With

---

2. In light of the stigma attached to serving time, to protect the identities of the incarcerated women at the center of this study I refer to them only by their first names. For all other people, places, and events I use their given names.

3. Batista is the stage name of David Michael Bautista, a former American football player and mixed martial artist turned professional wrestler and actor. To see his signature Machine Gun moves, watch https://youtu.be/oLO_q5NNd1k, accessed August 23, 2019.

their hands on the barrels of their machine guns, the *Serious Fun* cast issued what read to me as a collective warning about what could happen should South Africa refuse to adapt and the needs of the nation's women continue to go unmet.

CONTEXT AND METHODOLOGY

Unlike the women working with Demeter's Daughters at Midwestern who focused on individual self-repair as described in chapter 3 or those in the Big Water Drama Club who voiced their concerns about institutional change as described in chapter 4, the *Sun City* ensemble used their performance opportunity to demand revolution, a new social order.[4] As in the United States, in South Africa women have been largely invisible in crime discourses, having never been truly conceived of as the primary authors or objects of the law.[5] During the transition to multiracial democratic rule in the 1990s, women's organizations had to demand a seat at the negotiating table. Ultimately, they were successful in instituting one of the most gender-informed constitutions on the planet, but there is a difference between constitutional change and the reallocation of material resources required to bring about deep structural change. The fall of apartheid did not end the need to fight for equality, respect, and dignity.[6] In the post-(anti-)apartheid era, despite the ratification of one of the most progressive constitutions in the world, a masculinist bias continues to obfuscate both the contributions and the needs of the nation's women. Inadequate state responses to systemic problems like chronic unemployment and poor enforcement of laws prohibiting violence and discrimination against women have forced some to take matters into their own hands.[7]

---

4. Sun City is the nickname of the prison on the border between Johannesburg and Soweto in South Africa.

5. The lack of official judicial attention to Black South African women does not mean that women's behavior was unimportant or went completely unremarked. See Frances Bernault, "The Politics of Enclosure in Colonial and Post-Colonial Africa," in *A History of Prison and Confinement in Africa,* ed. Florence Benault, trans. Janet Roitman (Portsmouth, NH: Heinemann, 2003) for a history of the treatment of women by the criminal legal and prison systems during the colonial era. For a history of the criminalization of women in the twentieth century, see Shireen Ally, *From Servants to Workers: South African Domestic Workers and the Democratic State* (Ithaca, NY: Cornell University Press, 2009). For a comparative history of the use of incarceration in South Africa, see Dirk van Zyl Smit, "Public Policy and the Punishment of Crime in a Divided Society: A Historical Perspective on the South African Penal System," *Crime and Social Justice* 21/22 (1984): 146–62.

6. Cheryl McEwan, "Engendering Citizenship: Gendered Spaces of Democracy in South Africa," *Political Geography* 19, no. 5 (2000): 629.

7. Lisa Vetten and Kailash Bahana, "The Justice for Gender Campaign: Incarcerated Domestic Violence Survivors in Post-Apartheid South Africa," in *Global Lockdown: Race, Gender and the Prison-Industrial Complex,* ed. Julia Sudbury (New York: Routledge, 2005), 256–59.

The SADCS reports that women represent one of the fastest-growing segments of the prison population today. In the eight years following democratic elections in 1994, the number of women behind bars grew by 70 percent.[8] The women's prison population exploded by nearly 36 percent (3,380) between 2008 and 2013, coinciding with my fieldwork (2009–12).[9] These increases were not attributable solely to an escalation in illicit behavior on the part of women, but rather to shifts in policing and sentencing, which now mandated incarceration for the crimes that women are most likely to commit and to be convicted of, including nonviolent theft (shoplifting, robbery, burglary, fraud, embezzlement), narcotics (trafficking, sale, distribution), and sex work.[10]

In response to the rising numbers of women behind bars, the SADCS—an agency once internationally condemned for human rights violations, torture, and the execution of dissidents—has been tasked with rehabilitating and returning incarcerated people to civil society.[11] As SADCS has worked to transform its notorious prisons into "centers of learning" over the last three decades, community-based arts organizations have gained limited access. Where allowed, workshops in music, customary Black South African dance, and theater (acting, playwriting) often culminate in performances on a facility's grounds for other prisoners, visiting SADCS dignitaries, the media, and occasionally the general public. As in the United States, warders (corrections officers, police, or guards) offer such performances as evidence that they are doing their jobs; the prisoners are being rehabilitated.

South African teaching artists question whether these arts programs benefit the prisoners. They fear that warders value them for their ability to present "properly performative" (i.e., well-behaved and compliant) prisoners in entertaining displays that affirm and reaffirm state power, authority, and efficacy.[12] Compelling imprisoned men and women to perform in this manner does little to address the social, economic, and political structural problems that most prisoners identify as factors that contributed to their incarcerations. Instead of aiding the imprisoned, Kelly Gillespie warns, theater and dance programs for incarcerated people in their current iteration may obscure the "serious politics of race[,] . . . class," and gender embedded in South Africa's criminal legal

---

8. South Africa Department of Correctional Services (SADCS), *Annual Report* (2008–9).

9. SADCS, *Annual Report* (2012–13), 33.

10. SADCS *Annual Report* (2008–9), 20–22.

11. Bernault, "Politics of Enclosure," 11–39.

12. Alexandra Sutherland, "Now We Are Real Women: Playing with Gender in a Male Prison Theatre Programme in South Africa," *RiDE: Journal of Applied Theatre and Performance* 18, no. 2 (2013): 120–32; Miranda Young-Jahangeer, "'Less Than a Dog: Interrogating Theatre for Debate in Westville Female Correctional Centre, Durban, South Africa," *RiDE: The Journal of Applied Theatre and Performance* 18, no. 2 (2013): 200–203; Kelly Gillespie, "Moralizing Security: 'Corrections' and Post-Apartheid Prison," *Race/Ethnicity: Multidisciplinary Global Contexts* 2, no. 1 (2008): 69–87.

system, blocking the implementation of more effective interventions.[13] I too entered the work questioning what the show *Serious Fun at Sun City,* directed by Rhodessa Jones with Idris Ackamoor of the world-renowned San Francisco-based Medea Project: Theatre for Incarcerated Women, could contribute.

THE MEDEA PROJECT

Rhodessa Jones, a preeminent practitioner of theater for incarcerated women, has now nearly three decades of experience working behind bars in the San Francisco county jail system and in other carceral facilities in the United States and around the world.[14] In 2006, Roshnie Moonsammy of the Johannesburg-based Urban Voices Festival invited her and her creative partner, Idris Ackamoor, to join with other equally talented and dedicated South African artists to develop a theater piece at Sun City. The theater collaboration was the first of its kind at a women's facility led by African American and Black South African directors. Emerging from a broad continuum of Black women's activism, including social justice organizing against police brutality and sexual violence, Medea Project productions are known for using myth, song, dance, monologue, and scene work embedded in a distinct Black feminist performance praxis to restage the multiple interlocking social, economic, political, and judicial processes that cancel women's lives and place too many of them behind bars. Nina Billone writes that through Medea Project productions we come to understand how prison is performed.[15] Would their approach work in South Africa, a country with its own rich history of women's organizing and artistic protest?

I made three ethnographic fieldwork trips, the first in 2009 and the last in 2012, to find out. During my time there, I observed and participated in all facets of the rehearsal and production process to mount *Serious Fun in Sun City* four times at three locations.[16] My fieldwork was informed by my personal connection to Jones and Ackamoor as well as the everyday labor of a production assistant, which included providing support for the produc-

13. Gillespie, "Moralizing Security," 71.

14. For more about the Medea Project, see Rena Fraden, *Imagining Medea: Rhodessa Jones and Theater for Incarcerated Women* (Chapel Hill: University of North Carolina Press, 2001); Sara Warner, "The Medea Project: Mythic Theater for Incarcerated Women," *Feminist Studies* 30, no. 2 (2004): 483–509; Nina Billone, "Performing Civil Death: The Medea Project and Theater for Incarcerated Women," *Text and Performance Quarterly* 29, no. 3 (2009): 260–75.

15. Billone, "Performing Civil Death," 260–75.

16. In 2009 at Sun City in the women's small courtyard where rehearsals took place; in 2010, in a large vaulted auditorium for selected members of the general public, and then later, at the prestigious State Theatre in Pretoria; and finally, in 2012, returning to the women's prison's small courtyard.

tion while documenting the process. I met Jones in the 1990s when I participated in a solo performance workshop she taught and later performed with
Medea in San Francisco for a fundraiser. When I joined them in South Africa
in 2009, it was my first experience seeing Jones teach behind bars. To get
the most out of the experience, I lived with Jones and Ackamoor in a small
bed-and-breakfast in the (somewhat) racially mixed Johannesburg suburb of
Melville, commuting with them to and from the prison for intensive four-to-
fourteen-hour rehearsals five or six days a week for two to four weeks at a
time. I took handwritten notes about staging, transcribed scenes and monologues to build the script, learned songs and dances, participated in and occasionally led warm-up and closing acting exercises, and, to the extent allowed
by the SADCS, documented rehearsals and performances on video and in
photographs.[17] In 2010, at the State Theatre show, I additionally served as an
assistant stage manager and liaison between the directors, ushers and stage
hands, warders, and incarcerated artists. My fieldwork was supplemented by
opportunities to speak with the directors as well as with archival research and
correspondence with cast members who had been released.

I came away from my fieldwork with new questions as it became clear that
the group's evening-length production, *Serious Fun at Sun City,* invited audiences in Johannesburg, Pretoria, and across the country to (re)consider wom-
en's political, economic, and social value. Far more than asking the women to
act like "good prisoners," *Serious Fun* became an opportunity to stage a significant intervention in popular discourses about women, crime, sexual violence,
and justice at a time when South Africa was embroiled in discussions about
these issues at the highest level in the wake of then-President Jacob Zuma's
rape trial. Through performance, the ensemble issued a warning to the country to embrace new social modalities and perform to new standards or else
face unpleasant consequences. Their call is an example of *stage healing* performed to encourage radical change at the social or cultural level.

GETTING TO PRETORIA

Sun City was the only prison in Johannesburg for women, and it, like all prisons, was designed to make their lives miserable and their bodies hypervisible.

---

17. When the production moved to the performance phase, I helped prepare the theater spaces
by doing everything from picking up litter in the women's small courtyard to clearing dressing
rooms at the State Theatre and setting necessary props, microphones, and furniture in place. To further support the cast, I placed personal phone calls to friends and family members offering comple-
mentary tickets to the show. During each performance, I served as a core member of the backstage
crew; in fact, for the prison performances in 2009 and 2012, I was the only backstage crew.

Just beyond the front entryway near the warders' (corrections officers') offices, tired and anxious, overwhelmingly Black and Colored women in blue or red tracksuits (their uniform) waited along faded yellow walls for a chance to speak to a warder or counselor or to make a phone call. An unending chorus of women's voices appealed to the warders, "Open the gate, Miss?" To access our rehearsal space in a small courtyard, the production team had to wind up a long, spiraling, cement ramp through the center of the squat, red-brick building. As we walked, I caught glimpses of life. Down one walkway, a young woman stood over an unsteady toddler learning to walk in the Children and Mother's Unit. Another corridor revealed more women in long white aprons, gumboots, and lopsided hair-nets unloading heavy wooden crates of food into a white-washed kitchen. Newly sentenced women in their street clothes lined up anxiously before another gate, carrying heavy black trash bags stuffed with personal belongings. On many days, the disembodied voices of Christian gospel songs sung in complex harmonies found us as we treaded our way through carrying scripts, boom boxes, pencils, and paper, the tools of a theater project for incarcerated women in the works. The narrow side door that led to the interior courtyard at the center of the panopticon, however, enabled a shift. White metal bars set against a faded mural of flowers opened into an octagon-shaped, cement courtyard with brick walls so high only the blue sky could be seen above. Barred windows filled with broken glass were embedded at regular intervals into the bricks. Behind them, from their cellblocks, all day, every day, some of the 1,500 imprisoned women and girls watched us work.

When *Serious Fun at Sun City* premiered in November 2008 in the women's prison's central courtyard to an audience of over three hundred imprisoned women and SADCS officials, warders, members of the press, and other invited guests responded enthusiastically. The production wove customary African dances with monologues, scene work, song, and contemporary dances all developed by the cast into an evening-length performance piece. SADCS warders praised the play for allowing the cast to demonstrate that they were being "rehabilitated" as well as for providing the women with an opportunity for "emotional release" and to "showcase their talents."[18] In an interview with the *City Press* in 2009, Samantha Ramsewaki, then communications manager

---

18. These insights were gained through personal exchanges with SADCS warders during rehearsals in 2009 on the prison grounds. Warders expressed these comments about the women's "talents" with great sincerity and as a point of pride. I note that theater for incarcerated people in South Africa, like other performance forms, is confronted by the pervasive myth that Africans are natural-born entertainers. Repeated emphasis on the importance of the performance as a "showcase" for the women's "talents" evidenced for me not acceptance of the myth but instead a lack of knowledge or awareness of the hard work and professional expertise required to compose, stage, and present the piece.

for the prison, explained that SADCS considered the show a "dramatic success" because it "helped to teach restorative justice, the importance of forgiveness, and has helped them [the prisoners] address the emotional baggage they brought with them to prison and to make peace with it."[19] Local papers published laudatory feature articles that emphasized that the women were not the "monsters" the reporters expected to meet.[20] Many articles followed a narrative of redemptive suffering, emphasizing that the women had found their imprisonment productive—an opportunity to examine and better themselves and now seek forgiveness from the nation. This coverage seemed to offer rare, positive proof that SADCS, and by extension the entire government, were doing their jobs at a time when Johannesburg and the nation had developed a growing reputation for danger, crime, and corruption.[21]

South Africa's prison system is not unique in its appropriation of arts programs for rehabilitative purposes. In this climate every portrait, poem, song, dance, or scene produced by an imprisoned artist is presumed to be reflexive or confessional, an object presented to allow scrutiny of the "deviant's" soul. Rarely, if ever, is the work read as artistic or as an expression of an artists' thought, vision, intellect, or skill. Demonstrating that the SADCS is doing its new job has been extremely important. For the greater part of the twentieth century, South Africa's criminal legal system was explicitly calibrated to patrol and punish the movement (restricting both physical mobility and political activism) of the dispossessed Black majority.[22] When Dutch and English settler colonists began to occupy southern Africa in the seventeenth and eighteenth centuries, they adapted the penal practices of their homelands to subjugate the indigenous populations just as they did in North America. White political and economic elites used colonial judicial systems and the

---

19. Gail Smith, "Rogue Mothers and Deviant Daughters," *City Paper*, November 1, 2009, 25.

20. Smith, "Rogue Mothers," 25; see also David Smith, "Theatre of Burden," *Mail & Guardian*, November 13, 2009, http://mg.co.za/article/2009-11-13-theatre-of-burden.

21. There is also the very real possibility that crimes against whites have increased as Blacks—dissatisfied with the pace of change and the lack of real redistribution of material resources—have perhaps decided to seek reparations individually. The fear may also be the result of ongoing sensationalizing of Black crime by media outlets that remain disproportionately controlled by the former colonists.

22. Kelly Gillespie, "Containing the 'Wandering Native': Racial Jurisdiction and the Liberal Politics of Prison Reform in 1940s South Africa," *Journal of Southern African Studies* 37, no. 3 (2011): 509; see also Diana R. Gordon, "Side by Side: Neoliberalism and Crime Control in Post-Apartheid South Africa," *Social Justice* 28, no. 3 (2001): 57–67; Gary Kynoch, "Of Compounds and Cellblocks: The Foundations of Violence in Johannesburg, 1890s–1950s," *Journal of Southern African Studies* 37, no. 3 (2011): 463–77; Gail Super, "'Like Some Rough Beast Slouching Towards Bethlehem to Be Born': A Historical Perspective on the Institution of the Prison in South Africa, 1976–2004," *British Journal of Criminology* 51, no. 1 (2011): 201–21; Paul Williams and Ian Taylor, "Neoliberalism and the Political Economy of the 'New' South Africa," *New Political Economy* 5, no. 1 (2000): 21–40.

military to conquer southern Africans, whom they regarded as biologically inferior, criminal, primitive savages, and establish the independent Union of South Africa, the predecessor to the contemporary Republic.[23] As in the US, these processes invalidated and criminalized Africans' humanity, rights, cultures, and acts of resistance.[24] Under the pretext of preventing crimes against whites, the aggressive system of social control called apartheid was instituted in 1948. The apartheid state attempted to depoliticize all Black organizing by criminalizing any actions that defied racial segregation. The government attributed any and all Black organizing to local criminals known as *tsotsi*. Organizers of and participants in the Defiance Campaign Against Unjust Laws and other liberation movements of the twentieth century, including members of the African National Congress (ANC) and the South African Community Party (SACP), pushed back against the label. Black leaders understood that the authorities had criminalized the actions people took to survive apartheid's brutality, to resist oppression, and to liberate themselves. They coined the term *tsotsi-comrade* or *com-tsotsi* to reveal and invert the twisted logic of the state. A com-tsotsi is a person who is engaged in illicit activity to defend themselves and their community against apartheid rule because of a growing political awareness and the knowledge that other means of resistance were ineffective. While the state represented tsotsi as common criminals pretending to engage in political activism, the com-tsotsi engaged in criminal activity as a natural outgrowth of their critical analysis of the political and economic landscape.[25]

In the mid-1990s, the combination of local, national, and international pressure initiated a transition from white ethnic-nationalist apartheid rule to multiracial democratic elections. Observers of the transition predicted that the elected leaders of the transitional government would dismantle the existing judiciary, police, and penal systems which were notorious for violence and corruption. The South Africa police and penal systems were notorious for their use of kidnapping, torture, indefinite detentions without charge, false prosecutions, and for the murder of detainees. During the period of transition, hope soared that Black people would be able to participate as full citizens at every level of society. Activists imagined that as African men and women were elected to positions of government leadership that they would transform the judiciary, decriminalize Black life, and allow indigenous African forms of justice to be (re)incorporated into the criminal legal system, diverting most people away from penal facilities and into restorative social justice

23. Bernault, "Politics"; van Zyl Smit, "Public Policy"; and Gillespie, "Moralizing Security."

24. Bernault, "Politics," 11–39.

25. Gail Super, "The Spectacle of Crime in the 'New' South Africa: A Historical Perspective (1976–2004)," *British Journal of Criminology* 50, no. 2 (2010): 168–69.

initiatives.[26] In subsequent years, it has become clear that the "new" neoliberal South Africa has instead continued to rely upon the old penal infrastructure as a critical node of governance.[27]

Before democratic elections were held in 1994, South Africa's criminal legal system did undergo significant (albeit limited) restructuring. Former president Frederik Willem de Klerk ended the use of police and detention facilities for exclusively political purposes and dismantled some of the most sadistic security units.[28] The formal reorganization of the prison system under the 1998 Correctional Service Act did institute a new approach to penal discipline based on "behavior modification" rather than indiscriminate torture and death.[29] The structure of the police became less militaristic, a change that was accompanied by pledges of greater transparency and accountability, new uniforms, and the change of the prison system's name to the Department of Correctional Services.[30] Unfortunately, political and economic elites, including some leaders of the ANC—now the leading political party—continue to attribute most crime to organized and immoral Black gangsters who, they assert, choose to "live by the gun" because their "expectations were not met in the first years of democracy."[31] Individual moral "ineptitude" is considered the cause of crime, with roots traceable to the failure of the family—especially of mothers—to instill appropriate African Christian values.[32]

To modify prisoners' behavior, the state has recuperated the old prison system as the only reliable institution that can contain and control the threats posed by what amounts to a poor Black majority. This framing has enabled the "new" South Africa's government to deny its own role in implementing neoliberal economic policies that perpetuate the impoverishment of the majority. The recent adoption of "get-tough measures"—aggressive policing of targeted poor Black communities, longer sentences, higher bail, and supermax solitary confinement cells—evidences political decisions that prioritize the demands of the global free market over the needs of ordinary South Africans.[33]

In response to the rising number of incarcerated women in South Africa, the SADCS has initiated a "special focus" on the "upliftment of the female offender."[34] SADCS-sponsored educational, vocational, recreational, and reli-

26. Gordon, "Side by Side," 58.
27. Williams and Taylor, "Neoliberalism," 21–40.
28. Gordon, "Side by Side," 58–59.
29. Super, "Rough Beast," 211.
30. Super, "Rough Beast," 210–11.
31. Kynoch, "Compounds," 463.
32. Gillespie, "Moralizing Security," 79–83.
33. Gordon, "Side by Side," 60.
34. Super, "Rough Beast," 211.

gious "life-skills" programs are designed to return women to free society as properly moral citizens.[35] It is hoped that these measures will reestablish proper African Christian patriarchal authority and inoculate the mothers of the nation and their children from future criminality. The department has, however, been constrained in its ability to act as a result of rising imprisonment, crumbling infrastructure, overcrowding, and inadequate funding for staff training, programs, and supplies.[36] Because women make up only a small portion of the total prison population, they are often overlooked when already scarce resources are allocated. Teaching artists complain that their initiatives are not valued for teaching prisoners art history or art-making techniques, but instead are praised for their ability to provide gratifying entertainment for visiting dignitaries, often at the last minute. Warders point to the arts programs as proof that they themselves are performing up to the new standard. Kelly Gillespie warns that the "pageantry" of these staged events dangerously masks the state's role in the criminalization and incarceration of the poor Black majority, whose living conditions have not transformed substantially since the end of political apartheid.[37] Furthermore, by uncritically representing Black art and culture as an effective tool of the state's rehabilitative script, the SADCS obscures the actual role Black art, artists, and performance played in the anti-apartheid Struggle, underplaying its importance in forging a more democratic and inclusive nation.

Because *Serious Fun* made the SADCS look good, when the unprecedented opportunity to stage the work at the State Theatre in Pretoria as part of the National Women's Day Celebration arose in August 2010, they allowed it to take place. For cast and crew, the State Theatre performance promised a chance to communicate their perspective to a broader audience.

ATTENTION!

On a cool August evening in 2010 that had been set aside to commemorate the 1956 Pretoria Women's Anti-Pass Law March—the first large-scale interracial political action by South African women against apartheid—the Sun City women took their places on the State Theatre stage. As they clustered

---

35 The SADCS *Annual Report* (2012–13) defined its mission thus: "It is better to light a candle than to curse the darkness. We are turning our correctional centers into centers of learning. Offenders must read, study, and work. We must impact the hearts and minds of offenders so that, upon release, they are in possession of, at least, a certificate in one hand and a skill in the other" (12).

36. Super, "Rough Beast," 211.

37. Gillespie, "Moralizing Security," 70–71.

around a half dozen elementary school desks and chairs placed in a half circle at center stage to, Jones reminded them, "tell the truth." The State Theatre in Pretoria is a prestigious, six-theater multiplex built beginning in the late 1960s to commemorate the twentieth anniversary of the founding of the apartheid republic.[38] Located in the middle of Pretoria's once segregated downtown, the three-story, cement-and-mortar complex takes up a full city block with six performance spaces and four restaurants under one expansive roof.[39] Its Arena Stage seats over six hundred attendees in deep-red-upholstered, cinema-style seats and boasts a wide proscenium stage trimmed with a black dance floor, dark heavy curtains, sky-high riggings, and a flawless white scrim far upstage. It could not have been further from Sun City's meager accommodations.

Of course, the cast was not allowed to experience the posh. The SADCS transferred them in small, discretely marked security vans from Sun City in Johannesburg to the local women's jail in Pretoria for the duration of the show (August 5–17, 2010). They rode in SADCS vans across town from the Pretoria jail and entered the theater via the loading dock with warders clad in light brown uniforms directing their every move. On stage, spread evenly across the expansive black proscenium stage facing a full house of hundreds of school children, family members, curiosity seekers, and arts patrons as well as local, national, and international legislators and visiting dignitaries, they commanded the spotlight.

The multiracial, multiethnic cast, wearing facsimiles of customary Zulu, Tswana, Venda, Xhosa, and Pedi clothing interspersed with a few bright orange prison travel jumpsuits, established an elementary school classroom setting to start the show.[40] Sitting or standing, they formed a large half circle around a dozen chairs with desks attached and faced the audience. However, it quickly became clear that the students were not there simply to learn but also to teach. Once in place, the performers introduced themselves, shouting out their first names in a quick roll call. Then Xoliswa, a petite, thirty-ish woman, stepped into the role of Teacher atop of one the desks to call the ensemble

---

38. Bhekizizwe Peterson, "Apartheid and the Political Imagination in the Black South African Theatre," *Journal of Southern African Studies* 16, no. 2 (1990): 232.

39. David B. Coplan, *In Township Tonight!: South Africa's Black City Music and Theatre*, 2nd ed. (Chicago: University of Chicago Press, 2008), 375.

40. Less clear for audience members and the theater crew were the orange coveralls. These were SADCS uniforms assigned to be worn by incarcerated men or women when they were outside their cellblocks. A dignified elderly Black theater usher chastised me at one show for not using the appropriate doors to enter the house from backstage until I shared with him that they were locked, blocked, and guarded because the show did not consist of actors portraying a prison drama but of real women prisoners presenting a show about their lives. Thus a temporary carceral space now stretched from the front row of the auditorium to the backstage loading dock, with warders from Naturena, a suburb of Johannesburg, attentively on guard.

to "Attention!" as she executed a piece of gumboot choreography, slapping her ankle. They responded: "Mamela!" (Listen!) and repeated her gesture. The combination of sound and movement repeated across so many bodies reinforced the imperative to "Pay Attention," calling the cast to work well together and inviting audience members to engage, listen, and learn.[41]

Next, an *imbongi* (praise singer or poet) stepped forward with a short invocation, quickly followed by a trio of Zulu dancers. They executed a rapid series of straight-legged high frontal kicks that struck the ground like lightning with the downbeat of the music, embodying the Zulu concept of *isigqi!* (power!). Just as the performers appeared to tire, they were replaced in rapid succession by Xhosa, Pedi, and Tsonga dancers who showcased their own signature choreographies. A rump-shaking solo by Joyce, a boisterous Venda woman who served as the de facto captain of the ensemble, ended the sequence. With each dance, the women demonstrated that they knew their histories.[42]

Rehabilitation in South Africa, as at other sites around the world, begins with looking back, returning to what happened, revisiting what one did to wind up in prison. Just as imprisonment immobilizes the body, so too we imagine it stops the incarcerated from moving temporally, from advancing through time.[43] Incarceration queers time, stopping, even reversing it. Incarcerated women in South Africa, like prisoners the world over, are figuratively suspended in a state of backward looking. Because they must pay penance for past wrongdoing, they become divorced from the "prospect of a different future."[44] To compensate the state and other victims for injuries caused, their futures are stripped away, with prisons and jails the sites where both the removal and transference of time occurs.[45] To be released and returned to free society, they must reexperience their crimes again and again. Moreover, they must demonstrate remorse and convince others that they have acquired new values—African Christian values—and will not reoffend.

Although it is not rooted in Abrahamic faith traditions, customary dance is offered by the SADCS as a corrective for imprisoned peoples' presumed

41. Rhodessa Jones, dir., *Serious Fun at Sun City*, unpublished manuscript (2010), 3.

42. Louise Meintjes, "Shoot the Sergeant, Shatter the Mountain: The Production of Masculinity in Zulu Ngoma Song and Dance in Post-Apartheid South Africa," *Ethnomusicology Forum* 13, no. 2 (2004): 174.

43. Drew Leder, "Imprisoned Bodies: The Life-World of the Incarcerated," in *Prisons and Punishment: Reconsidering Global Penality*, ed. Mechthild Nagel and Seth N. Asumah (Trenton, NJ; Asmara, Eritrea: Africa World Press Inc., 2007), 64.

44. Jodi Kanter, *Performing Loss: Rebuilding Community through Theatre and Writing* (Carbondale: Southern Illinois University Press, 2007), 148–49.

45. Greg Moses, "Time and Punishment in an Anesthetic World Order," in *Prisons and Punishment: Reconsidering Global Penality*, ed. Mechthild Nagel and Seth N. Asumah (Trenton, NJ; Asmara, Eritrea: Africa World Press Inc., 2007), 71.

cultural ignorance as well as their lack of morals. "History instructs," as Timothy Snyder writes.[46] The dances discipline the imprisoned to move in ways deemed appropriate. Through choreography and the music that animates it, they demonstrate the ability to act right. Dance as a tool for learning history also reveals the consequences that ensue should they fail to comply. Women, as the symbolic conservators of South African customs, play a unique role in society. Their ability to perform customary song and dance is vital to the preservation and future of the nation.[47] Those who do not dance well or convincingly risk their freedom, social standing, and much more. The success of the nation dances with them.

The *Serious Fun* ensemble used customary dances to prove to the warders and spectators that they were being rehabilitated. Standing on their authority now as the "mothers of the nation," they could command "Attention!" and use their *isiqgi!* (power!) to tell the truth about what they have done and why. As *Serious Fun* unfolded, it became clear that the women did not lack moral values. To survive, they defied dominant expectations of appropriate South African women's behavior. In subsequent scenes and monologues, they told the audience—and the nation—why.

TESTIFY

After the opening montage, Jones called, "Who has homework?" from the edge of the stage, appearing briefly in her role as narrator and director.[48] Ms. Ellen, a round, thirty-something, dark-skinned woman with immaculate hair and nails that reflected her time working in the Sun City beauty salon, stepped forward as a special guest lecturer before the class. She began her monologue by asking the schoolgirls if they knew where drugs came from. They confidently shouted the names of places where illegal narcotics could be procured—"Brazil," "Columbia," "Afghanistan," "Pakistan," and Johannesburg's own "Hillbrow" neighborhood—and then transitioned into a moving

---

46. Timothy Snyder, *On Tyranny: Twenty Lessons from the Twentieth Century* (New York: Tim Duggan Books, 2017).

47. Deborah James, "'Babageŝu' (Those of My Home): Women Migrants, Ethnicity and Performance in South Africa," *American Ethnologist* 26, no. 1 (1999): 72.

48. Jones would on several occasions break the fourth wall to provide direction and encouragement to these novice performers. Her side-coaching from the edge of the stage galvanized the performers and emphasized to audiences that this was not an ensemble of professional actors playing prisoners but a production created by incarcerated women. While the show was complete, the seemingly open structure in which the director might give directions from the front row revealed that the show was live, in the process of being created before witnesses in the moment.

stage picture of an airport security line to demonstrate how drugs are transported. Two performers armed with imaginary scanner wands searched the cast (now playing airline passengers). They detected illegal drugs on each one and arrested them all. Against this backdrop, Ellen relayed her personal experience with international drug trafficking:

> Good morning, class! I am Ellen, mother of three beautiful daughters aged eleven, ten, and six. I'm in prison for drug trafficking and serving a ten-year sentence. I was arrested with 1.5 kg of cocaine on 21 January 2005. It felt like the end of the world. Let me tell you how it all fell apart. I fell in love with a Nigerian man, or so I thought. We had a child together. She was a beautiful bouncing baby girl. Wow, the guy was over the moon, it was his first baby. Little did I know that he'd drop this bomb on me—damn—the guy just up and left, never to return again. At this point the landlord came knocking on my door 24/7 demanding the rent. My kids and I started living like thieves. Life as we knew it was over. I had to sneak in everyday while the landlord was out to get clean clothes. No money for rent, no money for food, no money for school fees. A friend of mine, or so I thought, who knew of my predicament, introduced me to this game. She took my passport and started making bookings. I was also taken for a shopping trip and my hair was done, my nails and eyelashes and the works—very glamorous, or so I thought. I was about to fly all the way from S.A. to Sao Paulo, Brazil [and back]. I was promised 20,000 rand, which I never received a penny of.[49] I was arrested at Oliver Tambo International Airport [in Johannesburg]. Even the person I thought was my friend after my arrest immediately switched off her phone and I never heard from her again.[50]

With her concise narrative, Ellen appears to fulfill the state's demand that prisoners look back on their lives and confess. The confession is a formative and defining part of the rehabilitation process. The confession, Foucault theorized, is understood to produce or yield "intrinsic modifications in the person who articulates it" for the speech act "exonerates, redeems, and purifies him; it unburdens him of his wrongs, liberates him and promises him salvation."[51] Critical to the process is the role of the witness. Foucault explains: "One does not confess without the presence (or virtual presence) of a partner who is not simply [an] interlocutor but the authority who requires the confession, pre-

49. Twenty thousand rand was approx. $1,900.00 USD in 2013 and about $1,300.00 in 2022. The average South African earns about $50.00 a week.

50. Jones, *Serious Fun*, 11.

51. Michel Foucault, *Discipline and Punish: The Birth of the Prison*, trans. Alan Sheridan (New York: Pantheon Books, 1977), 59–60, 61–62.

scribes and appreciates it, and intervenes in order to judge, punish, forgive, console, and reconcile."[52] What is actually said means little.[53] As Franz Fanon found, what matters is that speakers acknowledge that the state has hailed—identified and classified—them as criminals, and that detainees recognize themselves as they are interpolated.[54] As Ellen recounted her crime, however, she evoked not the image of a dangerous gangster but that of a single mother who selectively engaged in international drug trafficking to provide the basics for herself and her kids—"rent," "clothes," "food," "school fees"—when abandoned by her partner. Ellen acknowledged her role in the scheme, but she was clearly the least knowledgeable person involved—nothing more than a mule set up to carry goods when convenient, easily disposed of when no longer needed. The monologue ends with a bewildered Ellen revealing that she was never even paid for her troubles. *Where were the "real" drug traffickers? I wondered, standing backstage every night. What drove them to traffic drugs internationally,* and, *why was Ellen the only one behind bars?* A monologue intended to demonstrate rehabilitation instead opened up questions about the legitimacy and efficacy of the police as well as the judiciary and penal systems.

With her subtle deviation from the rehab script, Ellen's monologue located *Serious Fun* along a continuum of Black political activism that critiques repressive governments and cultural practices, and calls for and enacts radical social change. Historically banned from giving testimony in judicial settings by white supremacists who argued they were incapable of telling the truth, Black South Africans developed a practice of personal narrative, a form of testimonial performance in which they recount their real-life experiences, inform listeners about the urgency of their political situation, and urge collective action. Nelson Mandela, Walter Sisulu, and other political prisoners used their public trials on charges of treason, incitement, and terrorism to challenge the apartheid government's legitimacy. They converted the state's mandate that they testify in court into opportunities to indict the court itself for human rights violations. Other artists and activists used song, dance, and dramatic texts to tell the truth about apartheid repression, subvert government discourse, and express their desire for an alternative, more inclusive nation-state to emerge.[55] So integral to the liberation Struggle and the constitution of the emerging, post-apartheid nation were Black rhetorical and per-

---

52. Michel Foucault, *The History of Sexuality: An Introduction* (New York: Vintage Books, 1990), 61–62.

53. See Elaine Scarry, *The Body in Pain: The Making and Unmaking of the World* (Cambridge: Oxford University Press, 1987).

54. Franz Fanon, *Black Skin, White Masks,* trans. Charles Lam Markmann (New York: Grove Press, 1967), 111–14.

55. Peterson, "Apartheid," 229–45; Coplan, *In Township Tonight!*; and Loren Kruger, *The Drama of South Africa: Plays, Pageants and Publics Since 1910* (London: Routledge, 1999).

formative practices of truth-telling that the 1996–98 Truth and Reconciliation Commission (TRC) hearings were designed by the transitional government to stage a symbolic reconciliation between the state and injured community members through acts of testimonial and personal narrative performance. Black South Africans relied heavily on these public speech acts with the hope that the ritual of truth-telling within the TRC's quasi-judicial settings would bring forth a "new" more democratic nation. Testifying publicly before the TRC and the nation restored the subjectivity, citizenry, and humanity of Black South Africans.[56]

Despite the vast scope of the hearings, the Commission was unable to create a substantial space in which women could recount their gendered experiences. Most women gave statements from their standpoint as wives and mothers who had witnessed or been impacted by the brutality suffered by male family members.[57] Testimony that fell outside this narrow purview was relegated to a special commission seated in Johannesburg that met for only two days in late July 1997. During those hearings, women told harrowing stories about personally encountering police and prison warders who used rape and other forms of sexual violence to control, inflict pain and suffering, and humiliate. Speakers also connected the brutality of the apartheid and colonial systems to present-day gender-based sexual violence in the home, workplace, and other community institutions. From the suburbs to the townships, the rural farms to the urban business districts, there was no space, the women declared, that apartheid's racist, sexist, and economic brutality did not reach.[58] Their testimony issued a collective warning that more had to be done. Yet decades later, women continue to be largely excluded from the South African political imaginary except as symbolic "mothers of the nation," a position that threatens to cancel past contributions and compromise their prospects for the future. Emerging from this complex genealogy of antiracist, antipatriarchal, judicial activism by "bad" Black women, *Serious Fun* became a vehicle through which the Sun City women might disrupt entrenched criminal legal discourse and practices and exercise their rights and abilities. Testifying to their true experiences under the guise of confessing wrongdoing, they moved the intervention onto the national stage and demanded radical change. By naming the problem and making it available for communal engagement and action, they set the stage for transformation.

56. Catherine Cole, *Performing South Africa's Truth Commission: Stage of Transition* (Bloomington: Indiana University Press, 2010), 164.

57. Analisa Oboe, "The TRC Women's Hearings as Performance and Protest in the New South Africa," *Research in African Literatures* 38, no. 3 (2007): 61.

58. Oboe, "TRC," 64.

Fifteen years after the last TRC hearings, Alouise, a light-skinned, forty-ish, almost frail-looking Colored woman with long braided hair, stepped out of the ensemble and moved to the microphone at the State Theatre moments after Ellen turned away. Alouise, like Ellen, had at one time worked as a drug smuggler but had been sentenced for murder. When she joined the ensemble in 2010, she was halfway through her fifteen-year sentence and had never shared with anyone at the facility the details about what happened the night her partner died. During one rehearsal Jones asked everyone to write, in response to the prompt, "Love Don't Love Nobody," to begin to get at how family dynamics, gendered obligations, and love relationships can entrap women. Alouise responded with the following monologue, which became one of the centerpieces of *Serious Fun* at the State Theatre. To stage her telling it, Jones and Ackamoor placed her alone before a microphone downstage left in a low spotlight. The cast scattered around the stage in a series of tableaux to enact aspects of her story—a group of children playing ring-around-the rosy, adults engaged in a violent argument, a few women huddled as if over an open fire in a barren field. Despite the separation, dressed now in identical bright orange prison travel uniforms, they read as one person, stood as one body, told one story. Alouise spoke:

> Love don't love nobody! I'm Alouise, a mother of three. When poverty stepped in, love stepped out. Fifteen years of marriage down the drain. I was living in a scrap yard with my kids for eight months. Then I met this guy, offering me a place to stay and a plate of food. We fell in love. He told me how much he loved me but little did I know what was in it for me. I had to hold on 'coz there was nowhere to go. I then became his personal slave and then the abuse started, all kinds of abuse including rape. My kids had to witness all these things. They too were abused in a way, still I had to hold on 'coz I loved him. I got to a point where I couldn't take it anymore. My body was tired of all the stabbing, the beatings, the hurt, the pain I had to go through. Let's not forget the rape. I was confused. I then went to the pillow where he kept his gun. I took it and threw the gun at him. It went off. A day later he died in hospital. And that, ladies and gentlemen, that's the reason I'm in prison. Love don't love nobody.[59]

Establishing herself as a mother and a respectable, married woman, Alouise's testimony details how impoverishment and abandonment by her husband forced her onto the streets and into the crime that landed her at Sun City.

---

59. Jones, *Serious Fun*, 17–18.

Homeless with three small children to care for, Alouise had few options in a society that lacked a deep network of institutional supports other than to accept the "plate of food" and "place to stay" offered by an unnamed stranger. She acknowledged that she stayed with him even after he became violent, but explains that there was "nowhere to go." In this post-(anti-)apartheid neoliberal state that champions economically self-reliant citizens, Alouise's choices and ability to act independently were circumscribed, rendering her in effect a prisoner in a violent home. She eventually defended herself with lethal force. Her description of grabbing the gun and throwing it at her former partner satisfied the penal system's expectation that she elocuted on her crime, but her personal narrative stopped short of admitting that she killed him.[60] While the gun "went off," Alouise did not admit to pulling the trigger. Instead, the man's death was framed as the result of unseen and unknown forces or actors— perhaps even divine intervention—that were beyond her power and control.[61]

Alouise thus elides the blame for the man's death and, from her telling, it is arguable whether any crime occurred. While on the surface her monologue fulfilled the form of a prisoner's confession, the content and the tone made her actions appear wholly justified. By *testifyin'* not to her own wrongdoing but to the injustices of South African society that left her and her children homeless, as well as to the man's brutality and the power of unknown, unseen, perhaps divine forces to intervene, Alouise subverted the state's mandate that she confess to prove she had been rehabilitated. Geneva Smitherman describes testifyin' as "a ritualized form of black communication in which the speaker gives verbal witness for the efficacy, truth, and power of some experience in which all blacks have shared."[62] Alouise recounted what happened to her and her children, but the production used her monologue as an example of the maltreatment of women in South African society. Alouise expressed deep regret that her actions led to her partner's death. But the production queries if, under the circumstances, she was wrong for defending her life. Alouise's monologue complicated the ritual of confession. She took responsibility for her actions and, before hundreds of spectators, expressed remorse, but in so doing she (re)established her personal dignity as well as the dignity of her young children, who witnessed the man's brutality and came to the show to hear her tell

---

60. In rehearsal, Alouise was more forthcoming about the specific circumstances behind her decision to retrieve the gun and pull the trigger. She chose not to detail them in her monologue, and I will only say, out of respect for her privacy, that she was once again engaged in a fight for her life.

61. Thanks to Austin Jackson for insights gained in conversation about this monologue.

62. Geneva Smitherman, *Talkin and Testifyin: The Language of Black America* (Boston: Houghton Mifflin Company, 1977), 58.

this story for the first time. Instead of the image of a repentant prisoner, on stage we see a woman who is behind bars for what she did to survive poverty and what she did to save herself and her children from interpersonal, domestic violence. We see a woman who, like so many others, made a choice that no one should have to make to defend herself and her family and who lived to tell the tale. Her final words, "Love don't love nobody," rang out with regret and too much loss.

The final monologue of this sequence picked up on the theme of women's survival but staged a more pointed critique of South African society. Lovely, a thirty-something Colored woman with a soft, round face, also smuggled drugs internationally. She joined the show for the 2009 production and was subsequently released after having completed her sentence. She was allowed to return and present a new monologue at the State Theatre that reflected on her time behind bars and, most importantly, on the experience of returning to her old neighborhood, Hillbrow, an infamous area known for a large immigrant population living in dangerous, high-density conditions. Jones, Ackamoor, and I picked up Lovely in the car at a taxi station or other meeting point daily on the way to rehearsals. As Ackamoor drove, Jones and Lovely would debate the content of her monologue while I took notes. In performance, Lovely improvised on the outline they crafted and interjected new thoughts as appropriate. In Pretoria, her monologue issued the most pointed critique of South African society. She greeted the audience with:

> Angicholwa ngiphumile (I do not believe I have come out). Am I out? Am I really out? . . . When I got out, the Members [corrections officers] when they saw me on the streets were the only ones who treated me in a respectful way. They're glad for me. Other people in the community, they called me Nelson Mandela. At first, I was proud, but then, I got angry. Nelson Mandela went to jail for you and for me, not for drug trafficking. Now you're using that freedom of speech he fought for to abuse. To have my child come to me and ask me, "Mommy, are you a bandit?" I'm not a bandit. My name is Lovely, and it is my duty to tell my child what has happened . . .

Lovely discusses how she has been treated by her Hillbrow community post-incarceration. Her neighbors deploy a well-known Black rhetorical practice called *signifyin'* to criticize and shame her. Geneva Smitherman defines *signifyin'* as a means of insulting or shaming another person using a clever, often humorous, turn of phrase. Although the practice is usually associated, like testifyin', with African American vernacular speech, the mocking hails of

Lovely's neighbors align. With their humorous criticisms, they "make a point" about Lovely's personal shortcomings by highlighting how far removed from dedication to the Struggle and the personal sacrifice symbolized by Mandela her illegal activities were.[63]

The State Theatre performance was an opportunity for Lovely to publicly answer back. She retorted to their criticism with a complex argument about women's rights, roles, responsibilities, and duties in the new South Africa that shifted the dialogue from the realm of the confessional into that of the political, challenging the depoliticization of "common" women's criminal acts in contemporary criminal legal discourse. Lovely argued that, by running their mouths against her, especially her child, the neighbors proved they were as far or farther removed from the values that animated the Struggle than they thought she was. Her claim to have a "duty" to tell her daughter what she had done activated an alternative repertoire of understanding about the responsibilities of mothering today and in the Struggle that exceeded the narrow parameters of parenting, citizenship, and productivity articulated by Hillbrow and, by implication, the rest of society. It is this wider "duty" to tell her child what happened that brought Lovely to the stage. There, she did not seek forgiveness, but instead called out those far-away Hillbrow neighbors and anyone else, arguably, who shared their opinions.

Like Ellen and Alouise, Lovely deviated from the anticipated confessional script, in this case both by eliding the details of her crime and by upbraiding society. Focusing more directly on the inappropriate actions of others and less directly on her own wrongdoing, she positioned herself—and by extension others in the ensemble—as women engaged in a much larger struggle for respect, dignity, and a better quality of life. Lovely's testimony interrupted and dispelled the clear-cut boundary between so-called common (immoral) criminals and those political prisoners whose (moral) actions were criminalized by an unjust state.[64] Her insistence that she had "a duty" to "introduce herself to her child" activated an alternative framework of motherhood, responsibility, community, and belonging that was often absent in popular criminal legal discourse and public policy. Her words reminded listeners that much work remains to be done and that the "bad girls" on stage are not the only ones with work to do.

---

63. Smitherman, *Talkin and Testifyin*, 118–19.

64. In the 1990s, with the prospect of large numbers of people being released from prisons, the country became embroiled in a heightened debate over the distinctions between "true crime" and "crimes committed against the apartheid regime" that might be framed as political and therefore legitimate acts; see Super, "Rough Beast," 208–9.

SONG AS A CALL TO ACTION

To reinforce the connections between contemporary incarcerated women and the legacy of political struggle without raising the ire of prison officials, the cast, with the assistance of Jones and Ackamoor, wove together songs that signified both a deep religious conviction and the Struggle throughout the script. They all sang "Malibongwe Amakhosikhazi," a religious hymn and a historic Struggle song that commemorates the 1956 Pretoria interracial women's march against the restrictive Pass Laws, underneath Ellen's monologue:

Igama lamakhosikazi malibongwe (Let thanks/praise be given to women)
Igama lamakhosikazi malibongwe
Malibongwe malibongwe malibongwe malibongwe (They must be thanked/praised)[65]

The song bears witness to women's activism and reminds listeners of their past contributions to the fight for freedom.[66] As a religious work, the song offers an alternative framework through which to approach everyday miseries on earth, reminding listeners that what we know in the material world is not all that there is. Like the songs US civil rights activists sang as they strode through hostile territory or were thrown into Southern jails, "Malibongwe" reminds singers and listeners of a time when the community was united against the apartheid regime and Struggle songs were deployed to sonically reoccupy segregated spaces, preparing the way for Black bodies to enter on their own terms and defiantly reclaim the ground on which to enact more inclusive ways of being in the world.[67] Singing "Malibongwe" at the State Theatre located the imprisoned women's stories within a trajectory of women's liberation work and reframed their current incarcerations as more than individual failings—rather, the result of both historic and ongoing inequality and injustice. It dared assert that the women's actions might be the latest front in an ongoing struggle for Black women's equality.

---

65. Thanks to Mbongeni Mtshali for help with this translation.

66. Shireen Hassim, *Women's Organizations and Democracy in South Africa: Contesting Authority* (Madison: University of Wisconsin Press, 2006), 26.

67. See Shirli Gilbert, "Singing against Apartheid: ANC Cultural Groups and the International Anti-Apartheid Struggle," *Journal of Southern African Studies* 33, no. 2 (2007): 421–41; Liz Gunner, "Jacob Zuma, the Social Body and the Unruly Power of Song," *African Affairs* 108, no. 430 (2008): 27–48; and Grant Olwage, ed., *Composing Apartheid: Music for and against Apartheid* (Johannesburg: Wits University Press, 2008).

As the cast raised their voices, they further activated a repertoire of Black vernacular and theatrical performance practices. In Black township theater, audiences expect to actively participate as cocreators of an event. At the State Theatre, hundreds joined in singing "Malibongwe" and other works throughout the show, such as the hymn "Moments of Trouble, Sing A Song" before Alouise's piece. In so doing, they dissolved the perceived distance between themselves and the performers, between themselves and the incarcerated. These moving, hopeful moments of *communitas,* of spontaneous collective belonging, evoked historic individual and collective acts to overthrow the regulatory power of the apartheid state and birth a new social order. By singing "Malibongwe" and other Struggle songs, the ensemble accessed a reservoir of shared knowledge embedded within themselves and the audience. In these moments, the production became a space for the actors and the audience to collectively reflect upon the past and to dream a future of greater inclusivity in which women were respected and valued. Working together, the songs, scenes, and monologues prepared the audience for the cast's final intervention, the Machine Gun, a dance that playfully but forcefully communicated the need to repair South African society.

MACHINE GUN

The Machine Gun choreography of the finale sent audiences at the State Theatre in Pretoria into a joyous uproar of recognition. It reminded attendees of the WWE wrestler Batista, certainly, and, I would argue, worked on another level to stage a critique of the government, in particular of then-President Jacob Zuma, by invoking his 2006 rape trial. On November 2, 2005, a thirty-one-year-old HIV-positive AIDS activist named Fezekile Ntsukela Kuzwayo (known as Khwezi, a pseudonym to protect her identity) went to Zuma's home in a Johannesburg suburb to conduct an interview.[68] Zuma, then Deputy President of the ANC, had known Khwezi's father when both were young men during the Struggle to end apartheid and had served time together at Robben Island, the nation's most infamous prison. Because of these close ties, after her father was killed in 1985 in a car accident Khwezi often turned to Zuma as

68. Until her death in October 2016 at age forty-one, Fezekile Ntsukela Kuzwayo was known in court documents and the media as Khwezi, a pseudonym used to protect her identity, not that it did much good. See Marianne Thamm, "'Khwezi, the Woman Who Accused Jacob Zuma of Rape, Dies," *Guardian,* October 10, 2016, accessed September 8, 2021, https://www.theguardian.com/world/2016/oct/10/khwezi-woman-accused-jacob-zuma-south-african-president-aids-activist-fezekile-ntsukela-kuzwayo.

her *umalune* (uncle) for advice. When he invited her to stay overnight rather than test her luck on Johannesburg's often dangerous roads, she accepted, not knowing that Zuma would enter the guest room where she slept and sexually assault her.

The rape trial that ensued would reveal deep fractures in South African society over the role of women. Judith Singleton writes that many men in South Africa "define rape as a premediated act committed only by strangers in the streets."[69] Discourses about rape there as in other parts of the world hinge on questions about consent. On the stand, Zuma admitted to the sex, but discredited Khwezi's accusations by operationalizing a working class, Black, nationalist, masculinist notion of Zulu culture. He insisted that Khwezi had invited him into a sexual encounter from the moment she entered his house by wearing a short skirt. He read her attire and the way that she sat—cross-legged so her thighs were visible—as an indication that she was aroused. He proclaimed, "In the Zulu culture, you cannot just leave a woman if she is ready. . . . To deny her sex, that would have been tantamount to rape."[70] As the cultural critic Nolwazi Mhkwanazi observed, Zuma and his supporters insisted, "If Khwezi had been a real Zulu woman . . . she would not have accused him of rape, and furthermore, she would have remained silent and submitted to his advances."[71] Subsequent witnesses further undermined her credibility. They testified that Khwezi had falsely accused several other men of rape prior to her allegations against Zuma. Finally, they pointed to a history of mental illness as proof of her instability, unreliability, and, ultimately, her inability to be raped.

Outside the courtroom, Zuma's supporters declared the trial a political smear campaign. They accused Khwezi of being paid to give false testimony and threatened to kill her. To reinforce their point, they reactivated a well-known Struggle song, "Awuleth umshini wami" (Bring Me My Machine Gun), at demonstrations. The act of singing it called on the nation to organize as they had done to end apartheid, with the enemy now recast as a young Zulu woman half Zuma's age. Liz Gunner writes that singing "Awuleth umshini wami" "marked off insiders from outsiders, the struggling righteous just from

69. Judith Singleton, "The South African Sexual Offences Act and Local Meanings of Coercion and Consent in KwaZulu Natal," *African Studies Review* 55, no. 2 (2012): 67.

70. Michael Wines, "Highly Charged Rape Trial Tests South African Ideals," *New York Times,* April 10, 2006, accessed September 13, 2021, https://www.nytimes.com/2006/04/10/world/africa/a-highly-charged-rape-trial-tests-south-africas-ideals.html?smid=url-share.

71. Nolwazi Mkhwanazi, "Miniskirts and Kangas: The Use of Culture in Constituting Postcolonial Sexuality," Dark Matter: In the Ruins of Imperial Culture, May 2, 2008, accessed September 13, 2021, http://www.darkmatter101.org/site/2008/05/02/miniskirts-and-kangas-the-use-of-culture-in-constituting-postcolonial-sexuality/.

the comfortable unjust, and . . . reached in a utopian gesture towards an inversion of this in a new and just social order yet to come, where the outsider/guerrilla fighter would become the insider/citizen."[72] Evoking a largely masculinist conception of militarism and nationalism, the machine gun song, sung in defense of the Deputy President, cast the rape prosecution as another in a long line of racist actions against Zuma, against Black South Africans, and the freedom struggle.

In the end, it worked. The judge assigned to the trial, Willem Van der Merwe, characterized Zuma's behavior as "totally unacceptable," but ultimately found it something short of rape. Zuma supporters sang "Awuleth umshini wami" in triumph when the not-guilty verdict was read. Soon after, Zuma was elected the fourth president of South Africa (2009–18). Khwezi was exiled. Fearing for her safety and for her family, she sought and was granted sanctuary in the Netherlands, where she lived until her death in 2016.[73]

With all these associations, why would a group of women prisoners, including many survivors of domestic violence and rape, take up the symbol of the machine gun in a performance about women, crime, punishment, and justice?

Why activate this repertoire with its controversial history?

To put it to new use.

Turning their gaze and guns forward toward the audience, the prisoners implicate all those present, in the hall and across the nation, in their call for a reconstitution of women's social and cultural positions in South African society. Performing the machine gun as a dance, not a song, activates the repertoire of the anti-apartheid movement. Audiences also cannot ignore the connections with Batista and the playful, intense world of wrestling he connotes. At the State Theatre, evoking Batista gave the women cover for what could otherwise be read as an act of domestic terrorism or revolution. As the women look over their shoulders before grasping their guns, it felt to me that they were looking beyond their own pasts toward each other and then beyond that to the bigger story of the nation. Looking over their shoulders for what lurks/lies/waits there acknowledged the presence of the past. Weapons in their hands, eyes forward, they cast themselves as part of the larger fight for their humanity. They signaled their willingness to take up real and symbolic arms to fight for and protect themselves. Taken together, the choreographer visually, viscerally, tied the women's fight for survival in the "new" South Africa to the war to end European settler colonialism, patriarchy, and their enduring

---

72. Gunner, "Jacob Zuma," 39.
73. Sapa Author, "Zuma Found Not Guilty," *Mail & Guardian*, May 8, 2006; Thamm, "Khwezi."

legacies. It insisted that racism, economic exploitation, and sexism needed to be acknowledged and ended, and that those who had been harmed by them, restored. To paraphrase D. Soyini Madison, their dance expressed their discontent with the status quo and articulated a desire for a more inclusive society with a sense of urgency that threatens violence if their needs continue to go unmet.[74] Eyes directed forward, they blow it all away, with playful, deadly, seriousness.

During the run, I again asked Sonia Radebe, the choreographer who helped the women shape the final dance, about the decision to end the work with the Machine Gun. Ever patient, she emphasized that the women enjoyed doing it. It gave them pleasure, which was reason enough to include it. But then she went a step further. She shared that the Machine Gun signified to her the struggle of many people who are relegated to the outside, the periphery, of society and must "battle their way in."[75] For her, the Machine Gun choreography communicated the struggle of these and all other artists to be included in the new social order.

TRAJECTORY

The need for violent upheaval and civil unrest like that staged by Nelson Mandela, Jacob Zuma, the 1956 Pretoria Women's Marchers, and other political prisoners and activists is presumed to no longer to exist since the multiracial elections began in the 1990s, yet the stories shared by Ellen, Alouise, and the other women in *Serious Fun* demonstrate that women continue to struggle. South African society, like many others, refuses to treat them as full human beings that are to be respected, seen, heard, and understood. The Sun City women's stories evidence the perils of relegating them to the status of rights-bearing individuals on paper only and of dismissing the efficacy of alternative prison-based arts programs like the Medea Project. Women fight back in the intimate spaces of the home as well as in public arenas, such as the theater. Poor, working women like those in the cast fight in these arenas because they have little access to the halls and spaces of economic and political power. Cultural practice, cultural production, is a site of power. So determined were these women to affirm the value of their own lives, they took over the script for prisoner rehabilitation to issue subtle but pointed demands for more respect, dignity, and resources as women in the "new" South Africa. Because

74. D. Soyini Madison, *Acts of Activism: Human Rights as Radical Performance* (Cambridge: Cambridge University Press, 2010), 12.

75. Conversation with author July 2012.

they made these claims using a recognizable repertoire of Black South African performance practices with sociocultural value, there was no sense that, as they made this call for radical change, they would abandon the histories, cultures, or communities that birthed them. They valued South African culture but demanded more from their government and from their countrymen.

Potentially facing penal prohibitions against explicit acts of defiance or criticisms of the state, the women of the Medea Project had to articulate their cause in acceptable, "maternalistic" terminology while simultaneously smuggling in an assertion of their rights to equality and full participation in society.[76] Their stories, songs, and dances exposed popular fictions about women who break the law and complicated the familiar, moralizing, positivist, and patriarchal approaches to crime, safety, security, and justice that predominate. Told again and again before larger and larger audiences of listeners, their testimonies, sung, danced, and spoken, undermined the authority of other tellers of tales about them. By challenging, disrupting, and complicating the SADCS's rehabilitative script and the undergirding epistemology and cultural practices that sustained it, the *Serious Fun* cast demonstrated the need for alternative responses to crime in South Africa with themselves, their lives, and their needs *for once* positioned at the center of the struggle.

Serious Fun demonstrates that individual self-repair and institutional and cultural change are not separate processes. In the next chapter, I return to the United States to consider how a small cohort of women known as Healing Justice Mamas employed theatrical storytelling and personal narrative performance practices to influence public policy on a national scale from their base in the US Mid-Atlantic region. Attending to this site demonstrates the importance of women's artistic work in shifting national public policies. The United States leads the world in the number of people that it incarcerates. Countries around the world look to it for leadership and innovation in policing and incarceration. Shifts in US prison policy impact individuals and have the potential to influence the landscape of incarceration worldwide.

76. Pamela E. Brooks, *Boycotts, Buses and Passes: Black Women's Resistance in the U.S. South and South Africa* (Amherst: University of Massachusetts Press, 2008), 210.

CHAPTER 6

It Has Been My Healing to Tell the Dirty Truth

It takes about thirty minutes to travel on public transportation from the Healing Justice Mamas offices to the Mid-Atlantic jail.[1] The well-lit, air-conditioned train races across town quietly in fits and starts, loading and unloading hundreds of middle-management business types leaning into cell phones; fresh-faced interns in ill-fitting suits, expensive headphones strapped to their heads; families of sweaty tourists; and me and Lolo. Lolo is a short, fifty-ish, nutmeg-brown African American woman with exquisitely manicured nails. In the blistering heat, she often wears sweeping chiffon skirts with conservatively cut V-necks and open-toe sandals to keep things cool and easy. I tower over her awkwardly in my "church girl" summer prison gear—loose-fitting black slacks, eggplant-colored nylon T-shirt, and yellow penny loafers. She has been facilitating the jail arts program at Mid-Atlantic for the Healing Justice Mamas for several years, drawing on lessons she learned in her eleven years in recovery from drug and alcohol abuse and from a series of workshops with Living Stage, where we met in the early 2000s.

---

1. To protect the identities of the incarcerated women at the center of this study, I use pseudonyms to identify all of the people, organizations, penal institutions, and settings where this research occurred. However, the names of public agencies, elected officials, and lawmakers that were in the public sphere are used where their inclusion would not harm the research subjects who are the focus of the study. The inclusion of those names and agencies is intended to demonstrate the scope of Healing Justice Mamas' activism and their commitment.

Lolo and several other Black women—Nadira, Affina, and Tafari—formed Healing Justice Mamas (the Mamas) as they healed and stabilized in recovery together. Healing Justice Mamas is a nonprofit organization that advances public-policy reform on behalf of women and girls in the United States and in Africa with histories of substance abuse, domestic violence, sexual victimization, and incarceration. They operate from their home base in a large Mid-Atlantic city near the nation's capital.

In this chapter I focus on five instances of public advocacy in which the Mamas used *testifyin'* to stage healing by interjecting stories about women and girls into popular crime and justice discourses. Testifyin' is, as noted above, a Black expressive cultural practice in which a speaker "gives verbal witness for the efficacy, truth, and power of some experience in which all Blacks have shared."[2] This kind of speech carries the weight of a confession in court or before the divine and is rooted in the Black church. The Mamas testify that they have healed themselves and done the hard work required of them by the state, by their families, and by their communities to make amends. Speaking with care and seriousness, the Mamas often begin their presentations by disclosing past drug use and other illegal activities. Their performances may include a moment in which they express remorse as is expected of a person who has broken the law. However, they do not seek forgiveness. They do not need it. Instead, they testify to the limits of carceral rehabilitative scripts and call upon elected officials, public policymakers, and the general public to invest more resources in proven treatment programs for women in order to address their physical and mental health needs and support the reconstruction of spiritual, familial, and communal ties.

The Mamas issue these demands based on what they call *sacred authority,* the wisdom and agency that comes from having survived violence, healed, and stepped into their own power. Some might call this authority faith, divine power, or the force that flows through the universe and binds us. Yes to all of that. By the grace of this higher power, the Mamas testify as Black women, survivors, mothers, and experts on maternal health and healing that women—mothers—need more help and they need it now. They testify because they want to transform society into a space that encourages and provides for maternal wellbeing, and from that care, promotes supportive human ties and relations.

The Mamas own healing demands this work. Understanding, as Stephanie Mitchem writes, that human life is embedded within the interconnected

---

2. Geneva Smitherman, *Talkin and Testifyin: The Language of Black America* (Boston: Houghton Mifflin Company, 1977), 58.

"web of the universe," they approach addiction as "sickness . . . derived not only from germs but also from situations that break relational connections."[3] Traumatic ruptures in their own family lives and communities contributed to the Mamas' problematic substance use. Their advocacy work is part of their own healing. It affords them opportunities to craft and tell stories about their experiences and connects them to community. For healing to occur, problems must be named and the story of how the dis-ease/disease occurred must be told. The Mamas testify because it furthers their own wellbeing and because other people need more supportive networks and more resources to feel balanced and whole.

The Mamas realize that they make these demands upon violent state institutions that produce inequality, ill health, and misery. They recognize that their words land on the ears of a skeptical, resistant, and frightened public. Nonetheless, they testify before anyone willing to listen that, to truly reduce crime and mitigate harm, our society must do more to foster cultural practices that prevent violence and that mend, suture, and bridge broken human ties and relationships where possible. Without these changes, there is no way to balance or renew individual, familial, and community life.

The Mamas use these opportunities to stage healing. They practice critical storytelling to advocate for new cultural practices and public policies that will impact Black women and all who reside under systems of governance that oppress, immiserate, exploit, and kill. Their practices connect spatially disparate sites—the drug treatment program at their local jail, the graduation ceremony at a drug court, a policy briefing for Congressional staffers, a meeting with members of the Black Congressional Caucus, and a public rally to stop sex trafficking held on the National Mall in Washington, DC. What emerges is a model of coalition-building that seeks to unite people across social, economic, and political divides to protect us all from interpersonal and state violence.

METHODOLOGY

Lolo and I met in 2000–2001 when I was a teaching artist at the Living Stage Theatre Company in Washington, DC. Founded in the mid-1960s by director Robert Alexander, for thirty-six years Living Stage was the community engagement or outreach arm of Arena Stage, the major regional theater in the area. Living Stage offered intensive, Viola Spolin–inspired improvisational

---

3. Stephanie Mitchem, *African American Folk Healing* (New York: New York University, 2007), 3.

theater workshops to participants aged 3 to 103 from the Washington, Maryland, and Virginia metro area. I met Lolo when Living Stage partnered with a comprehensive addiction and mental health treatment program for mothers entering recovery. Lolo was one of the beneficiaries of that collaboration. The theater workshops, cofacilitated by actress/playwright Rebecca Rice and poet/playwright Denise Kumani Gantt, worked in conjunction with counseling and other support services that the treatment center provided so Lolo and her children could stabilize in recovery and heal. Rice and Gantt approached their creative writing and performance-making workshops with the women from a Black feminist perspective. They used performance, including Black women's expressive culture (e.g., poetry, song, dance), to intervene in the numerous privileged discourses that undervalued Black women's lives, intellectual work, and creativity.[4] Poetry writing exercises and improvised scene and monologue work with workshop participants confronted and disrupted "derogatory stories" about Black women that circulated as truth.[5] The sessions offered participants a productive way to investigate and think about the breaks and breaches of everyday life as well as a supportive space to test the boundaries of the possible on stage and in real life. In their hands, theater was a site for sacred and secular work that put the wit and wisdom of Black women at the center of the narrative. I remember the workshops like they were yesterday. Lolo and the other mothers in recovery taught me more about being a Black woman than any other group with whom we worked.[6] Today, more than ten years later, she is again my teacher.

I accompanied Lolo to the workshops she led at a site I call the Mid-Atlantic jail for four months (June–September 2012). When I was not with Lolo at Mid-Atlantic, I joined her and the other Mamas at political policy briefings and public events they organized or to which they were invited. At these events, the group sought to educate women struggling with substance abuse issues, elected officials, law enforcement agents, and the general public about the need for effective, comprehensive treatment programs for women nationwide.

4. Lisa M. Anderson, *Black Feminism in Contemporary Drama* (Urbana: University of Illinois Press, 2008), 11–13.

5. Biggs, "Art Saves Lives: Rebecca Rice and the Performance of Black Feminist Improv," in *Black Acting Methods: Critical Approaches,* ed. Sharrell Luckett, 72–86 (New York: Routledge, 2016), 82.

6. For more about Living Stage, see Susan Haedicke, "The Challenge of Participation," in *Audience Participation: Essays on Inclusion in Performance,* ed. Susan Kattwinkel (Westport, CT: Praeger, 2003), 71–87; Lisa Biggs, "Art Saves Lives: Rebecca Rice and the Performance of Black Feminist Improv," in *Black Acting Methods: Critical Approaches,* ed. Sharrell Luckett (New York: Routledge, 2016), 72–86.

IS IT A TREATMENT CENTER OR A JAIL?

When Lolo and I finally emerge from the subway, the tourists and corporate types have disembarked. Heavy metal escalators with thick rubber handrails lift us, and a handful of other working-class African American passengers, up and out into a sleepy residential community. One side of the street is crammed with two-story red brick single-family houses. On the other side sits the sprawling, red-brick jail and public hospital complex. As Lolo leads the way, I see evergreen and white street signs directing visitors to the "Infectious Diseases" unit to the left and the "Treatment Facility" to the right. Lolo steers us to the right. I follow, confused. They call the jail a "Treatment Facility?" The only thing that distinguishes it from the hospital are the vehicles parked in front. A dark red food truck belches the fragrant perfume of BBQ at the hospital's front door while a white Police Canine Unit van idles before the jail.

In the lobby, Lolo explains that it is a privilege to be sentenced to the women's drug detox unit here. Those in detox are segregated from the general prisoner population, and they receive programming to address issues related to substance abuse. Many people struggling with problematic substance abuse disorders want treatment, but fewer than 3 percent of them receive any care. Even for those that do, what passes for treatment is often inadequate. Thirty-, sixty-, and ninety-day drug detox wards in prisons and jails like this offer a patchwork of twelve-step, peer-to-peer, and individual counseling; Alcoholics Anonymous and Narcotics Anonymous programs; and fundamentalist Christian teachings. For the hundreds of thousands of women like Lolo who began self-medicating with drugs and alcohol as teens to alleviate pain from untreated traumas, carceral detox interventions have had limited success. These units are often staffed by corrections personnel with limited training. With their support, women abstain from using and flush addictive substances from their bodies, but detoxing and healing are not the same thing. Healing from trauma requires addressing the past and building new supportive ties and behaviors. Few women feel safe and empowered enough to fully disclose personal feelings or experiences in carceral detox settings. After all, a jail detox unit is still a jail. Failure or refusal to comply with the officers' orders can result in a loss of privileges up to and including dismissal from the program and may have serious ramifications in terms of future sentencing. Looming threats of punishment can impair women's ability to heal. Behavioral health studies confirm Lolo's observation that imprisonment impedes Black women's efforts to complete treatment programs and further disadvantages a cohort that is already among the least likely to seek out or be offered treatment.[7] Detox units like those at the Mid-Atlantic jail may offer women a reprieve, but they rarely provide enough care to truly enable them to move into recovery and stabilize. Without adequate treatment and support, women relapse, and the cycle of problematic substance use and incarceration continues.

The failures in treatment and the lack of skilled, post-incarceration, care propelled Lolo, Nadira, Affina, and Tafari to come together as Healing Justice Mamas. At Mid-Atlantic, their poetry and performance program interjects powerful personal stories of women—mothers—like themselves who have struggled with substance abuse, family violence, sexual assault, and other traumatic experiences into the jail's detox curriculum. As survivors of domestic violence and sexual assault, community leaders, and experts in maternal addiction, they bring unique perspectives on healing to the detox program and are further able to connect women in Mid-Atlantic to a nationwide network of maternal health advocates. Their work bridges the divide between elected officials and low-income Black and Latino families in need of care. Lolo's first concern is with reaching the women.

Inside the detox unit, stark white walls meet hard linoleum floors. The two-story-high pod (cellblock) is glaringly bright. An officer seated to the immediate right of the door at an elementary schoolteacher-style desk signs us in. In the middle of the cellblock, the education/outreach coordinator, Ms. Williams, a mid-thirties Black woman with shoulder-length hair pulled back in a tight clip, is finishing up a session. Next to her sits another Black woman, a volunteer in her fifties, sporting Jheri-curls, a shapeless sweater, and dark pants and cradling a gigantic Bible. About fifteen women sitting in two rows of maroon plastic lawn chairs face each other and listen in as Ms. Williams speaks. They wear loose-fitting blue medical scrubs with white T-shirts underneath and puke-pink open-toe shower shoes. To a woman, they look exhausted.

Lolo and I wait for Ms. Williams and the volunteer to finish their session before moving into the unit. We then wait for permission to go up the stairs to the program room on the second story. There we wait still longer for the women to be escorted up the stairs to the room. After an officer counts us, the door finally closes. The women arrange themselves in maroon plastic lawn chairs against the walls, and Lolo begins class by handing out typed copies of poems they had written in previous weeks. She then asks everyone to help

---

7. George Pro, Ethan Sahker, and Julie Baldwin, "Incarceration as a Reason for US Alcohol and Drug Treatment Non-Completion: A Multilevel Analysis of Racial/Ethnic and Sex Disparities," *Journal of Behavioral Health Service Resources* 47 (2020): 464–75.

move the chairs into a large circle so we can see and meet each other as equals, a practice that I remember from our time together at Living Stage. Lolo greets everyone she knows and introduces herself and me to the new arrivals. Class this week consists of Lolo telling her story about how she transitioned from substance abuse into recovery. In my journal, I remember:

Lolo grew up in Maryland. She was raped at age thirteen, told no one, and "carried that silence" in her for years. For some twenty-six years she used crack cocaine, alcohol, and weed to self-medicate. She figured out a way to function. She was able to maintain a "normal" lifestyle working as an administrative assistant on Capitol Hill, but the birth of her fourth child pushed her to her bottom and later into recovery. Lolo used all through that pregnancy and the chaos got so bad that at some point she became homeless. Her aunt and uncle took her in, but the baby's father called social services to have the baby taken away when he was a newborn, about two weeks old. The boy was born with drugs in his system, and the father knew Lolo was still getting high. When the social worker came for the visit, one of Lolo's older boys let them in. Lolo got really angry, but the boy protested, reminding her that even if she disapproved, "they were the police and [he] had to." While the social worker was talking to Lolo, she was thinking about the $50 in her purse and how high she was going to get when they left. At some point the social worker asked to speak to the children alone, so Lolo went upstairs to the bathroom and got high while the woman was interviewing the children. They took away the baby (that night I think), but not the other children, at least not yet. It was December and after that stressful event, Lolo needed to get high again. She hit the streets and incredibly, after searching for hours, could not find any crack anywhere in a city renowned for its crack habit. About 4 a.m., still no crack in sight, she got down on her knees and prayed for help from God. It came, but not in the way that she thought it would. She saw the blue lights of a squad car. The cop was a guy who she knew from childhood. He stopped and he took her in. This was not the first time he had arrested her, but this time, she was able to access some treatment.

She did at least three attempts at treatment, including spending time at the jail where we are. That twenty-eight-day detox shit didn't work for her. While she was trying to heal, the kids were all taken away. That made things worse. The comprehensive, family-based treatment program that partnered with Living Stage, and that eventually gave birth to Healing Justice Mamas, did however work. She did a four-month in-patient treatment program with them followed by four months of out-patient, and a total of twenty-two months of treatment including intensive family and individual therapy. Lolo's been sober for almost eleven years, since the age of thirty-nine. She is fifty now.[8]

In the weeks that followed, I learned that Lolo regularly began class with a personal story and then invited the participants to ask her questions. Personal storytelling is essential to Lolo's pedagogy. Her ability to tell stories with ease and humor made her a riveting performer despite the jail's bleak surroundings. Harry Elam Jr. theorizes that Black performers like Lolo use solo performances to "explore, expose, and even explode" concepts of race, in particular how Blackness is "conceived and performed both on stage and in life."[9] Solo performance is an effective tool for this purpose because audiences understand the theatrical event as an opportunity for performers to take on or play other roles than they would in everyday life. For Black performers who don Black characters, performance provides an opportunity for them to mine the differences between their own personal experiences, audience perceptions and misperceptions of Black people, and social constructions of Blackness embedded in the performance text. Playing the alternative or "excess" Blacknesses allows performers to critique, "transcend, and even subvert" the known "socially patrolled boundaries of race," in particular the "political constructions and violent manifestations" that circulate at all levels of our society.[10] Lolo does not take on other characters in her story, but she makes a distinction between her present day self-as-narrator and the Lolos of the past. Most powerfully, she contrasts herself and her experiences with the most prevalent stereotype about Black mothers who use crack cocaine, the "crack (w)ho(re)." The stereotypical "crack ho" sells their body for drugs. They are considered one of the lowest, most shameful kinds of sex workers and addicts. Within American discourses about crime, they are among the most despised. Low-income Black mothers in particular who engage in sex work to procure drugs and alcohol are deemed unworthy of care. Instead, dominant discourses insist that incarceration will fix their "bad behavior." Recognizing how little people understand about addiction, Lolo tells this story to make a point. What women have been told about women, substance abuse, crime, and healing is false. The women assembled around the program room table need to know this because the lies, misperceptions, and shame associated with maternal substance abuse often prevents women from seeking treatment.

---

8. Fieldnotes, October 2015.

9. Harry J. Elam, "The Black Performer and the Performance of Blackness," in *African American Performance and Theater History: A Critical Reader,* ed. Harry J. Elam and David Krasner (Oxford: Oxford University Press, 2001), 288–89.

10. Elam, "Black Performer," 289.

Women who struggle with addiction often feel ashamed, angry, frightened, and alone. Stigmatizing public narratives, like that of the "crack ho," mischaracterize addiction in low-income Black women as an indicator of a lack of moral values and respectability as well as proof of racial degeneracy. Narratives spun by users and ex-users are replete with information about how they became addicted, yet our society effaces the difference between addiction-as-practice and addiction-as-identity. Women with histories of problematic substance use know how society views them. They also know how it feels to search "shameful places on the body to inject." They have felt the shame of lying to and manipulating others, of stealing from institutions and the people closest to them, and of having to brutalize and abuse others to maintain a high.[11] This shameful labor is integral to the social practice of addiction. Kathryn Hughes finds that shame is "part of the relational pull between addicts, ex-addict users, and non-users" and forms "the basis on which certain exchanges and intimacies occur."[12] As people become attuned to "junk time," the body clock that measures both how long it takes to metabolize a substance before painful withdrawal symptoms occur and one's temporal-spatial proximity to the next opportunity to use, they mobilize relationships with other users and nonusers to manage their addiction. These relationships offer women everything from financial assistance to secure drugs or alcohol to help in administering substances and a place to crash.[13] Further, social relationships help women obtain their drug or alcohol of choice while balancing the demands of everyday life (i.e., childcare, work, housing, family life, and so forth). In these ways, addicts, users, and nonusers care for themselves and for each other.

Just as addiction is a social practice dependent on human relationships, people need reliable support systems to recover.

No one heals alone.

Lolo's story explains how she recovered with the help of her former classmate turned cop and several unnamed professional mental health counselors. Back in the program room, her words carry the weight of one testifyin(g) or bearing witness before a court or before the divine, leaving me inspired. As Lolo speaks, I watch Lolo the present-day narrator/storyteller—eleven years removed from the events of the story—and experience the Lolo of the past—the drug-addicted mother that present-day Lolo brings to life. Her text and presentation, including the early reference to her childhood, enable me to imagine and to know her as more than a "crack ho," even though her story mirrors the stereotype of the insatiable predatory mother so fixated on get-

---

11. Kathryn Hughes, "Migrating Identities: The Relational Constitution of Drug Use and Addiction," *Sociology of Health & Illness* 29, no. 5 (2007): 684.

12. Hughes, "Migrating," 684.

13. Hughes, "Migrating," 678–80.

ting high that she will lose everything, including her own children, to feed her addiction.

Tracy Davis writes that dramatic texts enable "cross-temporal reflections" like this to occur because, in performance, "the present brokers past and future."[14] Performances fix audiences in their "own temporal moment" while their "imaginations are buffeted from one tense to another" as the script moves through time, from the dramatic past to the present to the future and so forth in linear and nonlinear fashions.[15] Davis notes, however, that while the actors are performing, spectators "do not so much suspend the ordinary rules of elapsing clock-based time but augment them with another set of principles," what she calls "theatrical time."[16] In "theatrical time" audiences have a "bi-dimensional and often dual-chronic experience of play attendance"; they experience the passage of "real time" concurrent with the elapsing of the "represented time" of the drama on stage.

Lolo's personal narrative performance enables me to also experience polychronicity and polyspatiality like a theater goer. I experience the elapse of "clock-based" forward-progressive time with the other women in the program room. I also am in sync with Lolo as the chronotopes of the story shift through time, moving from childhood sites in Maryland to her time on Capitol Hill as a young adult and into the chaotic biology-driven periods when she is most heavily into her crack use. I note the progression of time as she struggles to receive effective treatment and stabilize in recovery. And of course, I remember her from Living Stage. Her personal narrative reveals not a "crack ho" but an African American woman engaged in a sustained "performative struggle for agency" over time.[17]

But as I look around the program room, I realize my response may not be the norm. Lolo's narrative has been met by many down-turned stares. Half the group sits with their legs so tightly crossed they look like amputees; not only are they twisted like pretzels, they have slipped their arms inside their blue T-shirts and tucked their hands into their armpits. Others have slumped so far down into their uniforms they seem like boneless sacks, checked out altogether. There is a sense of disquiet in the room, but Lolo is undeterred.

"So that's my story," Lolo concludes. "Any questions?"

14. Tracy C. Davis, "Performative Time," in *Representing the Past: Essays in Performance Historiography,* ed. Charlotte Canning and Thomas Postlewait (Iowa City: University of Iowa Press, 2010), 144.

15. Davis, "Performative Time," 144.

16. Davis, "Performative Time," 147.

17. Kristin M. Langellier, "Personal Narrative, Performance, Performativity: Two or Three Things I Know for Sure," *Text and Performance Quarterly* 19, no. 2 (1999): 129.

A few people begin to unfold. Someone asks how long she was doing which drug; another wants to know which one got her going. Finally, someone asks her about her current perspective on those days.

"Oh, I knew I was all that!" she declares, with a saucy toss of her head and a snap that plants her hand onto her hip.

This cracks the room up. Lolo's final words, spoken in jest, accented by the snap, allow us to laugh, circumventing or disrupting the shame and silence that is meant to accompany such narratives about rape, addiction, mothering, crime, and Black women. Geneva Smitherman notes that African Americans often use "stylized, dramatic, [even] spectacular" dialogue to make a point.[18] Speakers "boast" to communicate how they survived or "got ovah," projecting themselves as "omnipotent fearless being[s], capable of doing the undoable." They triumph over impossible or insurmountable odds, Smitherman concludes, by tapping into unseen resources within themselves.[19] Lolo's concluding joke, "I knew I was all that!," instructs listeners that they too can "get ovah" problematic substance use. They can heal and stabilize in recovery by tapping into previously unknown resources within themselves. The pride and the joy with which Lolo snapped her reply reminds listeners that she, like they are, is more than her past. Like Lolo, they can find the resources they need to heal.

Sitting in the Treatment Center I also slowly realize that Lolo is using her story to signify on the jail's detox program, insulting it through verbal indirection and humor. How effective could this program be if Lolo completed it as well as one next door at the hospital and several others, all to no avail? After all, it was only at the comprehensive residential program that brought her to Living Stage that she was able to get well and stabilize in recovery. Lolo's story does more than recount her personal journey into recovery; it instructs listeners that recovery is a process that will require more than what the jail can provide. When the women are released, they will need more help because detox is not healing. Lolo wants everyone to know this and to understand that support is out there now through her, Healing Justice Mamas, and their nationwide network of providers.

We end class with a Living Stage ritual I had forgotten, but which we had used to conclude every workshop with Lolo's group. With it, Lolo extends the embodied practice of those long-ago workshops as well as the pedagogies and epistemologies that our teachers, Rebecca Rice and Denise Kumani Gantt, animated then, into this new framework. Standing, we form a circle. She turns

---

18. Geneva Smitherman, *Talk That Talk: Language, Culture and Education in African America* (New York: Routledge, 1999), 204–5.

19. Smitherman, *Talk That Talk,* 219.

to the person on her right and says, "I'm Lolo. I [say something affirming to the person next to me] and I give you my hand." Lolo grasps the hand of the woman next to her and holds it as she turns to the woman on her right and repeats the ritual. One woman after another, we turn, affirm the woman next to us, and take her hand until we are all standing together holding each other's hands. When my turn comes, I am overwhelmed with images and half-remembered names and faces of women with whom I have done this work over the years, all of them my teachers. When I turn to the woman next to me, I give her my hand, realizing that I know nothing about her. Nonetheless, I stumble through, saying something that hopefully was not too ridiculous. Despite my fumbles, as the session wraps up I feel that Lolo's storytelling and closing ritual brought the group closer together, if only for a moment, and communicated vital information about healing, opening up the possibility of more. In the days and weeks that follow, I witness Lolo and the other members of Healing Justice Mamas take the practices they learned in their recovery journeys to other sites to spread their message and to stage healing. Carrying these embodied performance practices with them, they advocate for effective healing at sites like Mid-Atlantic that often have no formal theatrical stages, but are spaces where people are gathered to learn and to act.

THE BRIEFING

Reaching the Rayburn House Office Building on Capitol Hill the next morning proves more difficult for me than getting to the jail. It requires two closely timed bus changes and a sweaty walk in ninety-plus-degree heat and humidity. I promised Lolo and Nadira, the executive director of Healing Justice Mamas, that I would meet them at 8:30 a.m. to help set up the briefing they are cosponsoring with Republican Congresswoman Mary Bono Mack. The briefing is designed to update Congressional staffers about current fronts of the ongoing War on Drugs and educate them about the excessive use of prescription drugs so that legislation can be passed to fund effective programs to help people heal. Nadira will be presenting along with high-ranking executives from President Barack Obama's Office of National Drug Control Policy (ONDCP) and two comprehensive, grassroots, family-based treatment facilities from New York and Florida. In the shining marble hallway outside our corner conference room, I meet Lolo attired in a smart, dark-colored suit. She asks me to sign in and hands me the briefing abstract before putting me to work unwrapping the pastries. The abstract reads:

In the United States, according to the Substance Abuse and Mental Health Services Administration, approximately 5.1 million persons are current abusers of prescription painkillers. According to the Centers for Disease Control (CDC), in 2009, about three out of four deaths due to prescription drug overdose were caused by prescription painkillers. The number of deaths due to this class of drugs in 2009 was nearly four times the number in 1999; this increase is paralleled by a quadrupling of the sales of prescription painkillers from 1999 to 2010. Overdose deaths due to prescription painkillers exceed those due to cocaine and heroin combined. Grim consequences of this opioid abuse are Maternal, Fetal and Infant Opioid Exposure and Neonatal Abstinence Syndrome. Investment in Family-Based Treatment maternal-addiction programs saves countless lives and families, because healing mothers with substance use disorder exponentially affects the child welfare system, juvenile justice and adult criminal justice systems. Family-based substance abuse treatment describes programs for pregnant or parenting mothers and their children that provide direct services or referrals for services including: substance abuse treatment, child early intervention, mental health, family counseling, trauma therapy, housing, medical care, nursery and preschool, parenting skills training, and educational or job training.[20]

From the podium Nadira welcomes about forty people to the gathering a few minutes after 9:00 a.m. She is a thin, stylishly dressed African American woman in a dark pantsuit. Long, tightly coiled dreadlocks curl over her shoulders. A mother of four and now a grandmother, she moves with ease and speaks with confidence. After thanking the Hon. Mary Bono Mack for her support, Nadira frames the event as an opportunity to make maternal addiction "an integral piece of the nation's drug policy." Critical to this initiative is the effort to change the "face of maternal addiction" from the stereotypical "crack ho." Like Lolo, Nadira emphasizes that most substance abusing mothers have suffered serious trauma, often physical, sexual violence. They self-medicate to manage pain, depression, posttraumatic stress disorder, and a host of other symptoms related to their untreated injuries. In the 1980s and '90s, hysteria regarding the manufactured crack "epidemic" prevented many women from accessing the care they needed even as methamphetamines and later prescription opioids flooded "nooks and crannies in the country that crack had never reached." The nation's determination to deny "crack hos" care contributed to disease and despair in urban, predominantly low-income Black

---

20. "Healing Justice Mamas Briefing Handout," fieldnotes 2012.

and Brown communities as well as in predominantly white urban, suburban, and rural parts of the country. By tapping into contemporary lawmakers' shared concerns about maternal health in their home districts, Healing Justice Mamas has been able to gather a diverse coalition to work on this issue. To truly change the face of maternal addiction, however, requires finding women who defy the "crack ho" stereotypes and are willing to speak.

A twenty-something, heavyset, dark-blond-haired white woman with a new baby in a portable car seat soon joins Nadira at the speakers' table. This young mother, Star, is in the early phases of recovery and receiving care from an intensive family-based treatment center about an hour away. Healing Justice Mamas works with her treatment center and has asked her to share her journey thus far. She is accompanied by a social worker and treatment specialist, an African American woman in her thirties, who has driven Star and her baby to the Capitol this morning and will stay with her for moral support. Star nervously joins the panelists. At Lolo's bidding, I place a chair at the end of the table next to her so the baby can be near. Star reads her handwritten notes from a well-worn sheet of white paper. My journal reads:

> This is the first time Star is telling her story. It begins with her witnessing her favorite aunt overdose in the bathroom on heroin. I think the aunt was screaming, "Please god, help me, I don't want this anymore" as she overdosed. Then at seven years old, Star was raped by her babysitter's son. Therapy was ineffective as the counselor just dismissed her as being slow instead of helping her out. At sixteen years old, her father offered her crack. He was an addict and she wanted a relationship with him so badly so she took it. She says he cared more about drugs than he did himself, something that she disapproves of, but despite his example, she soon found herself using drugs to "cover up and deal" with her own hard feelings. This continues until one day, several years later, a neighbor spotted her older child, a three-and-a-half year-old boy, all alone in the street. Social services intervened and the boy was taken into foster care. His loss and her anxiety lead to prescription drug abuse—OxyContin and Percocet. She is now in treatment and on methadone to address the pain. She is proud she has the baby with her and intends to stay clean because she wants to raise her own kids.

When she drops the paper, Star looks frazzled and flush. Tears brim in her eyes, but there is also a deep sense of relief. Learning how to identify, story, and share problems with others is an important step in the healing process. The social worker kindly hands her some tissue.

Star's personal narrative reveals a multilayered understanding of addiction. The reading enables Star to comment on the past with a self-reflexive tone that does not feel confessional to me, at least not in the legal sense. It feels to me like Star is testifyin', speaking a truth that is bigger than the law for all assembled to hear. It feels to me like she is telling this story to heal herself. While she acknowledges past wrongdoing, especially her failure to care for her children well, I understand that her substance abuse has roots in generations of mental health issues and family dysfunction as well as the inadequate responses of state actors (the therapist). Her presentation, like Lolo's at the Treatment Center, asserts that mothers struggling with addiction ought not be dismissed as criminal "crack hos" and bad mothers. Star has made mistakes and harmed other people, but she was not born bad. Until very recently, she was unable to access appropriate and effective care to heal. Now in treatment, Star is stabilizing in recovery and planning for a new future. Her story troubles the well-worn perpetrator/victim binary, revealing the instability of these "differentiated identities" and their relationship to the law and to justice.[21] Most importantly for this briefing, Star's story respatializes the War on Drugs. Her narrative expands the narrow historic focus on depressed Black urban enclaves to include white suburbs and rural communities, literally opening up a discussion on Capitol Hill about excessive drug and alcohol use, treatment and recovery nationwide. This creates an opportunity to investigate the myriad intersecting "power relations" that shaped Star's life and which continue to impact the lives of mothers struggling with addiction everywhere.[22] Star's story accomplishes this because it points to a larger truth. The War on Drugs has affected everyone. Despite all the hyperbole about predatory Black "crack hos," the punitive law-and-order approach has not stopped people from using, and it has not produced more safety, justice, or healing. Women and girls need more. Star, as an expert on her own experiences, delivers this message with clarity, and her remarks appear to have an immediate impact. Next, Nadira turns the microphone over to David Mineta, the director of ONDCP, a division that oversees both the Border Patrol and the development of drug-treatment programs. He begins his remarks by acknowledging Star, saying, "I hope my remarks do justice to Star's story and to her."

In subsequent conversations with Nadira, she indicates to me that facilitating these exchanges between the lawmakers and those directly affected by maternal addiction is one of their highest priorities. The Mamas hold ONDCP

21. Sidonie Smith and Kay Schaffer, *Human Rights and Narrated Lives: The Ethics of Recognition* (Gordonsville, VA: Palgrave Macmillan, 2004), 162.

22. Langellier, "Personal Narrative," 130.

Director Mineta in high regard because his past experience as a social worker in California brought him into close contact with real people with histories of substance abuse. Unlike other lawmakers who have shaped drug policy on the premise that substance abusers are inhuman monstrous "others," Mineta understands that this rhetoric induces panic, not effective programming. His approach complements that of Healing Justice Mamas because he seems to understand that "to see oneself as a subject and to see other people as *the other* or objects not only alienates oneself . . . but also enables the dehumanization inherent in oppression and domination."[23]

An opportunity to sit down with an ONDCP staff member weeks later confirms that the agency is trying to coordinate what feels like competing mandates. Mineta was charged by President Barack Obama, as the previous director was charged by George W. Bush, to find effective solutions that address addiction and promote the best law-enforcement technologies. On the one hand, the agency was expected to stop the flow of illegal drugs into the country. On the other, it was tasked with reducing demand. Obama authorized greater investment in effective treatment programs, but at the time I spoke with the ONDCP staff, they were waiting to implement new programs, contingent as they were on his reelection and the make-up of the Congress in 2013. Through its willingness to listen to the life stories of people who have lived with maternal addiction, the Office seemed poised to steer the Department in a direction that would make it possible to address real people's needs instead of perpetuating more harmful approaches. We all hoped it would contribute to mitigating the harm caused by sellers, problem users, and their enablers as well as by our "misogynist, racist and classist social structures," which set the stage for the problems to occur.[24]

THE GRADUATION

A week after the Congressional briefing, I climbed out of a cab and into a city park to witness a municipal Drug Court graduation. It is a balmy Thursday morning, the sun is shining, and there are only a few clouds on the distant horizon. As I climb the grassy ridge into the park, I hear a local radio station playing adult contemporary R&B hits and see several open-air cabanas

---

23. Kelly Oliver, *Witnessing: Beyond Recognition* (Minneapolis: University of Minnesota Press, 2001), 4; original emphasis.

24. Sara Warner, "Restoryative Justice: Theater as a Redressive Mechanism for Incarcerated Women," in *Razor Wire Women: Prisoners, Activists, Scholars and Artists*, ed. Jodie Michelle Lawston and Ashley E. Lucas (Albany: University of New York Press, 2011), 234.

interspersed among a grove of trees. Under one canopy, unopened bundles of chips, soda, and water await the start of the party. Two chefs turn chicken breasts and sausage links over the hot coals of mega grills, filling the air with the smell of barbeque. A third speakers' canopy has been set aside with a podium and microphones. Nearby, a table laden with plaques stands at the ready. It is a beautiful day to graduate from Drug Court.

The graduation ceremony begins with words of welcome from the Court staff, followed by salutations from the city's mayor. He situates the efforts of the Drug Court within the discourse of law enforcement and economic development:

> Being in the great outdoors nobody wants to hear any long speeches from me today . . . but I do want to congratulate those who are graduating today and have completed the program, and those who are early in the journey. Hopefully those who are early in the journey will look to those who are completing it as an inspiration that you can do it. Many people know that this program started in Miami in the late '80s . . . by one of our former Attorneys General Janet Reno, and came to the District of Columbia in 1993. We know that when programs are not successful they don't stay around very long. This has obviously been successful because next year it will celebrate its twentieth anniversary. . . . There are so many that have benefited mightily from it that the data are absolutely incredible. . . . Wal-Mart and Costco are coming to the city. You get to engage in not only your own personal development but the economic development of the city and it doesn't get any better than that. Thank you, guys, and congratulations!

The mayor draws parallels between the return of big box stores to the city and the changes that the court clients have made. The links are vague in his speech. Will the seeding of so many neoliberal corporations lift the city's struggling economy? Will they provide living-wage jobs that will reroute people from the illegal economy? Is their arrival meant to herald the coming of a rich and broad cultural ecosystem in which the Drug Court graduates will also be valued? Opportunities for gainful employment might deter some low-level drug dealers and alleviate distress on low-income families, but if people are self-medicating untreated traumas with alcohol and narcotics, a more comprehensive solution is called for. The next two speakers—one a Drug Court graduate, the other from Healing Justice Mamas—make this point.

The mayor is followed by a middle-aged man of Latin American descent who shares a letter he wrote on a pivotal day in his recovery journey. Late to one of his treatment-group sessions, he waited in the hall for a chance to join his class and penned the following reflection, which he now reads "on behalf of all the graduates." I jot down his speech:

> Letter of Resignation.
> Not Dear, but Undesirable Miss Cocaine. Extending my sincere feelings to your personnel Mr. Miller Lite, Mr. Jose Cuervo, Mrs. Maria Juana [for marijuana], Mr. Crack Daniels, the PCP office, and your unhealthy Heroin department. It is a pleasure for me to announce my life retirement from your trashy agency due to my following points:
>
> > 1. You are not providing me any benefits. Instead you are giving me a lot of deficits such as legal, mental, medical, and even worse financial problems.
> > 2. I am tired of your stupid agency taking away my family members, friends, my education, money, and my life.
>
> And finally let me finish here by letting you know that I now belong to a wonderful agency which is much better than yours which is called the drug court program, whose president, Judge Weisberg, worries over and helps all of us, the clients. And in conjunction with its marvelous personal case managers and the class facilitators who guide us to a path of well-being and accomplishments of positive things in our lives with drugs-free attitude and environment. Goodbye forever!

The reading elicits laughter from the audience of graduates, drug-court staff, and administrators. As the day progresses, I realize that this is but the first of many instances in which the graduates will take to the podium to acknowledge their achievements and declare with confidence that they are "done"—finished—with problematic drug use and with the Drug Court. Like Lolo and Star, this author frames his letter as the product of his individual journey to recovery, a spontaneous personal reflection that marks an end. Transposed into the environment of the graduation ceremony, however, where the accomplishments of the graduates, the case managers, and individual class facilitators are being scrutinized by no less than the mayor and the judge who runs the program, it raises questions in my mind about the readers' intent and the efficacy of the Drug Court program.

Graduations are public ceremonies meant to mark personal achievements and publicly signal graduates' transition from one phase of life to the next. The Drug Court graduation marks each client's successful completion of one of three phases of the six-month, mandatory treatment program. At this ceremony, clients are graduating from phase one to phase two, from two to three, or leaving the program completely. While every person's achievements are to be lauded, as in other carceral sites where prisoners must behave a certain way or else, the graduation ceremony does more than mark clients' accomplishments. It also uplifts this carceral model of health care. Underneath the celebratory veneer of the BBQ is the reality that folks are still under correctional control. Most people who have histories of substance abuse relapse multiple times. They catch new court cases when they do or when they simply fail to meet impossible parole expectations. Public policies that frame substance abuse as a crime and not a public health issue, including those enacted by the Drug Court, contribute to ill health and inequality. So while the writing of the letter may have been spontaneous and a personal marker of the writer's transition from one life phase into the next, there was a lot riding on his performance. The public reading affirms an internal, personal shift in the speaker, and purposefully acknowledges the work of the Drug Court staff and judge, who have the authority to withdraw support and to inflict punishment should a graduate fail or refuse to progress or to abstain. This is the bitter discursive ground on which the struggle for justice as care, as treatment, and as healing is fought. The "Letter of Resignation" sounds to me like a "thank you" and a "fuck you" to the Court, the surprising combination of which elicits our collective laughter.

When Nadira climbs to the podium to speak, people again fall quiet. Her speech draws parallels between her life and those of the graduates but situates her own substance abuse in a complex history of interpersonal violence, one that was exasperated by a lack of community-based, family-oriented, accessible care:

I'm a mother in recovery. I'm a Washingtonian, a native of Washington, DC. Born and raised . . . Coolidge [high school] alumni, graduate, and I was a young mother who experienced domestic violence. Most mothers who are substance abusing at first experience physical or sexual violence. Most folk—men and women—who are substance abusing have experienced some trauma in their lives, and are self-medicating to deal with that trauma. And so for me, I was self-medicating to the issues of unaddressed physical violence. I sought help. . . . It was very hard for me to find appropriate help for a mother, but finally I had access to a program that could help me. It was long term and . . . comprehensive. . . . It was in Anacostia DC. . . . I would sit and I would look across the Anacostia River and I would think, "This is a powerful place and powerful things can happen here." I wasn't, you know, talking about the work that I would eventually do with [Healing Justice Mamas]. I had no clue that that was in my future. I was only talking about my personal transformation.

At the time, the Washington monument was being resurfaced. I don't know if any of you remember that, but back in 1998 there was scaffolding going up around the Washington monument. I remember thinking as I watched that go up over my eighteen months of treatment that that scaffolding was mirroring what was happening in my personal life. [Nadira] was being restored. . . . Recovery involves change. Change means doing things differently. The problems that many of us face [are] not the problem; it is our resistance to the change and . . . fear of the unknown. What that meant for me in my personal recovery was that I didn't know what was ahead of me, but I knew what was behind me and I had gotten comfortable with those things that I liked that I knew I needed to change. . . . I want to talk about . . . embracing the unknown. I didn't know what was going to happen for me and my life. I only knew what had happened and I didn't want to go back there. My biggest hope was that I could become a responsible mother to my children. That I could become a loving and supportive daughter to my dad who was eighty-five years old at the time. . . . I wanted to be a productive member of the community. . . . I was marching forward and then facing my fears and facing the things that I needed to do.

What I know now is that courage is not absence of fear, but having fear and acting responsibly even in the face of that fear. When I think about the unknown I think about infinite possibilities. In recovery . . . if I had made a list of all the things I wanted, I would have shortchanged myself. And that's exactly where I was at. I just wanted to be a responsible citizen, but I didn't know that God had a plan for my life. And the very things that I thought were the worst things that could happen to me—being a mother and being a pregnant woman and not being able to stop using drugs—I thought that was the worst thing that could happen to anyone. But, that was the very thing that God used to make me uniquely qualified for the work that I do today.[25]

Nadira's speech lays bare her process of entering treatment, stabilizing in recovery, and then emerging into the next phase of her life as an advocate. Like Lolo's and Star's, Nadira's personal narrative operationalizes complex images of addiction across multiple, overlapping chronotopes that disrupt the logic of the War on Drugs and the "crack ho." She roots the narrative in local, recognizable landmarks that make the story accessible and familiar, including iconic spaces such as the Washington Monument. Like the other Healing Jus-

25. Fieldnotes, September 20, 2012.

tice Mamas moms, Nadira's personal narrative performance complicates the victim/perpetrator, innocent/guilty, good/bad girl binaries that dictate public policies and the assumption that justice means punitive retribution. She further operationalizes a new element, that of "God," the divine "higher power," to explain her transformation. This move connects Nadira to a long activist tradition enacted by African American women who operationalize a spiritual framework to authorize their political work. Melissa Harris-Perry theorizes:

> Faith in a benevolent and loving God is a common tool Black women employ to straighten out the crooked room of race and gender stereotypes. God provides an alternative measuring stick for judging their human worth. When judged against social values rooted in white beauty standards, economic success, political power or normative domestic arrangements, African American women consistently fall short. By focusing on a divine valuation based on their character, kindness, service and strength, Black women shift the angles of their crooked room and produce a new image for themselves. Faith is a resistance strategy.[26]

The Mamas' sacred authority empowers Nadira to address the Drug Court graduates, offer her perspective and some additional advice. Like Lolo, her presentation counteracts the reductive logic of law enforcement that equates criminality with Blackness. The "crack ho" is confronted with the local girl, high school graduate, and young mother trapped in an abusive relationship, and with the woman who found treatment for herself and her family, and who now advocates as a member of the recovery community. Drug Court administrators invited Nadira to speak because she is an excellent example. Like Lolo, she uses the opportunity to testify to her experience, smuggling in additional vital information that the graduates need to hear, namely that the best efforts of the Drug Court staff may not be sufficient to meet their treatment needs. Completing this program alone will not produce the healthy, safe, and dignified lives that graduates desire. More is needed. Nadira appropriates the familiar rhetoric of the confession endorsed by the penal system to testify and to communicate these ideas to the assembly. Rather than dampening the proceedings, Nadira's speech educates listeners about the important next steps Drug Court graduates may need to take to stabilize in recovery. She offers a way forward into the inclusive community of people in recovery, grounded in the multilayered story of a woman who has been where they were and stood

---

26. Melissa Harris-Perry, *Sister Citizen: Shame, Stereotypes and Black Women in America* (New Haven, CT: Yale University Press, 2011), 222–23.

exactly where they are (metaphorically, if not literally). Her performance is imbued with a sense of hope, futurity, and possibility. While it communicates vital information about the recovery process, it invites future actions for community and self-repair.

THE CAUCUS

The Congressional Black Caucus (CBC) comes to town a few days later. They are holding meetings at the 7th Street Convention Center, and we are attending a session convened by the Honorable Congresswoman Karen Bass of California on the "Impact of International and Domestic Human-Trafficking on African American Women and Girls." Inspired by Dr. Dorothy I. Height, Barbara Perkins, and Ka Flewellen, the International Black Women's Public Policy Institute is sponsoring this session, its fourth annual at the CBC annual convening. The Institute, I learn from the program, connects and advocates for Black women globally through "acts of kindness and public policy."[27] Their mission is to work in the United States and internationally to convene hearings and discussions to evaluate the impact of current public policies and to initiate new policies that address the major threats to the well-being of Black women and our families.

Without introduction, the program begins with a poem, delivered aloud from memory from the front row of the hall by a narrow, slightly stooped Black woman in her forties, wearing a long dark skirt and a headscarf that drapes down her back. I catch only a word or phrase here or there as I turn my ear to listen from across the room:

> Daily abuse destroys my youth . . . can anyone see me through this 1-way mirror? Caught by predators, sold to pedophiles, trapped by oppressors . . . I could never explain what I'm feeling without unearthing the traumas that need care . . . Emergency! Who can give us beauty for ashes?

The poetess has climbed the small dais during her presentation. As it concludes, Barbara Perkins meets her at the base of the stairs with a warm, full embrace. When she takes her seat, Perkins turns to the assemblage and welcomes us with a deep voice that reminds me of the best gospel church mother: "Though it is heavy, I stand encouraged, inspired, because instead of being anywhere else, you've chosen to be here." She turns to the poetess

---

27. International Black Women's Public Policy Institute program, 2015.

and acknowledges her contribution: "In an African tradition we form a circle around you to hold you up. The first year you came to us to tell the story of being an HIV+ mom who discovered with her first pregnancy she had the virus. Now you share with us your gift and your will, and we thank you." Perkins admits that sex trafficking was not an issue with which she had been familiar until people like the poet approached her. But she continues: "Once you know, you know you cannot ignore it anymore. . . . This is the civil rights issue of our time." So, for the next two hours, we peel back the layers to understand the issue, which the panel defines as modern-day slavery.

Brief welcoming remarks by a member of Congresswoman Bass's staff are followed by Karen E. Richardson, Associate Director of the White House Office of Public Engagement, who frames the issue as the continuation of slavery 150 years after the passage of the Emancipation Proclamation, with twenty million contemporary men, women, and children forced into labor in the well-structured "informal" economy. She emphasizes with an endearing sense of familiarity that President Obama is committed to investigating and prosecuting perpetrators. With some dismay, she recognizes that they are still woefully unaware of the networks and the casual relationships between traffickers and pedophiles. They have arrested a pitiful 125 people, the most ever, and have much more to do.

The session is then turned over to a panel of experts in the field of human trafficking broadly writ. The program includes Nadira along with a specialist in human trafficking from the American Federation of Labor and Congress of Industrial Organizations (AFL-CIO); the founder of a District of Columbia shelter for women and girls who have been trafficked into prostitution; the director of a New York City–based nonprofit that provides advocacy on behalf of LGBTQ youth of color to end "stop-and-frisk" and other forms of discriminatory, unlawful, and abusive policing; and a survivor of sex trafficking who is now an independent filmmaker.

The AFL-CIO representative emphasizes that, while the system today differs in many ways from historical US slavery, there are many entry points that have carryovers from historical times. Debt peonage continues to a limited degree, but the percentage of people who have been forced into labor for commercial sexual exploitation, manufacturing, farm, and domestic labor is staggering. This is how Wal-Mart can keep its prices so low. It is not only because they will hire only part-time employees and pay them low wages with no benefits. Sex trafficking makes up only a relatively small portion of the picture, but it soon becomes clear to me that the testifyings by and about women and girls that have been forced into prostitution or pornography are the ones that galvanize the audience to action.

The broad picture of national and international sex trafficking is grounded by the harrowing stories told by Tera, the founder of the shelter for women and girls who have been trafficked in the capital. She points out that only a few blocks from where we are sitting is the hottest spot in the city for sex trafficking. Weeknights between 2:00 a.m. and 7:00 a.m., she and her staff walk the intersection of 14th and K Streets to intercept girls and then head to 5th and K Streets for boys and transgender prostitutes. Another section of the staff hits the malls during the day because, as large commercial spaces where people cross paths and parents allow their children to roam unescorted, they are the perfect hunting ground for traffickers and pedophiles.

To demonstrate the myriad ways that traffickers manipulate children into prostitution, Tera reveals that her trafficker told her she was "DUMB" day after day, time and time again, to make her a slave and keep her a slave. Many times, she says, long before children encounter a trafficker, they have been primed by their families for the work. In some cases, parents and other family members exploit the kids themselves for money. Finally, there are criminal enterprises or gangs that force the children into sex work, not on street corners, but at the mall. Where else could teenage girls hang out all day with nobody questioning their presence? We expect them to be there, walking around, window-shopping. What we don't realize is that the girls are for sale. She concludes, "There is no space free of pedophiles," but steps can be taken to keep these children from harm. Like Richardson and the AFL-CIO representative, Tera advocates for the reauthorization of the 2000 Trafficking Victims Protection Act and the decriminalization of child sex workers. In conclusion, they make the point that this work is global, although we often discuss it in localized or provincial terms.

When Nadira's turn to speak arrives, she concurs with the previous speaker that sex trafficking is the "fastest-growing criminal industry in the world" today but emphasizes that we are not just talking about people being brought into the United States from other countries; most women and girls who are trafficked are American citizens, often runaways. Sexual exploitation in their homes primes girls and prompts them to run away. Usually within forty-eight hours of being on the streets, they are targeted by pimps, lured with promises of love and security (like a place to stay and a plate of food). Pimps recognize that sex trafficking is more profitable than selling drugs because there is less risk of being caught. The girls, usually ranging in age from twelve to fourteen years old, are criminalized for prostitution and solicitation, not the adult johns and pimps. Nadira concludes by saying, "We need zero tolerance for the sexual exploiters of minors. . . . Because let's face it, under the makeup and the high heels, regardless of what people say, I see a baby."

Nadira is followed by Briana, a woman who had been one of those exploited babies. Holding back tears, she says that she will not go into all the details of what was done to her because talking about it can be retraumatizing. Trauma disrupts our ability to communicate, yet Briana has found the support she needed to process the violence and move it into the realm of memory and then into the symbolic so that she can share her story with us. Through story, she restages the conflicts and human confrontations she endured and reveals to listeners their resolution. Here Briana extends a portion of her healing process—community building—to those of us in the room. Affirming that "it has been my healing to tell the dirty truth," she bravely shares some of her memories.

Trafficking victims, Briana emphasizes, "become wired for crazy." Traffickers teach their victims that they are "really are nothing" until that "distorted concept" becomes the victim's only frame of reference. I remember that she ran away from home seeking a better life, not realizing that her brain, especially the decision-making part, would not be fully mature until she reached her mid-twenties. Briana's traffickers taught her that she was "nothing," but she wants us to know something different. Moments later, she admonishes us that there is "no such thing as teenage prostitution" because teenage girls have no power, no volition or "desire" to have sex with a three-hundred-plus pound man. The girls are the ones being exploited. Black girls are the majority of the ones being exploited. They need our help now.

As I glance around the packed room, many in the audience are reaching into their purses and backpacks for tissues. Everyone on the dais seems shaken. My heart is heavy and my thoughts turn to the question of what to do next. The speakers have reoriented my sense of the city with new knowledge about the spaces and landscapes where the sexual exploitation of women and girls (and men and boys) occurs. I hear Briana's and Tera's demands to have their individual experiences recognized and their desire for other people to stand up and intervene, to fight, to resist and transform this sexual economy of Black women and girls. I want to do something—anything—*move*. I have heard Briana's story as a call to action from women who have been exploited within the sexual economy and a demand that their embodied knowledge of the "dirt" inform and shape future action. What happens next affirms that not only has Briana told this story but she has also created the conditions for us to sync up as a community, out of which sense of communal belonging there arises the possibility of additional collective action.

When Barbara Perkins returns to the podium, her words shift the room from immobilization by sorrow into resistance and activism. She observes that contemporary definitions of masculinity mark any girl who is prostituted as a "ho" while the men, the purveyors and pedophiles, skate off as the "good guys." The extent of street commercialization pales in comparison with the number of children and women being pimped at home so, "Talk ain't gonna do it," she says. I paraphrase her spontaneous closing remarks:

> We are smart women and we realize that we gotta roll up our sleeves and do more. This is gonna take much more [to get people to] wake up, stand up, and transform institutions, retool the family and rework the justice system. It may mean dismantling foster care as we know it, for the foster care system is preparing our children for exploitation and abuse. It is broken. . . . Wherever you see an on-ramp [join in and] help us lift it, for it looks too heavy to lift alone. There is no time for worrying about whose name goes on the marquee, no time for that foolishness. We are taking every little Briana, every little Tera, taking each one in . . . looking into the eyes of the people's souls, including the men perpetrators.[28]

In response to the personal narratives, Perkins stages an appeal for community engagement, one that embraces the children who are trafficked and those who have injured them. The survivor's stories alongside those from the Obama Administration and from the Mamas have made this topic not only "discussable" but also a site for activism. The organizers may have initiated this session out of a desire for "productive and embodied conversation" that could inform the direction of the CBC, but the power of the personal narratives has produced an opportunity for more.[29] The presentations have ignited "alternative imaginaries" that challenge established American social, familial, and legal "traditions." The scene has shifted.[30] Like the presentations enacted at other sites where Healing Justice Mamas activists infiltrate, the performance of these personal narratives has done more than inform listeners about past experiences or "express" dissent from the norm; they have "incite[d]" us to action.[31] We are physically and emotionally moved in the moment. Looking around the room, it seems like people are not only brimming with empathy and tears, they are fired up to do more. But how do we achieve healing and justice as the survivors' demands?

For the Mamas, the first step toward achieving this new modality has been to heal themselves and then to encourage the establishment of alternative

---

28. Fieldnotes, October 2015.

29. D. Soyini Madison, *Acts of Activism: Human Rights as Radical Performance* (Cambridge: Cambridge University Press, 2010), 49.

30. Madison, *Acts of Activism*, 49.

31. Madison, *Acts of Activism*, 49.

social modalities through individual grassroots interventions, advocacy work on Capitol Hill, and international collaborations. At each phase the women engage in a process of reframing and restorying their lives to redress the harms of the War on Drugs. They stage healing by interrupting performances of mastery and domination that pass for justice in the US. Most importantly, their work and their words encourage further activism.

To the streets we go.

THE MARCH

It is a bright sunny Thursday afternoon on the Mall in downtown Washington, DC, ten days after the Congressional Black Caucus events. When I step off the metro I see a sea of red STOP HUMAN SLAVERY T-shirts convening in the shadow of the Washington Monument. A large stage has been set up with its back to the Monument. Cars pass by hurriedly. At the meeting place between the lawn and the street, some forty tables have been arranged in a long, open rectangle. Organizations from around the world are laying out pamphlets, staking flags, unfolding lawn chairs, and settling in. Most of the workers are women, and they come in every shape, size, age, and accent. Healing Justice Mamas is a supporter and has a table set up somewhere on the lawn.

As I make my way over, I notice two African American women who have drawn a crowd around them at the main stage. The younger is dressed like a modern-day trafficked girl. She is in her early twenties and she wears bright red fishnet stockings, a pair of tight booty shorts, a pink tank top, and 4″ platform heels. On her head is an electric pink wig cut in a short style that falls just above her shoulders. She is sandwiched between two signs. The one across her chest reads, "Who is Stolen?" and the sign on her back says, "It Could be YOUR Child!!!" with a website (now inactive) linking the reader to their local campaign to end child sex trafficking. This young woman is accompanied by another young African American woman, Stacy Jewell, who I learn is an anti-slavery organizer and the founder of Who Is Stolen? Jewell takes to the stage. From the grass, I paraphrase her spoken-word poem:

> Every green light was a chance to please my daddy
> Because green lights mean the cars are coming
> And if I make the most I'll get the chance
> To sleep in the big girls' bed with him
> And not on the floor.
> The night rejoices in my captivity.

I will run to the sun . . . not be a vampire forever . . .

The night is thirsty for her and we must not be too tired to work.

He rips the clothes off.

You take his hand and say, "You don't have to take it. I will give it freely."

She's not weak enough so he turns to the daddy for a younger girl.

I cannot believe she is so young her breasts have not fully formed.

She's too young—in pigtails.

"Hey baby, you want a date?" the girl says

And she then turns away.

I'll come back for you, I say.

No you won't, no one ever comes back . . .

I want to be numb again like the drugs they once gave me to rape me.

Now I crave it to numb the pain of living.

The laugh is a lie . . .

Then one day, the sun invited me, a vampire, out into it—the sun!

I begin to walk, no, to run, to escape, when all the vampires were asleep.

It didn't burn me!

It took me . . .

Ten years to understand I was a victim,

One day to believe in the sun [Son].[32]

The crowd roars its applause. Jewell is testifyin'! Her poem is infused with the rhythms of the Black church and rings with a truth that too many of us in the crowd recognize. Jewell's poem ends with a sense of wonder at her discovery of the "sun/son," which aurally signify both as the sun of daylight and the son of God, Jesus Christ. I realize that she is operationalizing an alternative framework of geological time and of mythical, messianic, divine intervention. Both work to remind spectators that there is something more out there for people who are trapped in the sexual economy, even if that alternative world appears inaccessible or incomprehensible to them in the moment.

As I listen, I try to maintain a sense of optimism, of possibility. But all day long, women and girls who have been trafficked share stories like this. They talk about their desire to be loved; being raped, betrayed, and exploited for their youth and innocence; and somehow, often unexpectedly, finding a way out. The stories sicken and suffocate me, taking me imaginatively time and again to the horrifying spaces when and where the speakers endured the brutal abuse. The weight of the stories makes it hard to feel any hope, but the gathering does serve, like all the events in which Healing Justice Mamas is

---

32. Fieldnotes, October 2012.

involved, a purpose. Telling the "dirty truth" is vital. It helps expose the problem and contributes to establishing an inclusive community in which women and girls are valued. But after several hours of listening to the stories of exploitation, I can tolerate no more.

Salvation comes for me when I hear one of the organizers, a thin African American woman who is also a survivor of sex trafficking, rallying the crowd for a group walk around the Monument. Reflecting on her life journey thus far, she remembers that once she "never knew she had this kind of good in me."

"Freedom!" she declares.

"Freedom!" a thousand people answer back.

Before we leave, the woman asks us to hold a moment of silence for all the women and girls who survived, for those who died while enslaved that you never hear about, and for those who were unable to tell their stories. From this place of silent remembrance we move, making one slow loop around the Washington Monument. Along the way we pass dozens of curiosity seekers who ask why we are walking. Some people walk along with us to hear the answers while others stop to take in the eight-foot-high posters that have been mounted every three hundred feet or so along the walk route. These are images composed by survivors illustrating their lives before, their transformations, their rescues, their prayers for the future, and their determination to end the violence and the shame.

The stories of the women and girls gathered under the STOP MODERN SLAVERY banner on that day, like the oral histories Nadira and Lolo tell, are undergirded with a sense of hopefulness for a new future to emerge. Their personal narratives not only inform the listener of the individual speaker's past but also carry with them a wish, a prayer, a determination, and an incitement to produce another world by gathering people and building new relationships and new communities. Together they investigate some of the most pressing problems facing our society. Through the exchange of shared wisdom, they generate new possibilities and from them new social modalities. Testifying to the "dirty truth" becomes "a collective response to shared oppression," inciting performers and spectators to defend themselves "against the systemic forces" as well as the individual actors that have injured them.[33] Momentarily appropriating the Washington Monument as a conduit to this new world where Black women and girls are valued symbolically respatializes the Mall, and by extension, the nation. The march reminds me that activism can occur on a myriad of levels and through multiple, intersecting, and at

33. Nina Billone, "Performing Civil Death: The Medea Project and Theater for Incarcerated Women," *Text and Performance Quarterly* 29, no. 3 (2009): 272.

times even unseen practices. While I feel stymied, things may be moving in ways I cannot imagine. Alternative frameworks of time and of mythological, messianic, and divine intervention are at work here too. The collective labor of activists is making an impact, even if we cannot always immediately see or feel the change.

WHAT LIES AHEAD

The Mamas and their allies stage healing by relating personal narratives that challenge the well-worn "crack ho" stereotype and upset carceral logics and practices. The Mamas testify to denaturalize the idea that incarceration is rehabilitative and to open up the possibility for alternative, better informed, and more effective ways to mitigate suffering, heal disease, and strengthen human relationships. Imbued with a sense of optimism and futurity, their compelling oral histories affirm that healing is an individual and a communal process. More than merely telling people how healing works, the Mamas view opportunities to speak as healing work. Their stories cut through the violence, shame, and silencing to forge new coalitions to care for real Black women and girls. As is the case with Demeter's Daughters at Midwestern, the Big Water Drama Club, and the Medea Project in South Africa, the Mamas use performance to transform how we define crime, address human conflicts, and heal. This work continues in the final chapter which takes up the question of how to stage healing beyond prisons and jails.

Beyond Incarceration

"If I had a tree in my backyard, and it grew a seed with a balm inside that would heal all wounds, why would I keep that to myself? I would want everybody to have it if it works."

—Tarana Burke, speech at Michigan State University, 2018

Let me tell you about the power of story.

"There are 106 women serving life sentences in Louisiana," declared Ngozi, codirector of the Big Water prison theater program and one of the lead coordinators of the Beyond Incarceration Summit.[1] This three-day gathering of women and men in New Orleans in early April 2018 raised awareness of the effects of mass incarceration. At the Summit's closing ceremony, Ngozi addressed an audience of one hundred or so community members, including several formerly incarcerated women and men and their families, in a small, Black-owned community center in the shadow of the I-10 expressway. Like her, we all wore white. As she spoke, Ngozi beckoned several women to join her. The group of fifteen, ranging in age from their late twenties to their mid-sixties, formed a loose line across the stage, each holding a single handwritten white index card. On Ngozi's cue, they stepped up to the microphone to read aloud:

Mary. Sheila. Jeanie. Carolyn. Sharon. Terry. Patricia. Octavia. Ashley. Jill. Mable. Joy. Mary. Deborah. Angela. Betty. Amy. Selina. Michelle. Emma. Bobbie. Angellica. Dawn. Esta. Dessie. Bobbie. Lisa. Helen. Opal. Thea. Sandra. Edna. Gloria. Gail . . .

---

1. To protect the identities of the incarcerated women at the center of this study, I use pseudonyms to identify all of the people associated with the research project. However, the Beyond Incarceration Summit occurred in April 2018 in New Orleans.

As the names accumulated, voices broke and tears began to flow down faces, first on stage, and then all around me. Speakers placed hands on each other's shoulders to steady themselves. They whispered words of encouragement to one another until, finally, the list of all 106 women serving life sentences in Louisiana was done. Ngozi then stepped to the side and bent down to unveil a beautiful, handsewn, bright blue quilt with the women's names lying on the stage behind her. With an audible collective gasp, the audience moved as one to see.

Moments after the ceremony came to a close, Jodie, founder and codirector of the Big Water Drama Club and a coconvener of the Summit, found me at the end of the stage taking pictures of the quilt with my phone. She folded me into a warm hug, and declared through her own tears, "Ava is coming home!"

Stunned, I exclaimed, "When? Now?? Oh my god!!!" thinking I had somehow missed this major announcement. Ava was a "lifer" too and one of the original members of the Drama Club.

Noting my confusion, Jodie paused, took a breath, and shook her head. "Not today," she told me, "but some day. Ava is coming home. Ava is coming home."

"Ava is coming home," I repeated, at once realizing my mistake and the power of her conviction. "Ava is coming home."

As I repeated the phrase over and over again with Jodie standing next to the stage, I believed.

I was not alone. In the weeks and months to follow, a broad coalition of prisoner rights advocates, prison abolitionists, Black Lives Matter organizers, lawyers, filmmakers, church folk, and Drama Club Graduates (formerly incarcerated returned citizens) came together to tell Ava's story and fight for her release. Every time the opportunity arose to meet a public servant who worked on clemency requests for the governor, the Graduates told their own and Ava's story. And they kept telling it. Months later, the parole board reviewed her case and agreed she should be freed! This felt like a miracle, but the coalition knew that the governor still had to sign the paperwork. So, they told more and more people, including many who were close to the governor, about her case. Months and months passed without any word. Finally, a coalition member approached a person close to the governor again and asked them about the delay. They revealed that Ava's story had put them on their own "Damascus Road." In the biblical story of the "Damascus Road," Saul has a life-changing experience that compels him to stop persecuting the followers of Jesus. Ava's case was this staff person's "Damascus Road." Thinking about all the time she served—more time than the men who were convicted with her for the same crime—they had had a change of heart, but they still were reluctant to act. Speaking with Ava's supporter, a Drama Club Graduate who had known Ava behind bars and who had changed her own life, gave them the courage they needed to act. The next chance they had, the staff person put Ava's case in front of the governor, and this time he signed the paperwork! With the stroke of a pen, he moved her one step closer to freedom, if not to justice.[2]

Justice is not a fixed and tangible object but a powerful and elusive idea. As Dwight Conquergood reminds us, justice "lives only in performance" and "can be seen only when it is acted out."[3] Justice scripts, like other human ritual practices, are imbued with the power to transform relationships, to break lives, and to make people whole. We decide what justice is every day through our actions.

Theater stands in many people's minds at the opposite end of the spectrum, as a site for entertainment, release, relief. Theater should be engaging, always, but as I have tried to demonstrate throughout this book, theater can also do far more. Art is not the sole answer to the problems that plague the US justice system, but neither is more funding for police, more prosecutors, more prisons, and more jails. Despite all the money thrown at the criminal legal system, it has not stopped people from harming each other or helped most people who need to heal. To get the fairer, more just, equitable, and safer world we desire, we have to think beyond the current carceral and rehabilitative models, beyond patrol, punish, and control. We have to think beyond incarceration.

This means confronting poverty, racism, and sexism, and shutting down the derogatory images of and stories about Black women and girls that anchor and define our society. These depictions justify harassing, abusing, exploiting, starving, ignoring, celling, and killing Black women and girls with impunity. In addition to counteracting false images of and stories about Black women and girls, we have to animate new ways of behaving in the world. In prison abolitionist and in transformative and restorative justice circles, community members are working to identify and implement more supportive ways of addressing harm and holding people accountable for wrongdoing where desired and where possible. Yet there is still much work to be done to identify effective practices, disseminate that knowledge, and earn community buy-in. In the midst of the crisis, Black women and girls continue to be overpoliced and underprotected. Racialized, gender-based violence in popular media as well as in the courts, on the street, on the job, at school, in faith-based and

---

2. Phone call with Jodie, August 21, 2021.

3. Dwight Conquergood, "Lethal Theatre: Performance, Punishment and the Death Penalty," *Theatre Journal* 54, no. 2 (2002): 343.

other community institutions, and in the home has been a defining feature of life for too many Black women and girls for too long.

Enough.

Demeter's Daughters, the Big Water Drama Club, the Medea Project, and the Healing Justice Mamas demonstrate that performing artists have a vital role to play in the work to transform society. They can help reveal and tear down the false and harmful narratives that divide us, build more supportive communities, preserve and disseminate healing ways, disrupt violent and ineffective police and court systems through acts of creative activism, and incubate new practices of justice that actually encourage human wellbeing. This is especially true for those artists who are prepared to organize their creative work, in collaboration with participants, as sites at which to investigate the root causes of human conflict and disease. This is vital work that needs to happen and which is happening now. People have suffered enough. Rather than wait for others to act, they are working to move people and our society into a new phase of recovery and growth. This is the healing stage, where knowledgeable artists and their allies uproot old, harmful modalities, repair the damage done, and lay the foundation for a healthier and safer world.

Arts programs that *stage healing* can serve as sanctuary, shelter, and communion for this work because they ask something of those who participate in them and of those who witness the work. The support that prison-focused theater arts programs offer may look to some on the outside like fluff, a stopgap, a band-aid, even a diversion from the "real work" of prison abolition or of justice. But whom do we expect people will be when they come out of prison and jail if we offer no programming, no opportunities for personal growth? Recidivism metrics indicate that the limited educational, vocational, recreational, and religious programs currently available are largely ineffective. Many of these programs fall short because they, like the correctional institutions in which they are embedded, do not address the underlying causes of incarceration and offer little in terms of concrete support to enable and empower people to live in the world. People need much more support than they are receiving, and they need it now.

Moreover, whom do we expect we will be if no one tells the truth and if the old, violent ways are allowed to persist? Change cannot be expected to come only from inside prison walls. It has to happen everywhere. The status quo is not killing just Black women and girls. It is killing us all.

We need artists' help to dismantle the criminal legal system as we know it and to birth new cultural modalities that value Black women's lives and encourage safety, accountability, and well-being, three prerequisites for justice. No conversation about crime is complete without them. Currently and formerly incarcerated women artists and their allies are doing work that few others have been willing to do, and they are doing it exceptionally well. Moreover, they are *artists*. Having found a "healing balm," as Tarana Burke, founder of the #MeToo hashtag to support Black girl survivors of sexual assault, put it, they do not want to keep it to themselves.

Why would they?

It works.

They know it.

They are artists.

They want you to know it.

They want you to act.

Because Ava is coming home.

Ava is coming home.

Go do something beautiful with it.

BIBLIOGRAPHY

Aaron. "Director's Note." *Well-Behaved Women,* show program. August 31, 2010.

Abiodun, Rowland. "Ase: Verbalizing and Visualizing Creative Power through Art." *Journal of Religion in Africa* 24, no. 4 (1994): 309–22.

Adamson, Christopher R. "Punishment after Slavery: Southern State Penal Systems, 1865–1890." *Social Problems* 30, no. 5 (1983): 555–69.

Adhikari, Mohamed. *Not White Enough, Not Black Enough: Racial Identity in the South African Coloured Community.* Athens: Ohio University Press, 2005.

Alexander, Bryant K. "Performance Ethnography: The Reenacting and Inciting of Culture." In *The Sage Handbook of Qualitative Research,* edited by Norman K. and Yolanda S. Lincoln Denzin, 411–41. 3rd ed. Thousand Oaks, CA: Sage Publications, 2005.

Alexander, Michelle. *The New Jim Crow: Mass Incarceration in the Age of Colorblindness.* New York: New Press, 2012.

Ally, Shireen. *From Servants to Workers: South African Domestic Workers and the Democratic State.* Ithaca, NY: Cornell University Press, 2009.

Anderson, Carol. *White Rage: The Unspoken Truth of Our Racial Divide.* New York: Bloomsbury Publishing, 2017.

Anderson, Lisa M. *Black Feminism in Contemporary Drama.* Urbana: University of Illinois Press, 2008.

Angelou, Maya. *And Still I Rise.* Kindle ed. New York: Random House, 1978.

Anonymous. "Walk in the Day." Unpublished manuscript. Living Stage Theatre Company, Washington, DC.

Apetheker, Bettina. *The Morning Breaks: The Trial of Angela Davis.* Ithaca, NY: Cornell University Press, 2014.

Appleby, Joyce. *Inheriting the Revolution: The First Generation of Americans.* Cambridge, MA: Harvard University Press, 2000.

"Aretha Says She'll Go Angela's Bond If Permitted." *Jet Magazine,* December 3, 1970, 54.

Ashley, Lucas. "When I Run in My Bare Feet: Music, Writing, and Theater in a North Carolina Women's Prison." *American Music* 31, no. 2 (2013): 134–62.

Author, Sapa. "Zuma Found Not Guilty." *Mail & Guardian,* May 8, 2006.

Bailey, Moya. *Misogynoir Transformed: Black Women's Digital Resistance.* Kindle ed. New York: New York University Press, 2021.

Balfour, Michael. *Theatre in Prison: Theory and Practice.* Bristol, UK; Portland, OR: Intellect, 2004.

Balko, Radley. *Rise of the Warrior Cop: The Militarization of the American Police Force.* New York: Public Affairs, 2013.

Balogun, Oluwakemi M., and Melissa Graboyes. "Everyday Life in Africa: The Importance of Leisure and Fun." In *Africa Every Day: Fun, Leisure, and Expressive Culture on the Continent,* edited by Oluwakemi M. Balogun, Lisa Gilman, Melissa Graboyes, and Habib Iddrisu, 1–18. Athens: Ohio University Press, 2019.

Bates, Laura. *Shakespeare Saved My Life: Ten Years in Solitary with the Bard.* Chicago: Sourcebooks, 2013.

Beck, Dan, and Hal Cohen. "Cynthia Scott: 9 Versions of How She Died." *Detroit Free Press,* July 21, 1963, 3A, 4A.

Bernault, Frances. "The Politics of Enclosure in Colonial and Post-Colonial Africa." In *A History of Prison and Confinement in Africa,* translated by Janet Roitman, edited by Florence Benault, 1–53. Portsmouth, NH: Heinemann, 2003.

Bernstein, Robin. *Racial Innocence: Performing American Childhood from Slavery to Civil Rights.* Kindle ed. New York: New York University Press, 2011.

Berry, Daina Ramey, and Kali Nicole Gross. *A Black Women's History of the United States.* Boston: Beacon Press, 2020.

Berson, Jessica. "Baring and Bearing Life behind Bars: Pat Graney's 'Keeping the Faith' Prison Project." *TDR: The Drama Review* 52, no. 3 (2008): 79–93.

Beverley, Robert. *The History and Present State of Virginia, 1705.* Edited by Louis B. Wright. Chapel Hill: University of North Carolina Press. Accessed September 24, 2020, http://nationalhumanitiescenter.org/pds/amerbegin/power/text8/BeverlyServSlaves.pdf.

Bien, Laura. "In the Archives: Criminal Girls." *Ann Arbor Chronicle,* May 2, 2014.

Biggs, Lisa. "Art Saves Lives: Rebecca Rice and the Performance of Black Feminist Improv." In *Black Acting Methods: Critical Approaches,* edited by Sharrell Luckett, 72–86. New York: Routledge, 2016.

Billone, Nina. "Performing Civil Death: The Medea Project and Theatre for Incarcerated Women." *Text and Performance Quarterly* 29, no. 3 (2009): 260–75.

Blackwell, Orlando, dir. "Ain't Scared of Your Jails." *Eyes on the Prize.* Episode 3. Public Broadcasting Service, 1986.

Blain, Keisha N. *Until I Am Free: Fannie Lou Hamer's Enduring Message to America.* Boston: Beacon Press, 2021.

Boyd, Herb. *Black Detroit: A History of Self-Determination.* New York: Amistad, 2017.

Bosworth, Mary. *Explaining U.S. Imprisonment.* Thousand Oaks, CA: Sage Publications, 2009.

Bracey, John H., Jr., Sonia Sanchez, and James Smethurst, eds. *SOS—Calling All Black People: A Black Arts Movement Reader.* Amherst: University of Massachusetts Press, 2014.

Brooks, Pamela. *Boycotts, Buses and Passes: Black Women's Resistance in the US South and South Africa.* Amherst: University of Massachusetts Press, 2008.

Brown, J. M., and D. K. Gilliard. *Correctional Populations in the United States, 1994.* Washington, DC: Bureau of Justice Statistics, 1996.

Browne-Marshall, Gloria J. *Race, Law, and American Society: 1607–Present.* 2nd ed. New York; London: Taylor and Francis, 2013.

Buchanan, Kim Shayo. "Impunity: Sexual Abuse in Women's Prisons." *Harvard Civil Rights-Civil Liberties Law Review* 42, no. 1 (2007): 45–87.

Cacho, Lisa. *Social Death: Racialized Rightlessness and the Criminalization of the Unprotected.* New York: New York University Press, 2012.

Carby, Hazel V. *Reconstructing Womanhood: The Emergence of the Afro-American Woman Novelist.* New York: Oxford University Press, 1988.

Christie, Tanisha, and Ellie Walton, dir. *Walk with Me.* GoDigital. 2013. https://www.amazon.com/Walk-Me-Rebecca-Rice/dp/B00FNO85KU.

Cleveland, William. *Art in Other Places: Artists at Work in America's Communities and Social Institutions.* Westport, CT: Praeger, 1992.

Cohen, Cathy J. "Punks, Bulldaggers and Welfare Queens: The Radical Potential of Queer Politics?." In *Black Queer Studies: A Critical Anthology,* edited by E. Patrick Johnson, and Mae Henderson, 21–51. Durham, NC: Duke University Press, 2005.

Cole, Catherine. *Performing South Africa's Truth Commission: Stage of Transition.* Bloomington: Indiana University Press, 2010.

Colley, Zoe A. *Ain't Scared of Your Jail: Arrest, Imprisonment, and the Civil Rights Movement.* New Perspectives on the History of the South. Gainesville: University Press of Florida, 2012.

Conquergood, Dwight. "Lethal Theatre: Performance, Punishment and the Death Penalty." *Theatre Journal* 54, no. 2 (2002): 339–67.

Coplan, David B. *In Township Tonight!: South Africa's Black City Music and Theatre.* 2nd ed. Chicago: University of Chicago Press, 2008.

Correctional Populations in the United States, 1997. Washington, DC: Bureau of Justice Statistics, 2000.

Cox, Aimee Meredith. *Shapeshifters: Black Girls and the Choreography of Citizenship.* Durham, NC: Duke University Press, 2015.

Cullors, Patrisse. *Prayer to the Iyami.* Los Angeles: Broad Museum, 2020. https://www.youtube.com/watch?v=bco10-TKNlg.

Davis, Angela. "Angela Davis: Aretha Franklin Offered to Post Bail for Me, Saying 'Black People Will Be Free.'" By Amy Goodman, *Democracy Now!* August 18, 2018. https://www.democracynow.org/2018/8/17/angela_davis_remembers_aretha_franklin_who.

———. *Blues Legacies and Black Feminism: Gertrude 'Ma' Rainey, Bessie Smith and Billie Holiday.* New York: Vintage Books, 1999.

———. "Joan Little: The Dialectics of Rape." *Ms. Magazine,* 1975, 74–77, 106–8.

Davis, Tracy C. "Performative Time." In *Representing the Past: Essays in Performance Historiography,* edited by Charlotte Canning and Thomas Postlewait, 142–67. Iowa City: University of Iowa Press, 2010.

DeBow, J. D. B. *Statistical View of the United States.* Washington, DC: B. Tucker, 1854.

DeFrantz, Thomas F. "The Black Beat Made Visible: Hip Hop Dance and Body Power." In *Of the Presence of the Body: Essays on Dance and Performance Theory,* edited by André Lepecki, 64–81. Middletown, CT: Wesleyan University Press, 2004.

D'Emilio, John, and Estelle B. Freedman. *Intimate Matters: A History of Sexuality in America.* 3rd ed. Chicago: University of Chicago Press, 2012.

Derbes, Brett Josef. "'Secret Horrors': Enslaved Women and Children in the Louisiana State Penitentiary, 1833–1862." *Journal of African American History* 98, no. 2 (2013): 277–90.

Diamond, Elin. *Performance and Cultural Politics.* London: Routledge, 1996.

Du Bois, W. E. B. *The Philadelphia Negro: A Social Study.* Philadelphia: University of Pennsylvania Press, 1899.

Elam, Harry J. "The Black Performer and the Performance of Blackness." In *African American Performance and Theater History: A Critical Reader,* edited by Harry J. Elam and David Krasner. Oxford: Oxford University Press, 2001.

Ellis, Havelock. "The Results of Criminal Anthropology." In *The Origins of Criminology,* edited by Nicole Hahn Rafter, 184–85. New York: Routledge, 1999.

Ensler, Eve. "What I Want My Words to Do to You." Arlington, VA: Public Broadcasting Service, 2003.

Eskridge, William. *Gaylaw: Challenging the Apartheid of the Closet.* Cambridge, MA: Harvard University Press, 2009.

Extracts from the American Slave Code. Philadelphia: Philadelphia Female Anti-Slavery Society, 1820. https://www.loc.gov/item/12030696/.

"Family Driven from South by White Mob." *Chicago Defender,* Big Weekend edition, September 4, 1920.

Fanon, Franz. *Black Skin, White Masks.* Translated by Charles Lam Markmann. New York: Grove Press, 1967.

"Feb. 6, 1961: Jail, No Bail in Rock Hill, South Carolina Sit Ins." Zinn Education Project. Accessed August 24, 2021. https://www.zinnedproject.org/news/tdih/jail-no-bail/.

Fedock, Gina, with Christy Cummings and Sheryl Kubiak. "Incarcerated Women's Experiences of Staff-Perpetrated Rape: Racial Disparities and Justice Gaps in Institutional Responses." *Journal of Interpersonal Violence* 36, no. 17–18 (2021): 8668–92.

Ferrell, Jeff. *Crimes of Style: Urban Graffiti and the Politics of Criminality.* New York: Garland, 1993.

Ferrell, Jeff, and Clinton Sanders. *Cultural Criminology.* Boston: Northeastern University Press, 1995.

Fleetwood, Nicole R. *Marking Time: Art in the Age of Mass Incarceration.* Cambridge, MA: Harvard University Press, 2020.

Forman, James, Jr. *Locking up Our Own: Crime and Punishment in Black America.* New York: Farrar, Straus and Giroux, 2017.

Forsgren, La Donna L. *In Search of Our Warrior Mothers: Women Dramatists of the Black Arts Movement.* Evanston, IL: Northwestern University Press, 2018.

Foucault, Michel. *Discipline and Punish: The Birth of the Prison.* Translated by Alan Sheridan. New York: Vintage Books, 1995.

———. *The History of Sexuality: An Introduction.* New York: Vintage Books, 1990.

Fraden, Rena. *Imagining Medea: Rhodessa Jones and Theater for Incarcerated Women.* Chapel Hill: University of North Carolina Press, 2001.

Freedman, Estelle B. "The Prison Lesbian: Race, Class, and the Construction of the Aggressive Female Homosexual, 1915–1965." *Feminist Studies* 22, no. 2 (1996): 397–423.

———. *Their Sister's Keeper: Women's Prison Reform in America, 1830–1930.* Ann Arbor: University of Michigan Press, 1984.

Garland, David. *The Culture of Control: Crime and the Social Order in Contemporary Society.* Chicago: University of Chicago Press, 2001.

Gilbert, Shirli. "Singing against Apartheid: ANC Cultural Groups and the International Anti-Apartheid Struggle." *Journal of Southern African Studies* 33, no. 2 (2007): 421–41.

Gillespie, Kelly. "Containing the 'Wandering Native': Racial Jurisdiction and the Liberal Politics of Prison Reform in 1940s South Africa." *Journal of Southern African Studies* 37, no. 3 (2011): 499–515.

———. "Moralizing Security: 'Corrections' and Post-Apartheid Prison." *Race/Ethnicity: Multidisciplinary Global Contexts* 2, no. 1 (2008): 69–87.

Glaze, Lauren E., and Thomas P. Bonczar. *Probation and Parole in the United States, 2007—Statistical Tables.* Washington, DC: Bureau of Justice Statistics, 2008.

Glymph, Thavolia. *Out of the House of Bondage: The Transformation of the Plantation Household.* Cambridge: Cambridge University Press, 2008.

Goldstein, Donna. *Laughter out of Place: Race, Class, Violence and Sexuality in a Rio Shanty Town.* Oakland: University of California Press, 2013.

Gordon, Diana R. "Side by Side: Neoliberalism and Crime Control in Post-Apartheid South Africa." *Social Justice* 28, no. 3 (2001): 57–67.

Graber, Jennifer. *The Furnace of Affliction: Prisons and Religion in Antebellum America.* Chapel Hill: University of North Carolina Press, 2011.

Grant, Nicholas. *Winning Our Freedoms Together: African Americans and Apartheid, 1945–1960.* Chapel Hill: University of North Carolina Press, 2017.

Greene, Christina. "'She Ain't No Rosa Parks': The Joan Little Rape-Murder Case and Jim Crow Justice in the Post-Civil Rights South." *Journal of African American History* 100, no. 3 (2015): 428–27.

Gross, Kali N. "African American Women, Mass Incarceration and the Politics of Reform." *Journal of American History* 102, no. 1 (2015): 25–33.

Gunner, Liz. "Jacob Zuma, the Social Body and the Unruly Power of Song." *African Affairs* 108, no. 430 (2009): 27–48.

Haedicke, Susan C. "The Challenge of Participation." In *Audience Participation: Essays on Inclusion in Performance,* edited by Susan Kattwinkel, 71–87. Westport, CT: Praeger, 2003.

Hagen, Uta. *Respect for Acting.* 2nd ed. Hoboken, NJ: Wiley, 2009.

Haley, Sarah. *No Mercy Here: Gender, Punishment, and the Making of Jim Crow Modernity.* Kindle ed. Chapel Hill: University of North Carolina Press, 2016.

Hall, Stuart. "Notes on Deconstructing 'the Popular.'" In *Stuart Hall: Essential Essays,* edited by David Morley, 347–61. Durham, NC: Duke University Press, 2018.

Hansen, Karen Tranberg. "Introduction." In *African Dress: Fashion, Agency, Performance,* edited by Karen Tranberg Hansen and D. Soyini Madison, 1–12. London: Bloomsbury Academic Press, 2013.

Harris, LaShawn. *Sex Workers, Psychics, and Numbers Runners: Black Women in New York City's Underground Economy.* Champaign: University of Illinois Press, 2016.

Harris-Perry, Melissa. *Sister Citizen: Shame, Stereotypes, and Black Women in America.* New Haven, CT: Yale University Press, 2011.

Hart, Steven. "The Historical and Social Role of the Arts in Prison." *Prison Journal* 66, no. 11 (1986): 11–25.

Hartman, Saidiya. "Seduction and the Ruses of Power." *Callaloo* 19, no. 2 (1996): 537–60.

———. *Wayward Lives, Beautiful Experiments: Intimate Histories of Riotous Black Girls, Troublesome Women, and Queer Radicals.* New York: W. W. Norton, 2020.

Hassim, Shireen. *Women's Organizations and Democracy in South Africa: Contesting Authority.* Madison: University of Wisconsin Press, 2006.

Hawthorne, Nathaniel. *The Scarlet Letter.* Edited by Ross C. Murfin. Boston: Bedford Books of St. Martin's Press, 1991.

Hemphill, Prentiss. "Healing Justice Is How We Can Sustain Black Lives." *Huffington Post,* February 7, 2017. Accessed September 11, 2020. https://www.huffpost.com/entry/healing-justice_b _5899e8ade4boc1284f282ffe.

Hewitt, Andrew. *Social Choreography: Ideology as Performance in Dance and Everyday Movement.* Durham, NC: Duke University Press, 2005.

Higginbotham, A. Leon. *In the Matter of Color: Race and the American Legal Process.* 4th ed. Oxford: Oxford University Press, 1980.

Higginbotham, Evelyn Brooks. *Righteous Discontent: The Women's Movement in the Black Baptist Church 1880–1920.* Cambridge, MA: Harvard University Press, 1994.

Hill, Errol, and James V. Hatch. *A History of African American Theatre.* Cambridge: Cambridge University Press, 2003.

Hine, Darlene Clark. "Rape and the Inner Lives of Black Women in the Middle West." *Signs* 14, no. 4 (1989): 912–20.

Holliday, Ruth. "The Comfort of Identity." *Sexualities* 2, no. 4 (1999): 475–91.

Hornblum, Allen M. *Acres of Skin: Human Experiments at Holmesburg Prison: A True Story of Abuse and Exploitation in the Name of Medical Science.* New York: Routledge, 1998.

Hughes, Kathryn. "Migrating Identities: The Relational Constitution of Drug Use and Addiction." *Sociology of Health & Illness* 29, no. 5 (2007): 673–91.

Hurston, Zora Neale. *Dust on the Tracks.* Philadelphia: B. Lippincott Co., 1942.

Institute for Policy Studies. "Women and the Racial Wealth Divide." Accessed January 21, 2022. https://inequality.org/racial-wealth-divide-snapshot-women/.

James, Deborah. "'Babagešu' (Those of My Home): Women Migrants, Ethnicity and Performance in South Africa." *American Ethnologist* 26, no. 1 (1999): 69–89.

Jimoh, A. Yemisi, and Francoise N. Hamlin. *These Truly Are the Brave: An Anthology of African American Writings on War and Citizenship.* Gainesville: University Press of Florida, 2015.

"Joan Little Gets Job Outside Jail." *New York Times,* March 13, 1977, 26.

Johnson, E. Patrick. "Black Performance Studies: Genealogies, Politics, Futures." In *The Sage Handbook of Performance Studies,* edited by D. Soyini and Judith Hamera Madison, 446–63. Thousand Oaks, CA: Sage Publications, 2007.

———. "Quare Studies, or Almost Everything I Know About Queer Studies I Learned from My Grandmother." In *Black Queer Studies: A Critical Anthology,* edited by E. Patrick Johnson and Mae Henderson, 124–57. Durham, NC: Duke University Press, 2005.

Johnson, Georgia Douglas. "Blue-Eyed Black Boy." In *Black Female Playwrights: An Anthology of Plays before 1950,* edited by Kathy Perkins, 47–51. Bloomington; Indianapolis: Indiana University Press, 1990.

———. "A Sunday Morning in the South." In *Black Female Playwrights: An Anthology of Plays before 1950,* edited by Kathy Perkins, 31–37. Bloomington; Indianapolis: Indiana University Press, 1990.

Jones, Martha S. *Birthright Citizenship: A History of Race and Rights in Antebellum America.* Cambridge. Cambridge University Press, 2018.

Jones, Michelle, and Lori Record. "Magdalene Laundries: The First Prisons for Women in the United States." *Journal of the Indiana Academy of the Social Sciences* 17, no. 1 (2017): 166–79.

Jones, Omi Osun Joni L., and Sharon Bridgforth. "Black Desire, Theatrical Jazz, and *River See.*" *TDR: The Drama Review* 58, no. 4 (2014): 136–46.

Jones, Rhodessa, dir. *Serious Fun at Sun City.* Unpublished manuscript (2010).

Kanter, Jodi. *Performing Loss: Rebuilding Community through Theatre and Writing.* Carbondale: Southern Illinois University Press, 2007.

Kim, Mimi E. "Challenging the Pursuit of Criminalisation in an Era of Mass Incarceration: The Limitations of Social Work Responses to Domestic Violence in the USA." *British Journal of Social Work* 43, no. 7 (2013): 1276–93.

Kruger, Loren. *The Drama of South Africa: Plays, Pageants and Publics since 1910.* London: Routledge, 1999.

Kunzel, Regina G. *Criminal Intimacy: Prison and the Uneven History of Modern American Sexuality.* Chicago: University of Chicago Press, 2008.

Kynoch, Gary. "Of Compounds and Cellblocks: The Foundations of Violence in Johannesburg, 1890s–1950s." *Journal of Southern African Studies* 37, no. 3 (2011): 463–77.

Langellier, Kristin M. "Personal Narrative, Performance, Performativity: Two or Three Things I Know for Sure." *Text and Performance Quarterly* 19, no. 2 (1999): 125–44.

Lassiter, Matthew D., and the Policing and Social Justice HistoryLab. "UHURU Flyer." *Detroit Under Fire: Police Violence, Crime Politics, and the Struggle for Racial Justice in the Civil Rights Era.* Ann Arbor: University of Michigan Carceral State Project, 2021. Accessed January 3, 2022. https://policing.umhistorylabs.lsa.umich.edu/s/detroitunderfire/item/4928.

Leder, Drew. "Imprisoned Bodies: The Life-World of the Incarcerated." In *Prisons and Punishment: Reconsidering Global Penality,* edited by Mechthild Nagel and Seth N. Asumah, 55–69. Trenton, NJ; Asmara, Eritrea: Africa World Press, 2007.

LeFlouria, Talitha. *Chained in Silence: Black Women and Convict Labor in the New South.* Chapel Hill: University of North Carolina Press, 2016.

———. "'The Hand That Rocks the Cradle Cuts Cordwood': Exploring Black Women's Lives and Labor in Georgia's Convict Camps, 1865–1917." *Labor* 8, no. 3 (2011): 47–63.

———. "'Under the Sting of the Lash:' Gendered Violence, Terror, and Resistance in the South's Convict Camps." *Journal of African American History* 100, no. 3 (2015): 366–84.

Leonard, Nettie. *Annual Report of Women's Prison.* Albany: New York State Legislature, 1913.

Lewis, Edna. *Who Took the Weight? Black Voices from Norfolk Prison.* Boston: Little, Brown, 1972.

Lombroso, Cesare. "Criminal Craniums." In *The Origins of Criminology: A Reader,* edited by Nicole Hahn Rafter. New York: Routledge, 1999.

Lorde, Audre. "The Master's Tools Will Never Dismantle the Master's House." In *Sister Outsider: Essays and Speeches.* Berkeley, CA: Crossing Press, 1984.

Lordi, Emily J. *The Meaning of Soul: Black Music and Resilience Since the 1960s.* Refiguring American Music. Durham, NC: Duke University Press, 2020. https://doi.org/10.1515/9781478012245.

Lucas, Ashley. "When I Run in My Bare Feet: Music, Writing, and Theater in a North Carolina Women's Prison." *American Music* 31, no. 2 (2013): 134–62.

Madison, D. Soyini. *Acts of Activism: Human Rights as Radical Performance.* Cambridge: Cambridge University Press, 2010. https://doi.org/10.1017/cbo9780511675973.001.

———. "Co-Performative Witnessing." *Cultural Studies* 21, no. 6 (2007): 826–31.

———. *Critical Ethnography: Methods, Ethics, and Performance.* Thousand Oaks, CA: Sage Publications, 2019.

———. "Dressing Out-of-Place: From Ghama to Obama Commemorative Cloth on the US American Red Carpet." In *African Dress: Fashion, Agency, Performance,* edited by Karen Tranberg Hansen and D. Soyini Madison, 217–30. London: Bloomsbury Academic Press, 2013.

Marietta, Jack D., and G. S. Rowe. *Troubled Experiment: Crime and Justice in Pennsylvania, 1682–1800*. Philadelphia: University of Pennsylvania Press, 2006.

McEwan, Cheryl. "Engendering Citizenship: Gendered Spaces of Democracy in South Africa." *Political Geography* 19, no. 5 (2000): 627–51.

McGuire, Danielle L. *At the Dark End of the Street: Black Women, Rape and Resistance—A New History of the Civil Rights Movement from Rosa Parks to the Rise of Black Power*. New York: Vintage Books, 2010.

———. "'It Was Like All of Us Had Been Raped': Sexual Violence, Community Mobilization, and the African American Freedom Struggle." *Journal of American History* 91, no. 3 (2004): 906–31.

———. "Joan Little and the Triumph of Testimony." In *Freedom Rights: New Perspectives on the Civil Rights Movement*, edited by Danielle McGuire and John Dittmer, 191–221. Louisville: University of Kentucky Press, 2011.

Mead, Rebecca. "Behind Bars." *New Yorker*, October 25, 2010. https://www.newyorker.com/magazine/2010/10/25/behind-bars-rebecca-mead.

Meintjes, Louise. "Shoot the Sergeant, Shatter the Mountain: The Production of Masculinity in Zulu Ngoma Song and Dance in Post-Apartheid South Africa." *Ethnomusicology Forum* 13, no. 2 (2004): 173–201.

Mitchell, Charlene. *The Fight to Free Angela: Its Importance for the Working Class*. New York: New Outlook Publishers, 1972.

Mitchell, Koritha. "Keep Claiming Space!" *CLA Journal* 58, no. 3/4 (2015): 229–44.

———. "Love in Action: Noting Similarities between Lynching Then and Anti-LGBT Violence Now." *Callaloo* 36, no. 3 (2013): 687–717.

Mitchem, Stephanie. *African American Folk Healing*. New York: New York University Press, 2007.

Mkhwanazi, Nolwazi. "Miniskirts and Kangas: The Use of Culture in Constituting Postcolonial Sexuality." *Dark Matter: In the Ruins of Imperial Culture*, May 2, 2008. Accessed September 13, 2021. http://www.darkmatter101.org/site/2008/05/02/miniskirts-and-kangas-the-use-of-culture-in-constituting-postcolonial-sexuality/.

Morales, Aurora Levins. *Medicine Stories: Essays for Radicals*. Durham, NC: Duke University Press, 2019.

Morgan, Jennifer L. *Laboring Women: Reproduction and Gender in New World Slavery*. Philadelphia: University of Pennsylvania Press, 2004.

Morgan, Maia. "I Chose to Live: One Woman's Story of Surviving Sexual Abuse." *Glamour Magazine*, March 4, 2010. https://www.glamour.com/story/i-chose-to-live-one-womans-story-of-surviving-sexual-abuse.

Morris, Bob. "Faith Ringgold Will Keep Fighting Back." *New York Times*, June 11, 2020. https://www.nytimes.com/2020/06/11/arts/design/faith-ringgold-art.html?action=click.

Moses, Greg. "Time and Punishment in an Anesthetic World Order." In *Prisons and Punishment: Reconsidering Global Penality*, edited by Mechthild Nagel and Seth N. Asumah, 71–75. Trenton, NJ; Asmara, Eritrea: Africa World Press Inc., 2007.

Moss, Emily, Kriston McIntosh, Wendy Edelberg, and Kristen Broady "The Black-White Wealth Gap Left Black Households More Vulnerable." The Brookings Institute. Updated December 8, 2020. Accessed September 16, 2021. https://www.brookings.edu/blog/up-front/2020/12/08/the-black-white-wealth-gap-left-black-households-more-vulnerable/.

Moynihan, Daniel Patrick. *The Negro Family: The Case for National Action*. US Office of Policy Planning and Research. Washington, DC: United States Department of Labor, 1965.

National Association for the Advancement of Colored People (NAACP). "Criminal Justice Fact Sheet." 2022. https://www.naacp.org/criminal-justice-fact-sheet/.

National Prison Rape Elimination Commission Report. 2009. Accessed January 17, 2022. https://www.ojp.gov/pdffiles1/226680.pdf.

"Negro Women to Be Put to Work." *Greenville News* (Greenville, SC), October 2, 1918, 4.

Newton, Esther. *Mother Camp: Female Impersonators in America*. Chicago: University of Chicago Press, 1979.

Nguyen, Mimi Thi. "The Hoodie as Sign, Screen, Expectation, and Force." *Signs: Journal of Women in Culture and Society* 40, no. 4 (2015): 791–816.

Oboe, Analisa. "The TRC Women's Hearings as Performance and Protest in the New South Africa." *Research in African Literatures* 38, no. 3 (2007): 60–76.

Oliver, Kelly. *Witnessing: Beyond Recognition*. Minneapolis: University of Minnesota Press, 2001.

Olwage, Grant, ed. *Composing Apartheid: Music for and against Apartheid*. Johannesburg: Wits University Press, 2008.

Parchman Farm Women Singers. *Jailhouse Blues*. New York: Rosetta Records, 1988.

Patrick-Stamp, Leslie. "Ann Hinson: A Little-Known Woman in the Country's Premier Prison, Eastern Penitentiary, 1831." *Pennsylvania History: A Journal of Mid-Atlantic Studies* 67, no. 3 (2000): 361–75.

———. "Numbers That Are Not New: African Americans in the Country's First Prison, 1790–1835." *Pennsylvania Magazine of History and Biography* 119, no. 1/2 (1995): 95–128.

———. "The Prison Sentence Docket for 1795: Inmates at the Nation's First State Penitentiary." *Pennsylvania History: A Journal of Mid-Atlantic Studies* 60, no. 3 (1993): 353–82.

Pauperism and Crime in Michigan 1872–73: Message of Governor John J. Bagley. Lansing, MI: W. S. George & Co., State Printers and Binders, 1873.

Perkins, Sophie Huth. *The Colored Ladies' Political Club or the Colored Suffragettes*. Chicago: T. S. Denison and Company, 1910.

Perry, Imani. "She Changed Black Literature Forever. Then She Disappeared." *New York Times*, September 19, 2021. https://www.nytimes.com/2021/09/17/magazine/gayl-jones-novel-palmares.html.

Peterson, Bhekizizwe. "Apartheid and the Political Imagination in the Black South African Theatre." *Journal of Southern African Studies* 16, no. 2 (1990): 229–45.

Piepnza-Samarsinha, Leah Lakshimi. "A Not So Brief History of the Healing Justice Movement, 2010–2016." *Mice Magazine*, 2016. Accessed September 10, 2020. https://micemagazine.ca/issue-two/not-so-brief-personal-history-healing-justice-movement-2010%E2%80%932016.

"Police Brutality." *Illustrated News* (Detroit, MI) 3, no. 15. July 22, 1963, 2, 7.

Pollock, Della. *Remembering: Oral History Performance*. New York: Palgrave MacMillan, 2005.

Potter, Sarah. "'Undeserable Relations': Same-Sex Relationships and the Meaning of Sexual Desire at a Women's Reformatory During the Progressive Era." *Feminist Studies* 2 (2004): 394–415.

"Prison Population Growth: Rate (per 100,000 Resident Population) of Sentenced Prisoners under Jurisdiction of State and Federal Correctional Authorities on December 31, by Sex, United States, 1925–2012," Table 6.28.2012. *Sourcebook of Criminal Justice Statistics*. University of Albany, 2013. https://www.albany.edu/sourcebook/tost_6.html#6_a.

Pro, George, Ethan Sahker, and Julie Baldwin. "Incarceration as a Reason for US Alcohol and Drug Treatment Non-Completion: A Multilevel Analysis of Racial/Ethnic and Sex Disparities." *Journal of Behavioral Health Service Resources* 47 (2020): 464–75.

Quashie, Kevin E. *The Sovereignty of Quiet: Beyond Resistance in Black Culture*. New Brunswick, NJ: Rutgers University Press, 2012.

Rafter, Nicole Hahn. *Partial Justice: Women in State Prisons, 1800–1935.* Boston: Northeastern University Press, 1985.

——. "Prisons for Women, 1790–1980." *Crime and Justice* 5 (1983): 129–81. https://www.jstor.org/stable/1147471.

Reagon, Bernice Johnson, and Rosetta Reitz. "Liner Notes," *Jailhouse Blues.* New York: Rosetta Records, 1988.

Reagon, Bernice Johnson, and Sweet Honey in the Rock. *We Who Believe in Freedom: Sweet Honey in the Rock . . . Still on the Journey.* New York: Anchor Books, 1993.

Redmond, Shana. *Anthem: Social Movements and the Sound of Solidarity in the African Diaspora.* New York: New York University Press, 2013.

Reiss, Benjamin. *The Showman and the Slave: Race, Death, and Memory in Barnum's America.* Cambridge, MA: Harvard University Press, 2001.

Richie, Beth. *Arrested Justice: Black Women, Violence, and America's Prison Nation.* New York: New York University Press, 2012.

Ringgold, Faith. *We Flew over the Bridge: The Memoirs of Faith Ringgold.* Durham, NC: Duke University Press, 2005.

Robinson, Cedric J. *Black Marxism: The Making of the Black Radical Tradition.* 2nd ed. Chapel Hill: University of North Carolina Press, 2000.

Rousey, Dennis Charles. *Policing the Southern City: New Orleans, 1805–1889.* Baton Rouge: Louisiana State University Press, 1996.

Sabo, Donald F., Terry Allen Kupers, and Willie James London. *Prison Masculinities.* Philadelphia: Temple University Press, 2001.

Santamarina, Xiomara. "Elizabeth Freeman." In *African American Lives,* edited by Henry Louis Gates Jr. and Evelyn Brooks Higganbotham, 317–18. Oxford: Oxford University Press, 2004.

Santiago-Irizarry, Wilma. *Medicalizing Ethnicity: The Construction of Latino Identity in a Psychiatric Setting.* Ithaca, NY: Cornell University Press, 2001.

Sawyer, Wendy, and Wanda Bertram. "Jail Will Separate 2.3 Million Mothers from Their Children This Year." Prison Policy Initiative, May 13, 2018. https://www.prisonpolicy.org/blog/2018/05/13/mothers-day-2018/.

Scarry, Elaine. *The Body in Pain: The Making and Unmaking of the World.* Oxford: Oxford University Press, 1987.

Schechner, Richard. *Performance Studies: An Introduction.* 3rd ed. New York: Routledge, 2013.

Scott-Douglass, Amy. *Shakespeare Inside.* London: Continuum, 2007.

Sentencing Project, The. "Incarcerated Women and Girls Fact Sheet." The Sentencing Project. 2017. https://www.sentencingproject.org/wp-content/uploads/2016/02/Incarcerated-Women-and-Girls.pdf.

Shailor, Jonathan. *Performing New Lives: Prison Theatre.* London: Jessica Kingsley Publishers, 2011.

Shandell, Jonathan. "The Negro Little Theatre Movement." In *The Cambridge Companion to African American Theatre,* edited by Harvey Young, 103–17. Cambridge: Cambridge University Press, 2013.

Siegel, Micol. *Violence Work: State Power and the Limits of Police.* Durham, NC: Duke University Press, 2018.

Singleton, Judith. "The South African Sexual Offences Act and Local Meanings of Coercion and Consent in KwaZulu Natal." *African Studies Review* 55, no. 2 (2012): 59–75.

Smith, Christen A. *Afro-Paradise: Blackness, Violence and Performance in Brazil.* Urbana: University of Illinois Press, 2016.

Smith, David. "Theatre of Burden." *Mail & Guardian,* November 13, 2009. http://mg.co.za/article/2009-11-13-theatre-of-burden.

Smith, Gail. "Rogue Mothers and Deviant Daughters." *City Paper,* November 1, 2009, 25.

Smith, James M. *Ireland's Magdalen Laundries and the Nation's Architecture of Containment.* Notre Dame, IN: University of Notre Dame Press, 2007.

Smith, Sidonie, and Kay Schaffer. *Human Rights and Narrated Lives: The Ethics of Recognition.* Gordonsville, VA: Palgrave Macmillan, 2004.

Smitherman, Geneva. *Talk That Talk: Language, Culture and Education in African America.* New York: Routledge, 1999.

———. *Talkin and Testifyin: The Language of Black America.* Detroit: Wayne State University Press, 1986.

Snell, Tracy L., and Danielle C. Morton. *Women in Prison.* Washington, DC: Bureau of Justice Statistics, 1994.

Snorton, C. Riley. *Black on Both Sides: A Racial History of Trans Identity.* Minneapolis: University of Minneapolis Press, 2017.

Snyder, Timothy. *On Tyranny: Twenty Lessons from the Twentieth Century.* New York: Tim Duggan Books, 2017.

South Africa Department of Correctional Services (SADCS). *Annual Report* (2008–9). Pretoria: South Africa Department of Correctional Services, 2010.

———. *Annual Report* (2012–13). Pretoria: South Africa Department of Correctional Services, 2014.

Stanford, Ann Folwell. "More Than Just Words: Women's Poetry and Resistance at Cook County Jail." *Feminist Studies* 30, no. 2 (2004): 277–301.

Stevenson, Bryan. *Reconstruction in America: Racial Justice after the Civil War.* Montgomery, AL: Equal Justice Initiative, 2012. https://eji.org/reports/reconstruction-in-america-overview/.

Super, Gail. "'Like Some Rough Beast Slouching Towards Bethlehem to Be Born': A Historical Perspective on the Institution of the Prison in South Africa, 1976–2004." *British Journal of Criminology* 51, no. 1 (2011): 201–21.

———. "The Spectacle of Crime in the 'New' South Africa: A Historical Perspective (1976–2004)." *British Journal of Criminology* 50, no. 2 (2010): 165–84.

Sutherland, Alexandra. "Now We Are Real Women: Playing with Gender in a Male Prison Theatre Programme in South Africa." *RiDE: Journal of Applied Theatre and Performance* 18, no. 2 (2013): 120–32.

Swavola, Elizabeth, Kristi Riley, and Ram Subramanian. "Overlooked: Women in Jails in an Era of Reform." Vera Institute of Justice. 2016. https://www.vera.org/publications/overlooked-women-and-jails-report.

Sweeney, Megan. *Reading Is My Window: Books and the Art of Reading in Women's Prisons.* Chapel Hill: University of North Carolina Press, 2010.

Tate, Judy K. "Stargate: A Theatre Company of Imagination, Hope, Life Skills, and Quality Art for Justice-Involved Young Men." In *Applied Theatre with Youth: Education, Engagement, Activism,* edited by Lisa S. Brenner with Chris Ceraso and Evelyn Diaz Cruz, 197–205. New York: Routledge, 2022.

Taylor, Keeanga-Yamahtta, ed. *How We Get Free: Black Feminism and the Combahee River Collective.* Chicago: Haymarket Books, 2017.

Teeterly, Negley K. *The Cradle of the Penitentiary: The Walnut Street Jail at Philadelphia, 1773–1835.* Philadelphia: Pennsylvania Prison Society, 1955.

Terry, Charles M. "The Function of Humor for Prison Inmates." *Journal of Contemporary Criminal Justice* 13, no. 1 (1997): 23–40.

Thamm, Marianne. "'Khwezi, the Woman Who Accused Jacob Zuma of Rape, Dies." *Guardian*, October 10, 2016. Accessed September 8, 2021. https://www.theguardian.com/world/2016/oct/10/khwezi-woman-accused-jacob-zuma-south-african-president-aids-activist-fezekile-ntsukela-kuzwayo.

Thompson, James. "From the Stocks to the Stage: Prison Theater and the Theater of Prison." In *Theater in Prison: Theory and Practice,* edited by Michael Balfour, 57–76. Portland, OR: Intellect, 2004.

———. *Prison Theatre: Perspectives and Practices.* London; Philadelphia: Jessica Kingsley, 1998.

Tocci, Laurence. *The Proscenium Cage: Critical Case Studies in U.S. Prison Theatre Programs.* Youngstown, OH: Cambria, 2007.

Trounstine, Jean. *Shakespeare Behind Bars: One Teacher's Story of the Power of Drama in a Women's Prison.* Ann Arbor: University of Michigan Press, 2004.

Tucker, Jasmine, and Caitlin Lowell. *National Snapshot: Poverty Among Women & Families, 2015.* Washington, DC: National Women's Law Center, 2016.

US Department of Justice, Bureau of Justice Statistics. *Correctional Populations in the United States, 1994,* NCJ-160091. Washington, DC: Bureau of Justice Statistics, 1996.

———. *Correctional Populations in the United States, 1997,* NCJ 177613. Washington, DC: Bureau of Justice Statistics, 2000.

———. *Historical Corrections Statistics in the United States, 1850–1984.* Rockville, MD: Westat Inc., 1986.

———. *Jail Inmates at Midyear 2010—Statistical Tables.* Washington, DC: Bureau of Justice Statistics, 2011.

———. *Jail Inmates in 2015.* Washington, DC: Bureau of Justice Statistics, 2016.

———. *Jail Inmates in 2017.* Washington, DC: Bureau of Justice Statistics, 2019.

———. *Prison and Jail Inmates at Midyear 2000.* Washington, DC: Bureau of Justice Statistics, 2001.

———. *Prisoners in 1925–81.* Bulletin NCJ-8586. Washington, DC: Bureau of Justice Statistics, 1982.

———. *Prisoners in 1986.* Washington, DC: Bureau of Justice Statistics, 1987.

———. *Prisoners in 1989.* Washington, DC: Bureau of Justice Statistics, 1990.

———. *Prisoners in 1990.* Washington, DC: Bureau of Justice Statistics, 1991.

———. *Prisoners in 1994.* Washington, DC: Bureau of Justice Statistics, 1995.

———. *Prisoners in 1998,* Bulletin NCJ 175687. Washington, DC: US Department of Justice, 1999.

———. *Prisoners in 2000,* Bulletin NCJ 188207. Washington, DC: US Department of Justice, 2001.

———. *Prisoners in 2010.* Washington, DC: Bureau of Justice Statistics, 2012.

———. *Prisoners in 2012—Advance Counts,* Bulletin NCJ 242467. Washington, DC: US Department of Justice, 2013.

———. *Prisoners in 2017.* Washington, DC: Bureau of Justice Statistics, 2019.

———. *Prison Inmates at Midyear 2007.* Washington, DC: Bureau of Justice Statistics, 2008.

———. *Survey of State Prison Inmates, 1991.* Washington, DC: Bureau of Justice Statistics, 1993.

Van der Kolk, Bessel A. *The Body Keeps the Score: Brain, Mind, and Body in the Healing of Trauma.* New York: Penguin Books, 2014.

Van Zyl Smit, Dirk. "Public Policy and the Punishment of Crime in a Divided Society: A Historical Perspective on the South African Penal System." *Crime and Social Justice* 21/22 (1984): 146–62.

Vetten, Lisa, and Kailash Bahana. "The Justice for Gender Campaign: Incarcerated Domestic Violence Survivors in Post-Apartheid South Africa." In *Global Lockdown: Race, Gender and the Prison-Industrial Complex,* edited by Julia Sudbury, 255–70. New York: Routledge, 2005.

Wallace, Michele. "For the Women's House." *Feminist Art Journal* 1, no. 1 (1972): 14–15.

Walters, Wendy W. "'One of Dese Mornings, Bright and Fair / Take My Wings and Cleave De Air': The Legend of the Flying Africans and Diasporic Consciousness." *MELUS* 22, no. 3 (1997): 3–29.

Warner, Sara. "The Medea Project: Mythic Theater for Incarcerated Women." *Feminist Studies* 30, no. 2 (2004): 483–509.

———. "Restoryative Justice: Theater as a Redressive Mechanism for Incarcerated Women." In *Razor Wire Women: Prisoners, Activists, Scholars and Artists,* edited by Jodie Michelle Lawston and Ashley E. Lucas, 229–46. Albany: University of New York Press, 2011.

Wells-Barnett, Ida B. "Lynch Law in America." *Arena* 23, no. 1 (1900): 15–24.

West, Heather, and William J. Sabol. *Prison Inmates at Midyear—Statistical Tables, 2008.* Washington, DC: Department of Justice Statistics, 2009.

"Why Walk When You Can Fly?" The Living Stage Documentary. 1999. https://www.youtube.com/watch?v=OpgwtC6rdUk.

Wilkinson, Diana. "Faith Ringgold Captures the 'Long Road' Ahead for Women." National Museum of Women in the Arts. Accessed January 17, 2018. https://nmwa.org/blog/2013/09/26/faith-ringgold-captures-the-long-road-ahead-for-women/.

Williams, Paul, and Ian Taylor. "Neoliberalism and the Political Economy of the 'New' South Africa." *New Political Economy* 5, no. 1 (2000): 21–40.

Wines, Michael. "Highly Charged Rape Trial Tests South African Ideals." *New York Times,* April 10, 2006. Accessed September 13, 2021. https://www.nytimes.com/2006/04/10/world/africa/a-highly-charged-rape-trial-tests-south-africas-ideals.html?smid=url-share.

Wolff, Nancy, Jing Shi, and Jane A. Siegel. "Patterns of Victimization among Male and Female Inmates: Evidence of an Enduring Legacy." *Violence and Victims* 24, no. 4 (2009): 469–84. https://doi.org/10.1891/0886-6708.24.4.469.

Women and the Racial Wealth Divide. Washington, DC: Institute for Public Studies, 2018. https://ips-dc.org/women-racial-wealth-divide/.

Woods, Katelyn. *Cracking Up: Black Feminist Comedy in the Twentieth and Twenty-First Century United States.* Iowa City: University of Iowa Press, 2021.

Young, Harvey. *Embodying Black Experience: Stillness, Critical Memory, and the Black Body.* Ann Arbor: University of Michigan Press, 2010.

Wynter, Sylvia. "'No Humans Involved:' An Open Letter to My Colleagues." *Forum N.H.I. Knowledge for the 21st Century* 1, no. 1 (1994): 42–73.

Yancy, George. *Black Bodies, White Gazes: The Continuing Significance of Race in America.* 2nd ed. Kindle Edition. Lantham; London: Rowman & Littlefield Publishers, 2017.

Young-Jahangeer, Miranda. "'Less Than a Dog': Interrogating Theatre for Debate in Westville Female Correctional Centre, Durban, South Africa." *RiDE: The Journal of Applied Theatre and Performance* 18, no. 2 (2013): 200–203.

Yu, Henry. *Thinking Orientals: Migration, Contact, and Exoticism in Modern America.* New York: Oxford University Press, 2001.

INDEX

BLACK PERFORMANCE AND CULTURAL CRITICISM

E. PATRICK JOHNSON, SERIES EDITOR

VALERIE LEE, FOUNDING EDITOR EMERITA

The Black Performance and Cultural Criticism series includes monographs that draw on interdisciplinary methods to analyze, critique, and theorize black cultural production. Books in the series take as their object of intellectual inquiry the performances produced on the stage and on the page, stretching the boundaries of both black performance and literary criticism.

Printed in the USA
CPSIA information can be obtained
at www.ICGtesting.com
JSHW020140070124
54911JS00001B/35